Strategy and Defence Planning: Meeting the Challenge of Uncertainty explores and examines why and how security communities prepare purposefully for their future defence. The author explains that defence planning is the product of interplay among political process, historical experience, and the logic of strategy. The theory of strategy best reveals both the nature and the working of defence planning. Political 'ends', strategic 'ways', and military 'means' all fed by reigning, if not always recognized, assumptions, organize the subject well with a template that can serve any time, place, and circumstance. The book is designed to help understanding of what can appear to be a forbiddingly complex as well as technical subject.

A good part of the problem for officials charged with defence planning duties is expressed in the second part of the book's title. The real difficulty, which rarely is admitted by those tasked with defence planning duty, is that defence planning can only be guesswork. But, because defence preparation is always expensive, not untypically is politically unpopular, yet obviously can be supremely important, claims to knowledge about the truly unknowable persist. In truth, we cannot do defence planning competently, because our ignorance of the future precludes understanding of what our society will be shown by future events to need. The challenge faced by the author is to identify ways in which our problems with the inability to know the future in any detail in advance—the laws of nature, in other words—may best be met and mitigated. Professor Gray argues that our understanding of human nature, of politics, and of strategic history, does allow us to make prudent choices in defence planning that hopefully will prove 'good enough'.

Discarding Western analytic paradigm that kills unwar (ie: learn go)

JH - proto theory
reflexive CLASS. Europ/A in the whole
No hierarchially = ie. Eastern Tao

Strategy and Defence Planning

Meeting the Challenge of Uncertainty

COLIN S. GRAY

OXFORD
UNIVERSITY PRESS

OXFORD
UNIVERSITY PRESS

Great Clarendon Street, Oxford, OX2 6DP,
United Kingdom

Oxford University Press is a department of the University of Oxford.
It furthers the University's objective of excellence in research, scholarship,
and education by publishing worldwide. Oxford is a registered trade mark of
Oxford University Press in the UK and in certain other countries

First published 2014
First published in paperback 2016

Published in the United States of America by Oxford University Press
198 Madison Avenue, New York, NY 10016, United States of America

British Library Cataloguing in Publication Data
Data available

Library of Congress Cataloging in Publication Data
Data available

ISBN 978–0–19–870184–2 (Hbk.)
ISBN 978–0–19–877870–7 (Pbk.)

To Sir Michael Howard, with esteem and gratitude.

Preface

Strategy and Defence Planning: Meeting the Challenge of Uncertainty is the concluding volume in a strategy trilogy; the preceding works being *The Strategy Bridge: Theory for Practice* (2010), and *Perspectives on Strategy* (2013). Although each of these books can be understood standing alone, there is unity of argument binding them which advances cumulatively through the trilogy. The argument that binds these books into a single narrative is expressed in the title of the initial volume, which claims that the metaphorical bridge of strategy requires and employs theory for practice. In *Bridge* I sought to identify and explain the workings of fundamental elements in the general theory of strategy (in 21 dicta); these are the basic elements in the structure and dynamics of our subject. *Perspectives* provided very modest amendment to my general theory (a less than radical extra dictum was added to the original 21), and examined strategy in five perspectives that had not been explored in depth in *Bridge*: these five were the relationship between intellect and military muscle, culture, morality and its ethics, geography, and technology. This third book in the trilogy moves on both from and with the material of books one and two. *Strategy and Defence Planning* strives to answer *the* strategist's professionally most defining question, 'so what'? So, what does the strategist bring to the mission of planning for defence in the interest of future national security? If, as I have claimed in earlier books, strategic theory is for and therefore about strategic practice, what can strategy offer and how should it do so? The work is an endeavour to answer this question.

As flagged in my book title, the purpose of strategy and defence planning is to meet the challenge of uncertainty about the future. Unavoidably, analysis of this challenge dominates the whole text. Indeed, it is fair to say that any effort to understand and then respond to the challenge of uncertainty must begin with frank and honest recognition of the limits to human knowledge. The dilemma central to the argument is that we are obliged to undertake a critically important mission—defence planning—for conditions concerning which we cannot obtain any direct knowledge. We do not have, and will never obtain, evidence from the future about the future. To repeat, so what does this inconvenient scientific certainty mean for efforts to plan defence purposefully for our future national security? I find that the most promising answer to this conundrum lies in strategy with its general theory, understood inclusively as necessarily accommodating political 'ends' in its fundamental architecture. In practice the principal candidates to lead the approach to defence planning are strategy, politics, history, and (scientific) defence analysis. Critical examination of the relative and sometimes complementary merits and demerits of these 'big' categories constitute the working engine of this book.

If *Strategy and Defence Planning* has been enabled vitally by the preceding books in my trilogy, no less has it been facilitated by the generous financial support provided by the Earhart Foundation of Ann Arbor, Michigan. I am greatly indebted to the Trustees of the Foundation, and particularly to its President, Dr. Ingrid Gregg. I would like to have rewarded these good people with the discovery of a miraculous method for seeing the future reliably, but alas the impossible truly proved to be such.

As usual, I am grateful for access to the excellent work of others. In particular, I am very pleased to acknowledge the assistance that I have received from the glittering efforts of Williamson Murray, John Gaddis, Paul K. Davis, Stefan Fruehling, Nassim Taleb, and—most assuredly—Michael Howard. The range of principal disciplinary affiliations of these scholars all but define the challenge of this book, hovering as it must uneasily between history and social science (with some reference at least to aspirations for the certainty of science). Each of these scholars may well feel that I have done less than the necessary and deserved justice to their particular approach to the challenge of defence planning, and they could well be right.

Lest I have been unduly obscure, I must hasten to explain that the book jacket's depiction of Pericles' Funeral Oration has been selected in order to highlight my contention that defence planning is an eternal and ubiquitous necessity for our human political estate.

In addition to my intellectual debts to scholars distant from here, I am pleased to register the support and encouragement I have received from my home institution, the University of Reading. My head of department, Alan Cromartie, has been unfailingly encouraging, while I could hardly ask for better colleagues than I have here in my fellow strategists: Geoffrey Sloan, Patrick Porter, and Beatrice Heuser. Also, I wish to make special mention of my PhD student, Lukas Milevski, who will, I am confident, go on to trouble established beliefs in the field, undoubtedly to the benefit of us all.

My professional manuscript preparer, Barbara Watts, has been challenged to perform above and beyond the bounds of what is reasonable, and I am more than merely duly grateful. A similar judgement applies to my ever faithful and amazingly tolerant family. It was not always a joy to co-exist with *Strategy and Defence Planning*, I know, because Valerie and Tonia told me! I can only apologize—as usual.

Colin S. Gray

Wokingham
September 2013

Contents

List of Figures

Our record of learning from previous experience is poor; one reason is that we apply history simplistically, or ignore it altogether, as a result of wishful thinking that makes the future appear easier and fundamentally different from the past.

The best way to guard against a new version of wishful thinking is to understand three age-old truths about war and how our experiences in Afghanistan and Iraq validated their importance.

First, war is political.

Second, war is human. People fight today for the same fundamental reasons the Greek historian Thucydides identified nearly 2,500 years ago: fear, honor and interest.

Third, war is uncertain, precisely because it is political and human.

Major General H. R McMaster, US Army
(20 July 2013)

To defend a country is an art, in fact, not a science. The challenge is that we can train scientists, but we cannot teach students to be artists. We can only educate them to appreciate art.

Jakub Grygiel
(2013)

[handwritten notes in top margin:] Carpark ticket / VS c/z / VS RualZ +Receipt / hwz/Docs. / Fuel. / Route

Introduction: Defence Planning—
a Mission about Consequences

[handwritten:] Tx @ hunor planning x Ends/ways/means / Assumptions / & Behaviours?

INTRODUCTION

How can security communities plan prudently for their defence in a future
that in large part they do not understand? It is always advisable to be ready,
but ready for what? These are the questions that must shape and drive this
analysis. Defence planning needs context, because it cannot navigate itself. In a
sense defence planning is a grim, even possibly hopeless, struggle against the
laws of physics, because the future never comes and cannot be known with
certainty. The theory of strategy insists that time is the least forgiving of its
subject's dimensions.[1] Time lost cannot be recovered, while time to be, which is
to say the future, advances eternally beyond our grasp of detailed comprehension. The temporal context is a theme that has to be central to a study of defence
planning. This is not a counsel of despair, but it carries a warning that defence
planners are wont to ignore or forget, when they earnestly pursue knowledge
that is definitively unobtainable no matter how cunning their chosen methodology or well-polished their crystal balls. The fog that obscures the future is not
dispersible, though to a helpful degree it may be compensated for.

Strategy and defence planning communities think about and plan for
their future security. The purpose is to explore how people might cope well *[handwritten:]* =INNOV
enough with the challenge posed by uncertainty. The most important con- *[handwritten:]* STAAT
textual factor for national security is an ignorance about the future that is not *[handwritten:]* PURPOSE.
reliably reducible. It is necessary to emphasize the persistent fact of the lack of
knowledge about tomorrow, because attempts to alleviate that condition can
transform worthy aspiration for a tolerable tomorrow into a highly unreliable
belief that the future is substantially so foreseeable, miraculously perhaps, that
light has dawned already.

Of course, we know a great deal about the future. That important truth
granted, it remains the case that what we do not and cannot know is potentially
lethal. It is my purpose here to look critically at how polities can approach
defence planning in peace and war. This is a search for better understanding,

[handwritten at bottom:] esp for ft → org / (as defender for attacker

not for some chimerical potion or equation that will yield right answers. Since the fundamental practical question is 'how should we prepare for defence in the future', it is all but self-evident that there can be no objectively correct answer. None of the candidate answers are testable, save by the verdict of future events. We do not know with certainty either the effect of our defence behaviour on others, nor the merit in our defence choices in and for future conditions that are bound to be influenced, perhaps decisively, by accident as well as by chance.[2] The modest aim here is to identify what is knowable about the future, to distinguish that knowledge from those things that are not knowable and to explore the ways in which we can privilege what is knowable with only tolerable unreliability in order to achieve useful leverage in preparing to enhance future security.[3]

This study cannot locate miraculously ways and means to know that which is unknowable, but it can nonetheless aspire to help improve practical security performance. Conceptual keys to sound enough security performance may be found in understanding the utility of strategy and the salience of context. The logical and practical core of the whole subject of this work is, indeed has to be, politics. If this enduring reality is not appreciated, the challenge of uncertainty is not likely to command the analytical respect that it merits. Some readers will be acquainted with the professional literature that treats matters of defence planning and programming with great expertise. Process and method, organization and analysis, are explained in impressive detail. What often is lacking, though, is due notice of the dependence of the expert method and analysis upon the quality of the policy and its politics necessary for them to have meaning well enough fitted for their tasks. This is not to be critical of defence analysis, narrowly understood, rather only to insist that such analysis is utterly dependent for its ultimate and essential meaning upon the sense in the political missions it serves through defence policy, with its planning and programming.

In its higher realm of concern, defence planning substantially is guesswork, and it has to be such—educated guesswork one hopes, but still guesswork. Frank recognition of this would typically be politically embarrassing for a government. Indeed, one suspects that the effort and ingenuity usually required in the preparation of a grand design for future national defence itself tends to blur somewhat the reality of guesswork. When policymakers and senior officials, civilian and military, insist in public on their belief that the proposed defence budget is 'the right one'—an insistence that in Britain is often expressed as being 'absolutely the right one'—they can give the appearance of having convinced themselves that the product of their labours is indeed objectively correct. In contrast, this book insists that one cannot possibly identify the right defence budget, if for no better reason than that such knowledge is unknowable. Furthermore, it will not be possible to conduct an historical audit of past performance, because of the host of uncertainties that obscure causal relationships. Defence planning and budgeting entails guesswork about a future that we ourselves, by our choices, may well influence in unpredictable, or at least unanticipated, ways. The reason for this book is to help people cope prudently with a condition of much ignorance about the future. Defence planning has to be done, notably by guesswork, because there is no reliable expert methodology available we can employ. Much about defence can and needs to be analysed with quantitative methods. But the higher reaches of policy and strategy do not lend themselves to conclusive scientific analysis metrically verifiable by testing. Human political judgement, individual and collective, friendly and hostile, can make a mockery of rational process with its frequent domination by all too subjectively unreasonable intent.[4] The deceptively simple question, 'how much is enough?' begs many vital questions that are anything but simple. The beginning of analytical wisdom has to reside in appreciation of the logically proper question, 'enough to do what?' In order to understand the challenge posed by the uncertainty associated with the ignorance of makers of and actors in defence planning and actual military behaviour, one is obliged to seek to gain a grip upon the logical structure and the pragmatic realities of strategy. To attain such understanding is the goal of this exploratory journey into the jungle of defence planning.

I admit to a preference for intellectual inclusivity that can appear, and might prove, hazardous for the independent integrity of activities that may need to be understood distinctively on their own terms. Specifically, it is a working hypothesis here that, in the main, strategy and defence planning are the same subject. It is necessary to be unambiguous about the purpose of this analysis, and that mandates the definition of key terms and clear statement of the relationships between them. This enquiry and examination addresses an eminently practical question: 'how should polities approach the challenge of uncertainty that pertains to their future security?' The primary, though not exclusive, focus of attention here is upon military concerns for future security. The strategic function for security that is critical for this study accommodates all the elements in national assets, not only those usually controlled by ministries or departments of defence. It follows that although all activity that may be categorized as defence planning has to be included in the meaning of performance of the strategy function for a security community, all that is strategic is not defence planning. Definitions can be official and authoritative, but in truth they are arbitrary. The subjects treated here have attracted an array of concepts and terms-of-art from which one must select those best fitted to cover what lies at the heart of one's concerns. The overriding and most pervasive concern here is to examine the ways in which one can best meet the challenge posed by uncertainty, with non-exclusive emphasis on military dangers. A generous array of terms is on offer to categorize the subject. The choice of 'defence planning' is not beyond all reasonable contention, but it is the closest fit with my overall purpose. However, it is necessary that the shortlist of contending concepts be identified, and that the principal reason for non-selection should be appreciated. The following are the concepts that fail to make the grade for this analysis:

- *Strategic planning* carries too much controversial conceptual baggage (over what is, and what is not, strategic) that is apt to mislead, and also a small but notable risk of encouraging an undue diffusion of attention away from military matters, given that the military patent on strategy is now well and truly lapsed.

- *Military planning* is too exclusive in focus; were it the favoured concept wording it would endanger the inclusivity mandated by the nature and character of the subject.

- *War planning* is potently but inappropriately exclusive in focus, at least in the literal meaning of words; it is necessary to plan for peace (perhaps warlike peace) as well as for war.

In some contrast:

- *Defence planning* is usefully strongly indicative of a military focus, without being formally exclusive of non-military thought and activities. It would not be wholly unjust to regard defence planning as a concept that is a healthy compromise between the commonplace understandings of strategic and military planning

By defence planning I mean preparations for the defence of a polity in the future (near-, medium- and far-term). Understood inclusively, the behaviour thus defined is understood to cover, or at least relate closely to, the following activities which need to be considered as continuous processes in governance:

- Preparation of military advice relevant to the feasibility of options for political choice as policy;

- selection and design of grand and military strategies;

- the design, making, and administration of military programmes;

- the preparation of military plans;

- coordination with complementary social, economic, and political/diplomatic programmes and activities;

- the gathering and assessment of intelligence bearing on possible risks and threats to the polity;

- cooperation with allies (and co-belligerents, if not necessarily friends).

The inclusivity sought in the above understanding is not intended to be encyclopaedically inclusive, but rather hegemonic. By this, I mean to convey clearly the range of activities most relevant to a necessarily broad, yet unambiguous, organizing concept for a mission—the preparation for the defence of a polity in the future. Official wording varies over time and certainly across frontiers. All that is intended by the definitions and illustrations offered here is unambiguous indication of what I am most concerned to examine. Real-world porosity among categories of the activity is an actuality for the subject of this study.

The terms rejected here are not deemed incorrect but rather they do not best fit my primary concern with future peril that may include the threat and use of force. I have no quarrel with others who prefer different terms. What matters most is clarity of focus. There is much to be said in praise of Morton Halperin's rather ironically reductionist triptych which equated defence policy with 'capabilities, declarations, and actions'.[5] The preference revealed here for defence as the most vital descriptor is a choice fully compatible with recognition of the significance of context.[6] Choices made in the field of defence have to be exercised in support of ideas about a future quantity and quality of a national security that always contains much more than a military component. The challenge is not so much to recognize the salience of contexts for defence planning but to prevent relevant contextual factors from overwhelming the military core of defence considerations. As a matter of logic there always is yet more context to context. But, although the integrity of defence planning as a subject for analysis can be slain by undue contextuality, a robust commonsense should suffice to save us. The subject here has a firm centre of concern in the enduring need for political communities to plan, meaning to make systematic provision, for possible or probable menaces to their security that include the threat or use of military force. All polities are obliged to attempt to plan for their security in a future that will or strongly might contain peril in some military form. The subject is a unity. It is politics, strategy, and defence planning, with each contextual for the others, notwithstanding the authoritative descending rank-ordering of the three implied here syntactically. The conceptual chaos of alternative and often apparently competing terms, and the variety of linguistic and organizational forms that find favour in different locales, should not divert us from focusing upon the largely military concerns of defence planning, richly contextual though these concerns must be. The quest for prime causes makes logical sense, but is apt to enjoy only limited traction as an aid to national security understood in its sense of national defence. Although it should be useful to improve one's understanding of the contextual factors that might stimulate the growth of strategic menace, such comprehension does not equate to the ability to cope with the dangers perceived and, perhaps, anticipated.

This book is an exploration of strategy in action. It examines the relevance of the supply of strategic thought and method to the real world of politically-driven strategic demand. Ironically, among the virtues of the term defence planning for my purpose is the fact that it does not literally require any performance covered in its name to be strategic. In historical practice, all defence planning has strategic meaning, whether intended or not by its political sponsors and military executives, but the role of strategic logic frequently is more decorative for advisable legitimation than it characterizes behaviour functionally with accuracy. Because often the subject is human behaviour under stress in the particular form of defence planning, the focus here has to be on the art of the possible, aided by such science as may be pressed into service. One has to be alert to the biasing power of one's favoured enthymemes (arguments that depend upon unstated and therefore certainly explicitly unsubstantiated assumptions). The permanence of defence planning as a behaviour of government may or may not be regarded as insufficiently substantiated by historical evidence, but assuredly its prospective future is not an unstated assumption critical to this enquiry. It is an assumption for this book that all polities need to plan for their future security by conducting defence planning. By this I mean strictly the defence needs of the future, anticipated or not, in planning with variable accuracy or luck in foresight.

At some risk to my relationships with valued friends among historians, I need to register unambiguously the phenomena of reciprocal change in continuity and continuity in change. The important meaning of those ideas for this study is the proposition that the concepts central to this analysis are permanently relevant to the human security condition. I am arguing for the salience of functional rather than particular historical analogy. It may appear ironic, possibly even strange, that a book seeking to unwrap the often opaque subject of defence planning, should be concerned to establish historical contextualization. The thesis, the mantra perhaps, that there is change in continuity and also continuity in change, may seem banal. But, those ideas point accurately to the essential unity of the subject here, across time, space, politics, culture, and technology. Although this study temporally is forward-leaning, aspiring to aid understanding useful for security provision (through defence planning) in the future, it needs to rest upon comprehension of its subject educated by relevant contextual grasp.

The beginning of wisdom about defence planning is recognition of a necessity to discard the Western logical preference for sharp clarity of analytical distinctions (either/or reasoning). The subject is approached more suitably in an inclusive spirit and with tolerance of fuzzy boundaries, Continuity and change comprise essentially a unity of thought and behaviour in the unending stream of time. The details of choices in defence planning are always changing of course, because the contexts for choice are more or less dynamic. But, most significantly, that which is attempted in defence planning is functionally eternal; it is trans-historical. This exploration seeks to help educate, not to recommend or advise. Whether or not contemporary recommendations and advice are right enough in specifics will only be revealed, with arguable authority, by future events. But what can be attempted with some confidence in the integrity of the mission is sensible preparation of the minds both of those who attempt to perform as defence planners, and also of those who have to provide political guidance for the defence-planning function. *Strategy and Defence Planning* is policy relevant, but not policy-oriented. The demands, constraints, and possible opportunities of today are ever in flux, as circumstances change, both anticipated and often not. The educated strategist and defence planner, and hopefully his or her political leaders also, have to provide necessary security for the short-term, while not doing so in a manner likely to promote insecurity in the medium- and long-terms. It is a persisting, unavoidable truth about national security and defence planning that security in the future is always incalculably hostage to decisions made today for today and the near-term. But, as France and Britain discovered in May–June 1940, sound looking plans and preparations for the relatively long-term future necessarily are hostage to the adequacy of readiness for immediate trials.[7] In other words, while superior long-term planning is admirable, it requires near-term cover. For an earlier example illustrating the potency of temporal assumptions, consider 1914. In that year the satisfaction of France and Russia with the expected evolution in the balance of power towards an agreeably victory-probable condition anticipatable for several years thence, perhaps by 1916–17, was fundamentally vulnerable to the possible or probable consequences of contemporary German anticipation of the same predicted condition.[8] This is not quite to advance an immensely reductionist claim about the triggering of the First World War in 1914, but it is to argue for the potential strength of the temporal dimension to the subject here.

As usual I am obliged to acknowledge Carl von Clausewitz as being most influential in shaping my approach to this work. The intent here is to provide a proto-theory for the subject, an explanation of defence planning both in the light shone directly by strategic theory, and also when such planning is regarded as a form taken by strategic theory in action. The great Prussian thinker has much to say that bears upon the subject. It is probably unfortunate for us that Clausewitz chose to confine himself to fulfilling the promise in the relatively narrow, though, admirably focused title of his *magnum opus, On War.* Although he argues and asserts peerlessly the true unity of politics and war, the former is scarcely in evidence in his pages. He could hardly be more clear on the importance of policy (or politics), as the legitimizer, sponsor, and provider of purpose, providing guidance to the use of force. But, the political engine for war is not examined. The subject here is markedly different from that which was the all absorbing focus for Clausewitz, which is to say war itself. However, his explanation of the role and relevance of education in theory to the practice of warfare is thoroughly appropriate to my mission. He has cautionary words for those who believe that correct answers are determinable in the strategic realm, but nonetheless he affirms strongly his conviction that one can be prepared educationally for the challenges posed by events. He advises as follows:

> [A] theory need not be a positive doctrine, a sort of *manual* for action. Whenever an activity deals primarily with the same things again and again—with the same ends and the same means, even though there may be minor variations and an infinite diversity of combinations—these things are susceptible of rational study. It is precisely that inquiry which is the most essential part of any *theory*, and which may quite appropriately claim that title. It is an analytical investigation leading to a close *acquaintance* with the subject; applied to experience—in our case, to military history—it leads to thorough *familiarity* with it. The closer it comes to that goal, the more it proceeds from the objective form of a science to the subjective form of a skill, the more effective it will prove in areas where the nature of the case admits no arbiter but talent. Theory will have fulfilled its main task when it is used to analyse the constituent elements of war, to distinguish precisely what at first sight seems fused, to explain in full the properties of the means employed and to show their probable effects, to define clearly the nature of the means employed and to show their probable effects, to define clearly the nature of the ends in view, and to illuminate all phases of warfare in a thorough inquiry. Theory then becomes a guide to anyone who wants to learn about war from books; it will light his way, ease his progress, train his judgement, and help him to avoid pitfalls . . . [9]
>
> Theory exists so that one need not start afresh each time sorting out the material and plowing through it, but will find it ready to hand and in good order. It is meant to educate the mind of the future commander, or more accurately, to guide him in his self-education, not to accompany him to the battlefield.[10]

This reasoning applies to defence planning as much as it does to Clausewitz's subject exactly, the conduct of war. A little earlier in his text, Clausewitz had written tellingly about the meaning for the limits of theory of the nature of conflict and therefore of high command in it. Consider the relevance of these thoughts to the challenge of defence planning, even though they were written with combat most in mind:

> The second attribute of military action is that it must expect positive reactions, and the process of interaction that results. Here we are not concerned with the problem of calculating such reactions—that is really part of the already mentioned problem of calculating psychological forces—but rather with the fact that the very nature of interaction is bound to make it unpredictable. The effect that any measure will have on the enemy is the most singular factor among all the particulars of action. All theories, however, must stick to categories of phenomena and can never take account of a truly unique case; this must be left to judgement and talent. Thus it is natural that military activity, whose plans, based on general circumstances, are so frequently disrupted by unexpected particular events; should remain largely a matter of talent, and that theoretical directives tend to be less useful here than in any other sphere.[11]

Clausewitz proceeds to explain that while 'courage and self-sacrifice' is what is most needed 'in the lower ranks,' requirements are rather different as one climbs the pyramid of command. We are told that

> [T]he higher the rank, the more the problems [requiring solution by intelligence and imagination] multiply, reaching their highest point in the supreme commander. At this level, almost all solutions must be left to imaginative intellect.[12]

In peacetime, even if it is fraught with tension and alarm, it is exceedingly difficult to cope prudently with the 'imaginative intellect' of foreign adversaries, let alone of such adversaries when they are actively in the field as belligerents. The general theory of strategy insists that its subject is in its nature adversarial.[13] Often in times of war arguable errors in defence planning are made plain more and less painfully by the consequences of action. However, the painful clarity provided unmistakably by loss suffered in wartime, is an ironic condition of relative enlightenment not achievable in peacetime. Always contentiously, an exception would be the appropriate lessons that might be learnt from the contemporary wartime experience of other polities with their military establishments.

The challenges to adequate performance in our subject are rather more severe even than Clausewitz chose to flag, in good part because of his deliberate focus on the conduct of warfare itself, rather than on competitive preparation for its possibility. War itself is indeed a realm strongly characterized by chance and uncertainty, but in comparison with a pre- or interwar era it is also a period wherein the identities of adversaries are relatively certain, and much is revealed about enemy choices that necessarily was substantially opaque before the war began. The outbreak of war and often the opening military moves reveal actualities that either could not have been known for certain by defence planners before the start of hostilities, or which, even if anticipated by some, could not be assumed to be reliably accurate predictions. For example, before late May 1940, RAF Fighter Command could not know that it would have to contend with a Luftwaffe menace to the British homeland from bases primarily in northern France and Belgium. The strategic geography of war has a vital impact on the sense or otherwise in defence planners' choices. A German air threat across the North Sea from Germany was one thing, such a menace from airfields in Belgium and France was quite another. Only the unpredictable course of strategic history yet to come could reveal beyond argument the quality and quantity of the future German aerial threat. What could British defence planners through all of the 1930s have assumed as plausibly the most probable strategic geography of the next great European War, should there be such a dread event to anticipate?[14]

For another example of the value of the unexpected in wartime for the clarification of the minds of defence planners, consider the consequences of Japan's ultimately Pyrrhic partial operational success at Pearl Harbor on

7 December 1941. The US Navy was obliged to accelerate dramatically the pace of its emerging battle fleet revolution in favour of fast aircraft carriers and the style of sea warfare that they enabled and indeed mandated.[15] The tactical relationship between ships and aircraft remained arguable on the evidence available through much of 1941, but thereafter the proposition that sea power was operationally viable without cover by friendly air power was definitively discredited.

Given that defence planners cannot know that which is not knowable in advance about the future, it is all too plain to see that a leading challenge they must endeavour to meet well enough is coping with the consequences of (largely) pre-war planning errors. They require a hedging strategy by way of essential insurance against unexpectedly uncooperative events, particularly those fashioned cunningly and perhaps luckily in the future by enemies.[16] It is reasonably obvious that Clausewitz did indeed hit the centre of gravity of the problem field for defence planners when he laid emphasis upon the challenge posed by interaction between belligerents. His words on the matter bear repetition: 'The very nature of interaction is bound to make it unpredictable'.[17] This judgement should be a default-like screen-saving message on every defence planner's computer because it carries awesome implications for the content of good enough practice in defence planning. Those implications can be lethal to some fashionable approaches to the subject. It is not perverse to comment that unreasonable thought and behaviour is compatible with rational process and practice. The general theory of strategy is a rational construction, but it does make signal provision for the relevance of the rational exercise of unreason. Specifically, the theory identifies strategy as being necessarily human and value-charged. The rational architecture of strategic logic, with its interdependent ends, ways, and means—fuelled suitably by shaping and driving assumptions—in historical practice always is occupied and employed by human personalities with beliefs.[18]

There can be no evasion of the inconvenient reality of the adversarial nature of every general context for strategy and its defence planning function. In wartime, mistakes in planning usually are revealed fairly promptly by enemy action, albeit not always beyond argument. This should mean that course navigation aids for strategy are discernible in events because of the evidence provided by deeds. A downside of the certain knowledge that one has made a mistake is that one has taken damage that is as certain, though hopefully limited, as its most probable cause is likely to be arguable. In noteworthy contrast to the unhappy condition of the defence planner as strategist in wartime, who is obliged to contend with the consequences of the enemy's demonstration and exploitation of his errors, the planner in peacetime remains comfortably ignorant of the fallibility of his choices. In this book I strive to encompass the practical strategic realms of the defence planner both in times of peace and of war, recognizing that enough time for recovery may or

lack of real world clarity and/or ruinous errors + false +ves = 2008 Crash.

see Text.

may not be granted once the shooting begins. Not all wars are so structured so forgivingly as to allow civilized pauses for reflection on, and perhaps recovery from, errors revealed in pre-war defence preparation. The structural problem that must be of central concern to this analysis has to be the literal unavailability of thoroughly reliable evidence concerning future defence needs. The degree of uncertainty pertaining to the future defence requirements of polities might not unreasonably be judged to be show-stopping, were it not for the intractable fact that there is no choice other than to proceed with defence planning, no matter the reality of unavoidable ignorance.

Strategy, defence planning, and uncertainty are interdependent in the vital sense that one cannot understand any of them without simultaneously grappling with the meaning and implications of the others. That granted, the subject primarily is defence planning broadly understood literally as a function essential of performance for any and every polity. For that function strategy is a tool and uncertainty a permanent, if episodically alarming, contextual reality. For a Taoist rather than an Aristotelian thought it is not useful to try to think hierarchically about strategy and defence planning because their separate identities should not be obviously distinguishable; each should serve and hugely influence the other.[19] The Venn diagram in Figure 0.1 expresses the overlapping nature of the three concepts discussed here, together with the addition of politics as a hegemonic reality for all else.

The principal behaviours and conditions of interest expressed here elementally in Figure 0.1, are relevant to the whole history of humankind as a social and political being. If one temporarily sets aside consideration of period detail, and instead asks fundamental questions about the provenance of the behaviours and conditions portrayed in Figure 0.1, the answers have potent implications. To summarize collectively, each item in Figure 0.1 effectively has a boundary-free provenance. Functionally appreciated:

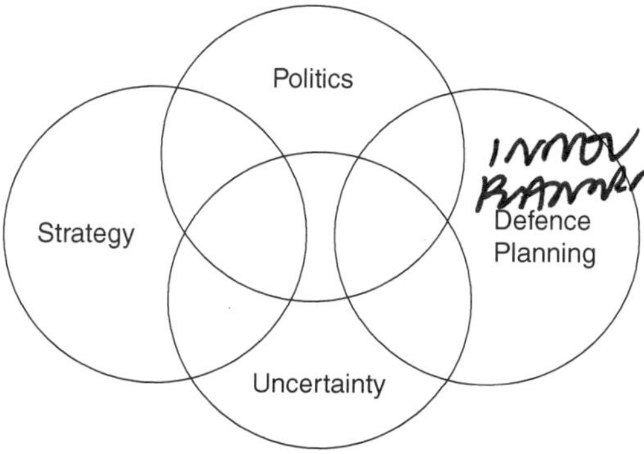

Figure 0.1 Principal Concepts

- *Politics* is a product of human nature and of the human need for order in society. Politics basically always is about relative power; its ubiquity and persistence speak conclusively to the functional necessity for governance.

- *Defence planning* is an eternal and ubiquitous necessity for all human societies; their particular political arrangements determine who does it, how, and exactly why.

- *Strategy* is a functional necessity for every human society, since all political communities need a security that must entail endeavour to match political ends with good enough available means employed in tolerably effective ways.

- *Uncertainty* is a condition of all human social and political life with respect to its future security.

If one applies Michael Howard's rule and examines the subject as one should in width, depth, and context, one is liberated from constraint by the limitations imposed by the restricted evidence of a narrowly contemporary focus.[20] The variety in detail of character across time and space is large, but the functions and conditions thematic to this study should not be considered in ways restricted by an unduly contemporary perspective on the future. Two historical illustrations are especially compelling in support of the argument for the potential contemporary value of history's rear-view mirror in order to aid navigation for the future. First, it is a matter of public record that Secretary of State and General of the Army George Catlin Marshall believed that familiarity with Thucydides' *History of the Peloponnesian War* was essential for an adequate grasp of contemporary political issues. In a speech delivered at Princeton University on 22 February 1947, Marshall spoke as follows: he said that he had doubts 'whether a man can think with full wisdom and with deep convictions regarding certain of the basic international issues of today who has not at least reviewed in his mind the period of the Peloponnesian War and the Fall of Athens'.[21] Second, there is little doubt that Winston Churchill derived extraordinary educational benefit from the effort expended in overseeing the research for, and then in writing in the 1930s, the million words of his history of his ancestor, the Duke of Marlborough. Marlborough arguably was England's greatest general of all time, while also he was an exemplary diplomat and an effective politician. It would be difficult to imagine an educational endeavour prospectively of more practical value for a coalition politician, as Churchill was required to be in the Second World War, than the gigantic literary historical project of *Marlborough: His Life and Times* (publication was completed in 1938).[22]

The two illustrations offered above highlight the important sense in the reciprocal theme of change in continuity and continuity in change. Athenians and Spartans, Englishmen and Frenchmen, had no prudent choice other than to conduct defence planning both as a tool for, and as an expression of strategy—in a political process for decision and action for which uncertainty about the future was a constant if varying condition. The subject of this study is housed temporally firmly in the early twenty-first century, but its nature has been and remains historically essentially enduring. That said, one needs to be watchful against the seductive lure of conceptual anachronism. While military historian Williamson Murray is almost contemptuously dismissive of the view held by some historians that ancient and medieval times were innocent of grand and military strategic understanding, he allows that 'there was no such concept as "strategic planning", at least as we conceive it, before the eighteenth century'.[23] My inclusive, heavily political understanding of defence planning, is much in accord with Murray's view of grand strategic sense, purposefully directed for future defence of the polity. In good part for reasons traceable to appreciation of geographical circumstances and opportunities, Murray sees modern strategic planning as having its more productive roots in the logistical needs of British and then American strategy in the eighteenth century.

The major questions and theme flagged in this Introduction are by and large employed at chapter length in the story arc for this book. The argument matures and advances cumulatively through chapters 1–6, and is digested and filtered as a whole in chapter 7. In the tersest of summaries by topics, the book proceeds as follows: definition of challenge; history; strategy; future fog; political process (and defence analysis); and conclusions about the need to be prudent and avoid paranoia. Each chapter is designed to pose and attempt to answer an important question. Those familiar questions have all been addressed in a substantial literature, sometimes to enlightening effect. However, typically the whole subject that this book seeks to reveal and understand is not deemed sufficiently relevant to be worthy of explicit consideration at length. Also, most writing about defence planning, or whatever is the precise conceptual titling for the subject preferred, is motivated by a desire to move the direction of policy and the substance of strategy and military preparation in a particularly favoured way. This literature tends to merge in content with the memoirs which advance political, strategic, and tactical, preferences, notably on the back of the authority of first-hand experience, often at the sharp end of conflict. Such works, mixing autobiography, current affairs, and advice on 'how to do it (presumably better)', are valuable and indeed necessary, but they have little in common with this book. My intention here is limited to an attempt to help those willing to be helped understand the problems of defence planning and how to approach them. The furthest that this book goes in meeting the problems and challenges it outlines, is to advise on how those problems and challenges can best be met. This is written for the purpose of education, not training; my guide is Clausewitz rather than Jomini.

This must begin with examination of the challenge to be addressed. It is particularly important that the mission be approached as a whole, and that its educational purpose intended to be of assistance to those who must practice defence planning, should not be lost on the voyage. These pages are not about choices that the author believes should be made in favour of specific actions and equipment, but they are about helping enable decision-makers make prudent choices.

In order to make progress towards understanding better how to approach the mysteries and dilemmas of defence planning, it is helpful to appreciate that just three masterful categories of ideas and experience must dominate the subject: strategy, history, and politics. Each of the three indispensably is vitally important, and all three provide cross-fertilization for the collective benefit, or to the detriment, of national defence planning. However, it is clear beyond substantial room for doubt that strategy, understood inclusively as to its theoretical architecture, deserves, needs, and requires recognition as the most masterful of the super-hero trinity identified. In the interest of optimum clarity of argument, these dicta explain simply the entire structure of all that follows:

- *Strategy* in its general theory identifies inclusively the pieces and workings that comprise the logical architecture for defence planning.

- *History* is the (only) archive of human experience that must serve as the database from which theory as explanation can or may be derived for the education of contemporary defence planners.

- *Politics* (and its then contemporary processes) yields the legitimate authority that provides decision over the substantive issues that must be addressed in defence planning.

All three categories are essential to defence planning, but as this work will argue, strategy when understood fully in its proper inclusivity among ends, ways, and means, should be understood to be at least the first among near equals in the trinity of conceptual and experiential oligarchs identified here.

NOTES

1. I explain this claim in my *Fighting Talk: Forty Maxims on War, Peace, and Strategy* (Westport, CT: Praeger Security International, 2007), 70–3.
2. Because irony would seem to be an iron law for international relations, not least for its many interacting security narratives between polities, this book must pay most careful attention to the subject examined admirably in Ken Booth and Nicholas J. Wheeler, *The Security Dilemma: Fear, Cooperation and Trust in World Politics* (Basingstoke: Palgrave Macmillan, 2008).

3. We have reason to be grateful to former US Secretary of Defence Donald Rumsfeld for his usefully terse categorization of our knowledge. He has said and written as follows: 'Reports that say something hasn't happened are always interesting to me because as we know, there are known knowns: there are things we know we know. We also know there are known unknowns: that is to say we know there are some things [we know] we do not know. But there are also unknown unknowns—the ones we don't know we don't know'. Donald Rumsfeld, *Known and Unknown: A Memoir* (New York: Sentinel, 2011), xiii. He proceeds to observe that '[t]here are many things of which we are completely unaware—in fact, there are things of which we are so unaware, we don't even know we are unaware of them.' (xiii). There is much sense in Rumsfeld's suitably humble categorization. The only offer I can make by way of possible improvement is to suggest an additional category of those things that we believe we know, but which, alas, in truth we do not.

4. The human nature and variable character of the people who must conduct all aspects of defence planning compels recognition of the vital distinction between rationality and reason. This text has to cope with the reality that people, their intentions, and their well-ordered processes of government, may proceed rationally to attempt to achieve policy goals that are wholly unreasonable in the eyes of others. It is possible to behave rationally in pursuit of ambitions that derive from a vision of the desirable that flows from values that many of us find absurd and even morally reprehensible. Such ambitions and their policy goals should be impossible to realize rationally, but we dare not assume that that is a law of history, or indeed that anything is infeasible because of the implications of its immoral enormity by our reasoning.

5. Morton Halperin, 'Nuclear Weapons and Limited War', *The Journal of Conflict Resolution*, 5 (June 1961), 161.

6. The importance of context for strategy is explained briefly in Colin S. Gray, *The Strategy Bridge: Theory for Practice* (Oxford: Oxford University Press, 2010), 38–41.

7. See N. H. Gibbs, *History of the Second World War, Grand Strategy: vol. 1, Rearmaments Policy* (London: Her Majesty's Stationery Office, 1976), ch. xxi, and Brian Bond, *British Military Policy between the Two World Wars* (Oxford: Oxford University Press, 1980), ch. 11 and Conclusion.

8. Robert A. Doughty argues credibly that 'French strategic planners [from 1892 until the outbreak of war in 1914] believed the Germans could not prevail on both fronts [east against Russia and west against France] and, even if France or Russia were beaten, the other would prevail and assure the eventual victory of the two allies'. Doughty, 'France', in Richard F. Hamilton and Holger H. Herwig, eds., *War Planning 1914* (Cambridge: Cambridge University Press, 2010), 146. Also see David Stevenson, *Armaments and the Coming of War: Europe, 1904–1914* (Oxford: Clarendon Press, 1996), ch. 6, and id., 'Strategic and Military Planning, 1871–1914', in Talbot C. Imlay and Monica Duffy Toft, eds., *The Fog of Peace and War Planning: Military and Strategic Planning under Uncertainty* (Abingdon: Routledge, 2006), 93–4.

9. Carl von Clausewitz, *On War*, tr., Michael Howard and Peter Paret (1832–4: Princeton, NJ: Princeton University Press, 1976), 141.

10. Clausewitz (1976).

11. Clausewitz (1976), 139–40.
12. Clausewitz (1976), 140.
13. Clausewitz (1976), 75, and Gray, *The Strategy Bridge*, 33–4.
14. See Paul Kennedy, 'British "Net Assessment" and the Coming of the Second World War', in Williamson Murray and Allan R. Millett, eds., *Calculations: Net Assessment and the Coming of World War II* (New York: Free Press, 1992), 19–60.
15. Andrew F. Krepinevich Jr, 'Transforming to Victory: the US Navy, Carrier Aviation, and Preparing for War in the Pacific', in Imlay and Toft, eds., *The Fog of Peace and War Planning*, 179–204, is persuasive.
16. The merit in a hedging strategy for coping with uncertainty is argued in Colin S. Gray, 'Strategic Thoughts for Defence Planners', *Survival*, 52 (June–July 2010), 159–78. While the prudence in such a strategy should be obvious, decisions on specifically how to do it (i.e. hedge against what, when and how, exactly?) can be awesomely difficult to make. I am grateful to Professor Yakov Ben-Harim, of Technion–Israel Institute of Technology, for the relevant insight in his paper, 'Strategy and Uncertainty' (2012).
17. Clausewitz, *On War*, 139.
18. I endeavour to press this point in *The Strategy Bridge*, 36–8.
19. An outstanding wide-ranging but user friendly guide to Aristotle's voluminous and hugely influential canon is Christopher Shields, 'Aristotle', in the *Stanford Encyclopaedia of Philosophy* <http://plato.stanford.edu/entries/aristotle-ethics/>. Another helpful guide to Aristotle is Alan Ryan, *On Politics: A History of Political Thought from Herodotus to the Present* (London: Allen Lane, 2012), ch. 3. In notable contrast to the Aristotelian, which became largely the Western scientific insistence upon correct classification and the making of clear choices as to what is correct and incorrect in particular cases, the holistic Oriental inclusivity of Taoism encompasses and probably helps enable a more subtle, if more complex, way of thinking and behaving. See Ralph D. Sawyer (tr.), *The Tao of War: The Martial 'Tao Te Ching'* (Boulder, CO: Westview Press, 1999), and Derek M. C. Yuen, 'The System of Chinese Strategic Thought', *Comparative Strategy*, 29 (July–August 2010), 245–59.
20. Michael Howard, *The Causes of Wars and other essays* (London: Counterpoint, 1983), 215–17.
21. Paul A. Rahe, 'Thucydides as educator', in Williamson Murray and Richard Hart Sinnreich, eds., *The Past as Prologue: The Importance of History to the Military Profession* (New York: Cambridge University Press, 2006), 99.
22. Winston S. Churchill, *Marlborough: His Life and Times,* 4 volumes in 2 books (1933–8; London, George G. Harrap, 1947). My view, that Winston Churchill derived considerable practical benefit from his study of Marlborough, also is to be found in Geoffrey Best, *Churchill and War* (London: Hambledon and London, 2005), 260–6, and Williamson Murray, 'Thoughts on Grand Strategy', in Murray, Richard Hart Sinnreich, and James Lacey, eds., *The Shaping of Grand Strategy: Policy, diplomacy, and war* (New York, Cambridge University Press, 2011), 27–80.
23. Williamson Murray, *War, Strategy and Military Effectiveness* (Cambridge: Cambridge University Press), 8. Also see his ch. 6, 'History and Strategic Planning: From Rome to 1945'.

Q: Is there an Red of industry link here?

1

Defining the Challenge

Preparation, Not (Only) Plans

FOREIGN PARTS: THE FUTURE

The theory of bureaucratic politics claims with much evidence in its support that where one stands largely determines where one sits.[1] That near truism can usefully be joined as an aphorism held in high regard by the proposition that what one stands for is notably determined by where one is sitting. The centre of gravity of a study of defence planning has to be the black hole from which no light can escape that is the future. Particular strategies are designed, developed, executed, and fine-tuned not only in ways and for outcomes that reflect approximately the balance of power among the stake-holding contributors, but also by beliefs, including assumptions, then current about the future. It is one thing to bring a person to recognize fully enough that his knowledge of the future is unreliable, but it can be handier still to trigger recognition that particular definition of a desirable future will be influenced critically by the contemporary contexts of ideas and circumstances.

There is no choice other than to plan defence for tomorrow on the basis of assumptions made today, as well as with some of the legacy of consequences from yesterday's assumptions. Of course, today is ever shifting, but it is not entirely plausible to believe that it will be revealed to be ever more friendly by the events of tomorrow. Alas, neither today nor tomorrow have fixed properties. Because theoretical physics cannot be of practical assistance to the defence planner who must struggle with a future that is as dynamic as the present and the past, it is only prudent for one to admit as necessary to such ignorance as is irreducible, and seek ways to cope well enough with that lack of knowledge. Ignorance of the future is unavoidable and is a condition that cannot be reduced reliably, but behaviour in this ignorant state is in useful measure discretionary. This is contentious, one must confess, given the power of the understanding of today manifested as a 'presentist' cloud that is contextual for the reasoning that conducts defence planning, even be it ever so rationally performed. Because future defence planning has to be done today, it is contemporary attitudes and beliefs that rule. Interpretation of very recent experience tends to hold dominant sway over planning for the future, even though it will reflect a serious lack of historical perspective. Policymakers and military strategists may well reject recent, perhaps current, negative experience as a model for the future, probably not realizing that the model in disfavour possibly is accorded too much weight as an option, even when its value for the future is denied. American examples of this phenomenon were the clear rejection of limited conventional warfare after Korea (1950–3), of more irregular war and counterinsurgency (COIN) after Vietnam (1965–73), and today—again—of more protracted episodes of counterinsurgency (COIN) and attempted nation-building after Afghanistan and Iraq (2001–2014?).[2] Pain aversion is both a familiar and an easily understandable reality in the politics of defence planning. Defeat or overly expensive success (i.e. 1914–18 for Britain and France) is an unpleasant reality that defence planners understandably seek to avoid. However, the 'never again' resolve can lack strategic sense to the point of its being an absurdity, given the absence of plausible historical contextuality. The context that rules the aversion extant is of course the recent past and the present.

In each of the historical cases just cited, the primary reason for the rejection of a particular kind of national strategic experience in the future was scarcely military-strategic at all. Clausewitz was right when he wrote that 'war is not a mere act of policy but a true political instrument, a continuation of political activity by other means'.[3] The US polity rejected, seriatim, limited conventional war in the 1950s, irregular war in the 1970s, and currently is in the process of rejecting irregular war of the COIN variety again, in the 2010s. The repeated American political decisions not to wage a particular unfavoured kind of war and warfare ever again, meaning commonly in practice for a generation (of approximately twenty years, at least), is not usually bereft of forward-looking strategic reasoning and military analysis. But one should not be misled into believing that post-war debate over future defence plans is primarily shaped by competing visions of the future. Such visions will be real enough in public discourse, but their traction in the political process that conducts defence planning and selects strategies tends to owe far more to the influence of recent experience than to arguably prudent prescience in statecraft and strategic thought.

Defence planning needs recognition as a profoundly political endeavour, as well as one conducted sometimes in the light of military-strategic reason, should that be unmistakeably on offer, and by expert analytical method. To focus near exclusively on the apparent logic of strategic prudence and sound methods of defence analysis would be to risk misunderstanding this subject. America's failures in the 2000s by its own domestic political definition, to secure political victory out of military success, resulted in policy and strategy choices that, in effect, denied the particular contextual integrity of the rejected recent past and present. Each of the historical cases cited was distinctive in detail, but similarly each demonstrates the potency of 'today' (1953, 1973, 2013) over choices in defence preparation for tomorrow. The aphorism that claims that generals (and other strategists and defence analysts) are inclined to plan to refight the last war, is wrong on several grounds, but nonetheless it is useful in registering the high relevance of the recent past to expectation of the future. While it is true that much is learnt about war by its conduct, it is also true to claim that particular experience of war educates by what is currently believed to be negative example. Many Americans thought that they had learnt by bitter and frustrating experience in Korea how not to wage modern warfare, especially of a limited conventional kind. Vietnam, Iraq, and Afghanistan, similarly have educated or mis-educated by the deed in the field.

Limited conventional war could not be, at least it was not, tailored success-fully to the strategic needs of America's mission in Vietnam, and the profes-sional worth in the enduring basics of COIN rediscovered by an unmistakeably failing America in Iraq and Afghanistan in the late 2000s, were sufficient neither to pacify abroad, nor to produce evidence of success adequate to sustain support at home. Societies and their political representatives assess their future strategic requirements based not so much on the needs estimated for the future cases that are identified speculatively, for those needs are unknown, but rather what is believed to be known today. This distinctly 'presentist' perspective is the product of contemporary attitudes and opinions formed or reinforced by very recent experience. In addition, it is important to be aware of persisting cultural attitudes that have significant calorific value for strategic choices about the future.

Although defence planning in a vital sense must be about the future, in practice it cannot help but be dominated by people whose whole knowledge and experience is only of the past. Even when some vivid experience is explicitly rejected as a model for future behaviour, it may well have played a large shaping role in planning for the future. Both victories won and victories denied persist as ghostly analogies, influencing efforts in the present to prepare well enough for the future. In their anticipation of the future it is important for defence planners to be aware of their dependence on what they believe they know from the past and the present.

It is tempting to characterize the future as ungoverned space, but to do so would be a serious error. The defence planner has to recognize that the future will no more be ungoverned than was the past or is today. Unknown and unknowable in detail, does not mean ungoverned, let alone ungovernable. The challenge for the planner is to guess prudently as to the identity and relative weight of influence among the elements that will be prominent in the governing of the future. Political power assuredly will fill any temporary vacuums in future space significant for our security. In political terms, the security space for the defence planner is ever contextually adversarial; this is the substantially anarchical reality of world politics and is therefore a given for the defence planner. Even when no plausibly dominant enemy is credibly predictable, it is only prudent to assume that enemies lurk currently undetectable in the future. Because they always have done so, it would be an irresponsible defence planner who would be sufficiently bold as to suggest their functional irrelevance. It is true that card-carrying defence analysts can be trusted to find future dangers to the nation, and if they cannot be found they certainly can be created by our catalytic action. The character of war has changed radically, but it continues unaltered in its nature. The proposition that war has a future of indefinite duration is among the safer predictions that can be offered.[4]

CALCULATIONS?

People can be surprised, if not shocked, to learn that planning for national defence should be regarded and approached more accurately, certainly more honestly, as an art than a science or even a social science. This book is about politics and people. The ubiquity and pervasiveness of human agents in and doing politics guarantees a range of potential individual and collective behaviours that makes a mockery of pretentious efforts to render the subject here fit for exploration by quantitative methods. If history demonstrates anything conclusively, it is that politics is not a science, except arguably in the relaxed sense of social science. This readily explained and easily verifiable fact is in danger of being forgotten, or perhaps not grasped at all, by societies that license people as political scientists without appreciating realistically what the term does and does not mean. Considered positively, a political scientist is a person who studies political phenomena scientifically. The descriptor means that political phenomena are examined on objective principles in a systemic way, for the purpose of explanation, which is the role of theory.[5] These points are not advanced as argument, rather are they authoritative according to the superior contemporary dictionary of the English language. However, the authentically stark differences between the physical and mathematical sciences on the one hand, and the social sciences on the other, are nowhere near as well understood as they need to be if the challenges to the defence planning function are to be appreciated as they should.

To risk undue reductionism in the interest of clarity:

1. To be *scientific* means to pursue truth in the form of (repeatedly demonstrable) reliably correct answers derived from application of correct theory to specified problems.

2. To be social scientific means to pursue usable truth in the form of explanation of phenomena that generally is true, though some exceptions usually are admitted and condoned.

3. To be artistic means to pursue truth by creative responses to unique, if generically familiar, challenges. Artists may behave systematically, but they are likely to rewrite theory to suit the circumstances and their imagination.

The whole subject of this text is plagued with the ill consequences that follow misunderstanding of the differences between science, social science, and art. Because defence planning in most aspects is characterized by metric applications, it is not hard to be persuaded that the numbers that often function in effect as the lingua franca of national security have an authority largely on their own terms. For example, it can come to be believed that there is a correct number of capital ships, army divisions, air wings, or ICBMs (suitably deployed and possibly defended actively). Countries in the Western world have public cultures deeply respectful of science. Moreover many of the people in the extended defence communities of the West have professional skills that are largely technical. Especially is this true for the United States, but by no means is it dominantly characteristic only there. The problem is not with defence numeracy per se; indeed, how could it be, with so many matters important to defence planning needing careful, including sceptically critical, quantitative analysis. The problem is rather that which occurs when a significant cohort of technical (defence) issues is approached by its most dedicated functionaries (defence professionals) as if it were a set of scientific challenges that could be met with analytical methodology capable of yielding objectively correct answers.

What can usefully be calculated, should be so treated. But, the sense in the calculations is hostage to the answer provided to the strategist's basic question, 'so what?' As operations research is dependent on the quality in the systems analysis to which it should be subordinate, so systems analysis needs validation by strategy, policy, and politics.[6] What is argued here was claimed with admirable directness by Clausewitz in words already quoted in the Introduction. He claimed that 'the higher the rank, the more the problems multiply, reaching their highest point in the supreme commander. At this level, almost all solutions must be left to imaginative intellect'.[7] Although Clausewitz was writing with generalship in war uppermost in his mind, we can adapt and apply his powerful general argument to the field of defence planning. For example, episodically from the early 1700s until today, in war after war, and sometimes in rather warlike peacetime also, Britain had to decide on the scale and character of a military continental commitment with an Expeditionary Force (BEF).[8] Often there was controversy over the political, and especially the strategic, utility of such a Force. From Tories in the War of Spanish Succession

(1702–14) who favoured a fairly strictly maritime, colonial, and coastal raiding amphibious strategy to oppose the menace of French hegemony, to the apostles of victory through strategic air power in the 1930s, it was obvious that largely contextual matters of policy and strategy needed to be settled, before defence planning could proceed with any expectation of continuity of effort being politically sustainable. What kind of a war does one wish to wage, if one finds one must fight one?[9] Should one plan for war to be won by the navy, with the army in a strictly supporting role? Large questions of that sort assuredly mandate the conduct of detailed defence planning. But, that planning has to proceed with guidance given continuously, or for a generous gloss, dynamically, by a strategic, including a grand strategic, sense that has to enjoy the authority of high policy and the politics that make, sustain, and may change it.

An important difficulty with and for defence planning is the necessity for a polity's defence effort to have both internal and external integrity. The internal integrity of the effort is far easier to understand and maintain correctly than the external. If, by analogy, one thinks of defence planning as an architectural challenge, it is easy to appreciate the range of difficulties that need to be addressed and mastered. The national defence effort requires the internal integrity that allows it to work well enough as a system, indeed as a system of systems. 'Teeth' and 'tail' need to match, while the entire military machine depends upon strategic guidance in defence planning that has a reasonably settled view as to the probable, certainly the desirable, character of future military operations. A classic example of contrasting endeavours in defence planning is the case of RAF Fighter Command versus the Luftwaffe in the summer of 1940. The RAF was proved by events to have achieved both internal and external integrity.[10] With regard to its internal integrity as a system of systems, RAF Fighter Command worked well, while its external integrity also was demonstrated by events to be fit for strategic purpose. The contrast with the Luftwaffe is startling, notwithstanding the popular fallacy that the Battle of Britain was won only by a 'narrow margin'. The margin was not narrow. Fighter Command had the resources that it needed to succeed in its primary combat task of homeland air defence in daylight, and also, as important, the system was large enough to achieve strategic victory. In other words, Hugh Dowding's Fighter Command had internal integrity as a complex system-of-systems that functioned well enough. In addition, in vital strategic regard, the Command had external integrity in its proven ability to see off history's first independent strategic air campaign.[11]

Of particular significance for the subject here is the clarity and strength of the connection between Dowding's strategic concept for the guidance of the air defence campaign, and the excellence for their day of most of the programmed efforts that delivered the Fighter Command of summer 1940.[12] Dowding planned, indeed had long prepared, a sustainable combat effort keyed to his ability to rotate fatigued pilots, provide adequate (if barely) operational training for novice replacements, replace lost aircraft, repair damaged ones, and have ample reserves of spare parts, fuel and ammunition. The RAF was always likely to win an air battle over Britain, provided the Germans were poorly directed strategically; equipped inadequately for the campaign; unwilling or unable to learn rapidly from their mistakes—and so long as the RAF did not commit gross operational error, and was not required to fight at a great disadvantage over the continent. It is important to note just how complementary the two perspectives on integrity were shown to be. Dowding's strategic sense was crucial for the guidance he provided to Air Vice Marshal Keith Park, who waged the Battle of Britain operationally as Commander of 11 Group RAF Fighter Command. But, the high competence of those two senior officers would not have sufficed to ensure victory, had defence planning in the 1930s not chosen, programmed, manufactured, and trained, the various parts of the system that needed to work together in 1940. In critical contrast, although the Luftwaffe had excellent air crew and aircraft, it was not well equipped for the kind of campaign it was ordered to conduct in August and September 1940. Even had the Luftwaffe been better equipped and trained than it was for the coercive mission against the British homeland in 1940, it is more likely than not that the lack of strategic sense in and behind German political and military operational choices would have proved lethal to the prospects for campaign success.

The defence planner faces inescapable challenges from two directions. His future plot for defence provision must serve well enough internally, meaning as a military system (of systems), while simultaneously it will have to be able to serve the polity adequately in combat. It is a truth generally under acknowledged that foreign policy must work well enough at home, whence it originates, before it can be effective abroad. This same near truism holds with abundant force for defence planning. Such plans and their implementing material programmes are not immaculately strategic designs settled prudently strictly on the basis of prescient anticipation of external risks, threat, and danger.

Although perceived danger from abroad is vital, if not quite essential, fuel for defence planning, debate over the probable reality of such danger, as well as of how best to cope with it should it materialize, is hostage to domestic politics inclusively understood. It is not impossible to conduct defence planning in the absence of an obviously dominant enemy, but to do so tests the credibility of politicians and their voters in democracies, usually beyond the bounds of prudence. When plain apparent evidence of menace is lacking, strategies of hope and goodwill are favoured, duly blessed by the absence of current evidence of the need for defence. There are severe limits to the extent to which government is able persuasively to argue for defence planning as insurance against the certainty of danger in a future that currently is uncertain in nearly all important respects. The historical record shows that typically democracies need to have serious menace demonstrated to be such before they will choose to believe in it. Teleological, Whiggish assumptions about an allegedly inexorable improvement in human political behaviour are quite widespread among decent liberal-minded people, including scholars who should know better. If, by definition, tomorrow must be brighter than yester-day or today, it is extraordinarily challenging to attempt to argue conserva-tively for prudence in defence planning. Threats that are only imagined and anticipated in the abstract tend not to play well to taxpayers today. Hope for moral progress elides mystically into substantial faith in its likelihood.

The external integrity of the product of defence planning is partnered by an internal integrity that has two components: the military system itself and also its domestic political context. Outlined here in the briefest manner is the basic structure of the subject. Defence planning, though only generally, can be said to face abroad, but having said that one must not fail to acknowledge the facts that it must both function effectively internally as a system and be politically tolerable at home. Everything connects to everything else.

1. Politics behind governance must license defence effort in general, and endorse or condone particular defence choices.
2. Strategy should guide defence planning and military execution in at-tempted realization of future political objectives.
3. Defence planning must translate strategic guidance into a capable range of feasible ways to be employed by achievable military means in the service of politics and its policy.

The Gold Standard

This book argues that the concept of good enough defence planning is both meaningful and in practice should be attainable. The intention here is to help define the mission of defence planning in a way useful for practice. It is essential to recognize the nature of the challenge that defence planning seeks to meet. That challenge is not to pick the future defence posture, and hence the plans to secure it that might be celebrated with a gold medal only in the future. The medal would be merited by defence plans proved by events to have been good enough to support adequately national security by reasonable definition.

The task set here is difficult, but not impossible in the way that analytical pursuit of allegedly discretely correct defence posture would have to be. Defence planning is good enough when it enables a polity to meet successfully the challenges that future politics throws its way. Because defence planning functionally is needed by all polities all of the time, though admittedly with varying intensity of need over time, any and every possible context of per-ceived and misperceived threat is relevant to this examination. The writ of this enquiry is by no means limited to a particular condition of world political disorder. There have been many reasons declared and otherwise for enmities and wars in world politics; self-evidently the character and degree of the challenge posed by uncertainty has varied widely. For illustration by recent example, consider the abrupt alteration in principal challenges to American defence planning since 1945. In summary form, the principal threat architec-ture perceived by the United States shifted as follows:

1. January–May 1945: Germany and Japan.
2. May–August 1945: Japan.
3. September 1945–1989 (arguably December 1991): the Soviet Union.
4. 1990–September 2001: no dominant threat.
5. September 2001–2013: 'Terror', Al Qaeda in particular; violent Islamism (Jihadism).
6. 2013–: new nuclear-weapon states (NWS), and China.

For notably, though not exclusively, geopolitical reasons there have been many relatively stable relationships of conflict between polities.[13] Long-term enmi-ties simplify the task of the defence planner, though they can also miseducate when they feed assumptions about probable future belligerency that cannot shift adaptively to changing circumstances. The essential structure of the challenge of uncertainty to defence planning is immune to change in political and strategic contexts. Some uncertainties certainly are strategically more significant than are others, but the fog that is the product of ignorance about the future is present in all historical cases. Even when adversaries are stable in identity, political and most strategic geography, and technology, so numerous and possibly potent are the contributing dimensions to politics and strategy that uncertainties abound.[14]

Although much attention in these pages is addressed to the identification of approaches that should maximize the prospects for success in defence plan-ning, two kinds of sovereignty are capable of ensuring failure. These sover-eignties must never be forgotten as one proceeds in pursuit of promising methodology—politics and strategy. While the two unquestionably are hier-archically tiered in favour of politics, each, independently, can exercise lethal practical sway over the effectiveness of defence planning. Politics, strategy, and defence planning do not constitute three discrete activities, plainly distinctive though each certainly is in its core function. The activities overlap, indeed interfuse, with implications that should be troubling to those who try to insist on sharp impermeable boundaries between categories, regardless of fuzzy actualities. Defence planning employs, and in a fundamental sense is, strategy in order to do politics. This highly reductive characterization of the broad subject here carries complicating baggage for understanding. Even the most prudent and technically all but impeccable exercise in defence planning cannot be protected reliably against folly or even just bad luck of kinds largely existentially contextual to the planner's responsibilities. It is necessary to register the interdependencies among politics, strategy, and defence planning, because the third ranked item (defence planning) cannot otherwise be analysed usefully. Politics and strategy are not simply episodic contextual sources of harassment to defence planning as a permanent function and process of government, rather are they integral and vital components of that process.

When one considers the uncertainties that do or plausibly could frustrate a defence planning process, those definable expansively as political and strategic loom large indeed. Contrary though it is to the professional military ethos in some polities—the United States for a prominent example—the soldier's subject is politics, and the inescapable political meaning of what he does is the product of strategic effect. *Ab extensio*, defence planning in peace and war is by reasonable definition, substantially political and strategic effort. This is the reality expressed unmistakeably in the geometry of the Venn diagram presented as Figure 0.1 in the Introduction. Political choices made at home and abroad often have little basis in competent strategic reasoning, while such strategic purpose as they do command may bear no close relation to the material products of defence planning. However, it is only fair to recognize that the large measure of art, of creative design in the inspired imagination, in politics and its violent expression in war, renders futile a search for certainty in making prudent defence planning choices.

The gold standard for competent defence planning has to be one that accepts **as** givens the uncertainties of politics, domestic and foreign, and also the sheer range of potentially troubling influences that lurk permanently in the nature of strategy in all its dimensions. Above all else one should point to the vagaries of politics fuelled by human beings who can be notably diverse in their risk aversion. The defence planner's task should be understood to be the mission of making good enough provision for the national security, most especially, though not exclusively, in its military aspects.[15] The relevance of non-military considerations to the defence planning process is explained in substantial part by the inclusive logic of grand strategy as contrasted with military strategy. That logic finds both military and other support for national defence planning in the forming of alliances and coalitions. For example, there was a crucial sense in which the Soviet (Red) Army played the leading part in the team effort essential to the winning of the Second World War for Britain and America, as well as for its political masters at home in the USSR. Defence planning always has political context; its content cannot be appreciated soundly if political circumstances are neglected.

The golden rule that advises the pursuit of defence planning goals deemed good enough to cope adequately with the uncertainties of politics and strategy is all very well as an airy generalization, but what should it mean in practice?

What is Good Enough?

The central challenge to the process of defence planning is the need to be sufficiently correct on matters that might prove to be important for future national security. There can be no simple answer to the general question for the planner concerning what may be good enough, though the reasons why such indeterminacy is a fact tend not to be understood as clearly as they should. Some among those who both propose defence plans and pass (domestic) political judgement on them, believe sincerely, but alas erroneously, that national defence is a subject that poses definite questions capable of being answered directly and exactly with confidence. Such a mindset is tolerable only when it is held by those who understand that the definite details they are considering are isolated and arguably significantly fixed items in what otherwise in the main is concealed by a fog of uncertainty. Because politicians and officials understandably are reluctant to disclose the true quantity and quality of their inescapable ignorance, they are obliged to defend defence planning decisions with claims for wisdom that cannot be judged with reliable accuracy at the time they are made. Strictly—if ungenerously—regarded, public debate on future defence tends to be a case of the blind leading—or almost as likely misleading—those who are also blind. That said, defence planning has to be conducted, regardless of the inconvenient fact that the future is substantially unknowable, and not even capable of being anticipated with much confidence. The mission here is to appreciate the nature of uncertainty about the future for the purpose of helping enable better understanding of the defence planning function and challenge. Defence planning only becomes mission impossible if one foolishly demands a certainty of knowledge that is unattainable. Accepting some risk of premature disclosure, I need to register confidence in the proposition that the most useful source of assistance to those who guide future defence planning can only be the historical record, frequently ambiguous and contestable though it is. Argument for this belief, though with reference to grand strategy rather than the somewhat more narrowly-focused realm of defence planning, has been advanced with characteristic clarity by the historian Williamson Murray. He advises as follows:

> History provides a number of crucial elements necessary to craft realistic strategic expectations. It is not so much the direct lessons of the past that are germane to think about the future; rather it is the understanding of the ambiguities and

uncertainties that political and military leaders have confronted in the past and will confront in the future that is the basis of any successful grand strategy.[16]

If one substitutes defence planning for Murray's grand strategy, the fit of his reasoning with my subject is all but exact. In part because most issues in and pertaining directly to defence planning lend themselves to numerical representation such as numbers of men and women, items of equipment, missile accuracy and reliability, and have an almost reassuring physicality, reference to them conveys an aura of confidence, even familiarity, which may obscure the real uncertainties. A citizen listening to and perhaps participating personally in public debate about future defence plans, might well be shocked were the true extent of ignorance made plain. The public policy issue of the day may be framed and organized with reductive economy simply in the following question; will the proposed defence plans be good enough to meet our future security needs? It is almost frightening to recognize the distinguishable, if probably interacting, sources of uncertainty thus posed. To be specific though not exhaustive:

1. How far into the future need concern us seriously today?
2. Who or what in the future might make us feel insecure?
3. How much security do we need, can we afford, and might we advance through our defence planning?
4. What will be the character of our future security environment?
5. What will conflict, war, and warfare, be like in the future?
6. How proficient will our national military forces be in the future, quantitatively and qualitatively?
7. Given that every conflict and war with its warfare is unique in its character, though not in its nature, how confident can we be that our armed forces will be tactically, strategically, and ultimately politically effective?

The questions above are deployed in illustration of the facts of a notably dynamic uncertainty. When defence plans are made for the future, it cannot be known with high confidence when such plans may be needed; where they will be needed; against who they may be needed; how hard the resources planned for will be required to fight; or what the 'grammar' of future warfare will be like.[17] These are not trivial sources of doubt.

The more closely one looks at the defence planning mission, the less stable the whole context is recognized to be. Everything is a work in progress, with many of the elements vital to performance in defence planning being by their nature unstable. If one seeks a good enough defence, how can that arguably modest goal be attained when one cannot know reliably what our defences should be planned to be good enough to achieve? As an important addition to the foci of uncertainty itemized above, it is important to remember that the content of each of the seven sources of concern is in temporal motion. As time moves on, the 'now' and the 'then' in lockstep, both parties to the relationship will be shifting, sometimes in surprising ways and at unanticipated speed. The perception of threat changes, as both perceiver and perceived alter in characteristics that can be significant. While there are major continuities in attitudes and behaviour over time towards statecraft and its defence planning, it is unusual, though not unprecedented, for them to be all but immobile for a long period. To comprehend the problems for defence planning for the purpose of locating prudent, affordable, and appropriate solutions or partial answers, first it is necessary to be honest in recognizing Donald Rumsfeld's known unknowns, the predictable fact that there are unknown (and unknowable) unknowns, and there are unknowns that are falsely known.[18] The defence planner in effect is a practising strategic theorist. Of necessity, he is obliged to express through plans with their derivative programmes, how national security in the future should be able to support the nation's safety. The defence planning function provides explanation of anticipated future national security—and that is theory. To do this, even to attempt it, is a heroic task.[19]

Preparation, Plans, and Planning

Some readers will be familiar with Harry R. Yarger's excellent book, *Strategy and the National Security Professional*.[20] Ironically, perhaps, I find little in Yarger's book with which to disagree, even though we may appear to have significant differences. The key distinction between my intellectual framework and that of Yarger is my preference for treating the defence planning function more rather than less inclusively. Yarger argues that

> *Strategy is not planning.* As described above, it partakes of a different mind-set. Planning makes strategy actionable. It relies on a high degree of certainty—a world that is concrete and can be addressed in explicit terms. In essence it takes a grey world and makes it black and white through its analysis of the facts and assumptions about the unknown. Planning is essentially linear and deterministic, focusing heavily on first-order causes and effect. It assumes that the future results can be precisely known if enough is known about the facts and the conditions affecting the undertaking. The planning process is essential to reduce uncertainty at the operational and tactical levels—it allows detailed actions to be prescribed.[21]

Yarger goes on to claim, unexceptionally, that

> *Planning is not strategy.* It is essential for the successful execution of a strategy—making strategy actionable, but requires a different mind-set. Most national security professionals are *trained* for the certainty of planning, but must be *educated* for uncertainty as they enter the strategic realm.[22]

Yarger's view is both admirably clear and sensible. However, it does risk overly sharp categorization. It is my preference to take conceptual and, by implication, practical risks of a contrasting kind. This book argues that defence planning most accurately and usefully should be regarded as a function that in effect achieves a fusion of strategy and planning. This fusion can be understood appropriately more in terms of preparation to protect in the future, rather than as plans ready enough for implementation should they fit the strategy chosen in that future. Possibly contrary to appearances, this perspective is not intended to imply any demotion in the essentiality of concrete plans that need to be definite in relevant detail for efficient execution. What I am arguing is for a more inclusive understanding of strategy than usually is the case. It is damaging to strategic performance if one holds that while strategists create and may guide the execution of strategy, planners produce the plans required to provide purpose and order through definite instructions for operational commanders and their tactical forces. This conceptual architecture is not really incorrect, but it endangers comprehension of the essential unity of the subject.

Strategies are theories, which is to say they are purported explanations of how desired effects can be achieved by selected causes of threat and action applied in a particular sequence. The full title of my first book in this trilogy, *The Strategy Bridge: Theory For Practice*, may have risked understating the connections between strategic theory and strategic practice, because there is a vital sense in which all strategy must be done tactically. The unavoidable logical implication of this argument is that all behaviour, which is tactical by definition, also is strategic. A number of people have stumbled upon the high plausibility of this claim, as the popularity of the novel-sounding concept of the 'strategic corporal' attests.[23] Theorists have responded to the changing character of most contemporary conflict simply by applying incorrectly the standard adjectival label, 'strategic', to ever lower levels of tactical effort. Arguments favouring corporals with the badge of strategy have in truth been correct, but not for the reason usually offered. Corporals are strategic because all military behaviour (tactics in action) has some strategic weight, be it net positive or negative in consequence, great or small.[24]

When strategically viewed, the world does not encourage the neat categories that can appear sharp and distinctive in PowerPoint™ presentations. Politics are not always strictly domestic or international, wars and warfare are not conveniently divisible into regular or irregular types, and strategies cannot usually be labelled as exclusively offensive or defensive. The components of strategy itself—ends, ways, and means—are so interdependent in practice that an insistence upon conceptual clarity threatens misunderstanding of its true unity.[25] The fairly recent rediscovery of the concept of grand strategy reflects a belated appreciation of the integrity of the belief that national security is a whole subject, even though it needs to be approached with due attention to the distinctive natures of its several principal parts (e.g. diplo-macy, politics, economics, intelligence, military capabilities). The inclusivity favoured here commands a respect for grand strategy, unduly ambitious though this very big idea tends to be when one searches for historical cases of its creation and possibly reasonably consistent practice.[26]

Among the merits of grand strategy as a conceptually inspiring and guiding light is its definitional insistence upon recognition of the entire scale and scope of the context for defence planning. The conception, design, and purposefully attempted practice of grand strategy is probably historically unusual. Indeed Murray goes so far as to claim that

> [d]uring much of the past, a strategic framework, much less a grand strategy, has rarely guided those responsible for the long-term survival of polities either in a political or military sense.[27]

The principal reasons for its rarity lie in the complexity of its relevant concerns and the persistent reality of unanticipated contingency.[28] The historical reality is that polities most typically attempt to do what they need to do only when events, actual or unarguably desperately imminent, seem to mandate action. However, it can be an error to focus unduly upon a notion of rational choice in grand strategy. Culture and custom play roles in strategic choice, often as preferences apparently exercised with minimum fresh effort by the momentum of inertia. Habit and tradition, which may or may not be evi-denced persuasively by more than expediency and current convenience, are players in strategic history.[29]

Although this author is Anglo–American and the content of the text somewhat favours the national experiences of Britain and the United States, the questions addressed here have eternal universal relevance. All polities, everywhere and at all times, have needed to plan for their defence in the future. The uncontroversial fact that most polities in history did not create and maintain defence planning staffs on the model of the Great General Staff of nineteenth-century Prussia, let alone the humungous bureaucracy of today's Pentagon, is beside the essential point. Indeed, modern defence planning is exactly that, modern. However, the function of defence planning has been of permanent, if contextually variable, importance at all times in the past. Provided one is able to see Helmuth von Moltke (the elder) in full historical context, which is to say in the entire stream of time, illustration of argument with modern examples need not mislead.[30] It is necessary to recognize that the concept of the defence planning function was not invented in nineteenth-century Prussia, even though military planning changed radically then, and continued to expand in quantity, if not always in quality, for the next two centuries. As the general theory of strategy insists, 'strategy is logistical'.[31] No matter which strategy is chosen, which geographical environments are ex-ploited, and which period in history is one's subject of most concern, the narratives of supply and movement that comprise logistics explain essential enablers or disablers for statecraft and generalship. Obviously, the character of the logistical detail in defence planning varies widely for reason of all the factors that in specific terms translate strategy's general theory into particular strategies. Those specific strategies were only feasible when they were meaningful explanation of what was necessary or at least advisable in a particular period. Strategy was always in large part a logistical story.[32] Military planning staffs inspired by the Prussian model became the norm by the late nineteenth-century. Belatedly the United States, and even more belatedly Britain, bowed somewhat reluctantly to the need for professional planning revealed in the British case by the evidence of experience in the Boer War.

The industrial revolution had implications for war that mandated defence planning on a scale and to a professional standard that certainly was novel. Most specifically, the coming and the maturing of the railway permitted logistical quantities that states could not decline to attempt to exploit: the railway age was not discretionary.[33] This is not to suggest or even imply that the function and concept of defence planning employed here is synonymous with war planning; it is not. Nonetheless, there can be no evading the sense in General McMaster's judgement that 'war is the final audit of military institutions'.[34] As a codicil to those words one could add that the final audit of war should be its political consequences. That said, McMaster is right to emphasize the fact that warfare is the final test of how good an army is demonstrated to be in meeting its most defining of challenges. Armies are maintained for several reasons, but the most core of their necessary competencies has to be combat. Defence planning is not only about the military instrument in war, but fitness for possible or probable war must be one test that should not be eschewed. The challenge of defence planning is amply shown by the evidence provided in the set-piece multinational experiences of 1914.[35] The scale and duration of the First World War were possible only because of the tolerable competence of military and civilian planners; that competence was essential if the contemporary technology for supply and movement was to be exploited. The fate of the rival war plans in action, from mobilization, to assembly and concentration in forward deployment, through initial operational manoeuvre, illustrates all too well the reasons why this book elects to regard defence planning with high inclusivity. The early course of the war in 1914 showed both the triumphs and severe limitations of pre-war military planning. Holger H. Herwig paints a memorable word picture of the German mobilization as follows.

> Europe was on the move by early August 1914. The Military Telegraph Section of the German General Staff mobilized 3,822,450 men and 119,754 officers as well as 600,000 horses. This gigantic force transported to the front in 312 hours by 11,000 trains. More than 2,150 54-car trains crossed the Rhine River over the Hohenzollern Bridge at Cologne in 10-minute intervals between 2 and 18 August.

The west army, consisting of 1.6 million men organized into 23 active and 11 reserve corps (or 950 infantry battalions and 498 cavalry squadrons), thundered across the various Rhine bridges at a rate of 560 trains per day, travelling at the then almost unheard-of speed of 20 miles per hour.[36]

Whether or not Alfred von Schlieffen's (unduly?) grand war planning design of December 1905 was logistically feasible and possessed operational integrity, there are no plausible grounds for disputing the efficiency of the German *Aufmarsch*.[37] With characteristic inconvenience the warfare launched with such initial administrative competence, at least by the Germans, the French, and the British, proved rapidly to be an inconclusive nightmare that could not be concluded triumphantly by cunning operational manoeuvre. All states' pre-war military planning was soon demonstrated by events to be too hopelessly narrowly militarily exclusive to guide the conduct of a modern great coalition war. The focus in this text on defence planning writ large encourages and enables examination of matters that the military planners for 1914 did not consider adequately, if at all. This does not imply dismissal of real-time operational decisions in 1914 as matters of little importance. One must strive to be alert to the perils inherent in unduly structuralist historical explanation. It is important to register the nature and changing character of challenges to defence planning, but it is scarcely less necessary to remain alert to the power of particular people at particular times to act, and especially interact, in ways and with consequences that could not be predicted with confidence at the time. Although the analysis here is obliged to be more than somewhat general in the explanation it seeks as theory, the significance of individuals with their unique personalities is ever to the fore in my mind, notwithstanding the potency of circumstance. History is moved by what people do and fail to do in contexts by and large not of their own making. Adolf Hitler did not make the relevant world for his ambitions in the 1930s and early 1940s, though personally he exploited both real and apparent opportunities in ways and with consequences that justly can bear his name.

Strategic history does not permit its executive agents imprudently to take a narrow view of defence planning, at least not if they are to merit strategic and, possibly in consequence, political success. An argument that runs through these pages is the claim that good enough understanding of the likely character of war and its warfare in the relevant future is critically important for effectively appropriate defence planning. This uncontroversial argument is illustrated amply by strategic contexts both recent and distant. Directly stated in question form, it is, 'how well is future war and warfare understood?' This essential question unfortunately begs an obvious, but frustrating follow-on challenge; 'how can we know with high confidence what future war will be like'? The answer has to be that only the passage of time will reveal the future of war. That rather unhelpful answer might obscure for the unwary the strong probability that actually there is not a single discrete future out there in the time to come. Instead, there are almost certainly an unknowable number of possible futures, with the character of the one that discretely will occur being in part the product of our choices today and tomorrow in the interactive process of eternal historical change. The past is singular, notwithstanding the contending pasts that are the historical stories told by historians. Considered from today, the future, in sharpest contrast, assuredly is plural. This is the unclimbable mountain situated at the core of the structure of the challenge for defence planning.

If statesmen and strategists have good enough understanding of the character of war and warfare for their most relevant time, even approximation to the multiple and multinational disasters of 1914–18 can, though may not, be avoided. It is well to bear in mind that the absence of evidence of war in a period is not synonymous with any proof concerning reasons for that absence. Negative evidence should be understood only to be proof of non-existentiality, not of proof of cause of such. For much of history the continuities in context for politics, diplomacy, and warfare were sufficiently stable as to allow defence planning to be conducted with considerable confidence as to its suitability for purpose. But what could be assumed much less often to be reliable knowledge about contemporary politics and warfare were the choices that people would make, such as, shall we fight, how hard will we fight, ought we to make peace? Defence planning should be understood as entailing preparation for the future that cannot be confined narrowly to the military, and most assuredly not solely to the operational inspiration expressed in war plans (or plans of campaign, operational manoeuvre). Operational excellence in design of manoeuvre and educated assessment of tactical effectiveness are largely irrelevant, if not actually hazardous, in the absence of sound inclusive understanding of contemporary war in the circumstances of the particular conflict of the day. As one must keep insisting in noble company with Clausewitz, war is politically purposeful violence.[38] The logistical enabler of military campaigning initially is political. Of course, administrative incompetence or ill chance like bad weather can frustrate the tidy execution even of plans that have been conceived and designed by genius. However, if defence planning is approached and treated inclusively, military mobilization and subsequent operational manoeuvre can be supported as required. What will matter profoundly is for the strategists and operational commanders of the period to comprehend the contemporary character of warfare, notwithstanding the unavoidable uncertainties that must pertain to individual (and some collective) human choices.

In practice, logistics always are disciplinary in effect, whether or not strategists and campaigning commanders elect to be so constrained in their operational ambition. The ill consequences for their authors of the great German adventures on the offensive in the West in 1914 and 1918 are powerfully supportive of the view that the gods of logistical truth should not be mocked. When Germany repeated its logistical sins in the Second World War on the Eastern Front, one considers what could appear to be a national style, a pattern of professional misbehaviour as fatally reckless as it was traditional and even cultural.[39] It is worth recalling that Prussia and Germany enjoyed an enviable reputation for leading the way in modern staff work, and particularly for professional military mastery of the railway system and its timetables as the key enabler for advantageous exploitation of Germany's central geostrategic location in Europe. But, when the numbers do not compute well for acceptable outcomes, one can always change the assumptions unilaterally about the expected duration of the war and the character of its warfare. Even apparently intractable logistic challenges may be rendered irrelevant, provided one assumes that in its timing, duration, and character, the war will be permissive of what could prove to be lethal logistical constraints. Russian distances, poor communications infrastructure, and weather, should not have been a surprise to a German Army that had occupied southern Russia as far as the Caucasus as recently as in 1918. The dominant problems in 1941–3, were, first, that the Germans believed that they had unbeatable armed forces who waged an unstoppable character of warfare; second, they were convinced that their Soviet enemy was so feeble in its fighting power that German errors would be forgiven in practice. Errors in assumptions of this magnitude tend not to be permissive of correction when their falsehood is revealed by experience. The commission of error in defence planning is entirely normal; this is the reason why planners need to be ruthless in the avoidance of Plan 'A's that are naked of Plan 'B's, just in case . . .

Logistical competence and incompetence can be found in any age, only the details of their characters differ, not their nature. Even logistical defence planning of a severely restrictive kind need not preclude military effort intended to achieve decision. Adolf Hitler would invite and duly receive strategic catastrophe in part because he believed that his will, military skill in generalship, and even simply the racial merit of pure-bred Germans, must triumph over tediously non-permissive facts of physical geography and the inconvenience of an enemy who declines to collapse. Nonetheless the unarguable facts of German failure in 1914, 1918, and 1941–3, should not mislead one into adopting an undue determinism. Men, horses, and machines all need to be fuelled, rested, possibly repaired, and mileage is mileage. The defence planner needs to beware of apparent comforting certainties which, though undoubtedly true in themselves, are necessarily flawed if they are expected to explain more than they are able. Bread, fodder, and oil all have calculable meaning for practicable military action. But, human will (morale), and skill (strategic, operational, and tactical), vary widely. Even if one knows for certain the quantities that can be measured in war, how confident can one be that their military (strategic and political) meaning is grasped suitably? Winston S. Churchill may be quoted aphoristically in advising that '[w]hen in contact with immeasurable events it is always dangerous to have fixed opinions'.[40] Even though much pertaining to national defence and its planning needs to be measured, the use to which those measurable quantities (men, machines, budgets) will be put, and the ways in which that will be done, assuredly are beyond metrically calculable certainty. Military capability and feasibility confines strategy to the art of the practicably possible, but unfortunately for the structure of the challenge to defence planning that confinement typically is compatible with a range of possibilities. During the Cold War, American defence analysts sought with grim earnestness to build and sustain a nuclear force posture that assuredly would deter the Soviet adversary from adventure in any and all circumstances. But, what was the value in deterrent effect of particular levels of particular kinds and amounts of putative nuclear damage? Large numbers were chosen and were analytically defensible, though only if one chose to accept the analysts' assumptions. Did the technically credible military threat of assured destruction convert into political coin as assured deterrence?[41] The most vital issue was not the extent and kind of damage that could be inflicted, but rather the relationship between Soviet anticipation of being the recipient of such action and deterrent effect on their behaviour. Many professional defence analysts appeared not to understand that the deterrent worth of military posture cannot be measured quantitatively. The key variable is the choice to be made by individuals at a particular time; this is not quantifiably calculable, even though educated guesses about it may have to be made.

In the War of Spanish Succession, physical constraints and moral norms and customs effectively were as common to both sides as was the relevant technology and indeed the tactical style in warfare.[42] But, despite the common contemporary 'knowns' of military planning, the Duke of Marlborough succeeded admirably in outmanoeuvring the French and their allies in campaign after campaign. The consequence was that as Commander in Chief of the Coalition Army he was able to lure the enemy into battle where and when it would be at a significant disadvantage. There was no shortage of professional military expertise among the French, indeed quite the contrary. Logistical limitations in the late seventeenth and early eighteenth centuries necessarily restricted the boundary of what was operationally, strategically, and politically possible, but this has always been true. The contemporary logistical dependence of NATO forces upon poor (frequently contested) communications from the port of Karachi through Pakistan to Afghanistan, in essence is simply an example of an eternal challenge to defence planning. Details always are unique to period, but the defence planning function has not differed in its nature among such distinctive cases as the march of the army of the First Crusade to the Holy Land in 1097–8, the wars of Napoleon, and indeed of every conflict anticipated and actual. Defence planning broadly and campaign planning narrowly, always have had to cope with known, at least knowable, constraints, as well as with the uncertain possibilities of will, skill, and sheer accident of fortune. Even in a period that was not physically or morally readily permissive of heroic strategic endeavour, meaningful success still was practicable to those few who were able to tolerate the constraints and risks. Marlborough's unbroken succession of victories in battle from 1704 until 1711 demonstrated what could be done when extraordinary talent and a personality not strongly averse to risk was combined with a professional respect for the conditions of the period. David Chandler is helpfully direct in addressing the practical limitations that constrained Marlborough as defence planner and command-ing general.

> Yet these wars [especially the Nine Years' War, 1688–97; and the War of the Spanish Succession, 1701–11] were undoubtedly 'limited' [despite their extrava-gant political stakes and aims] in a very real sense—namely in the restricted ability of armed forces to carry out the grand strategic or political aims ordered by their rulers and governments. Schemes of vast manoeuvre and rapid decision were beyond their scope. Campaigns and even wars were therefore largely controlled by logistical factors: an army was only operationally viable for areas over which it could carry its bread. Magazines of pre-stocked supplies were essential, but this reliance placed obstructions on the freedom of strategic movement. No army dared to advance more than a week's march from its latest magazines. Then it had to halt to establish a new depot, re-site the ovens, and bake a fresh bread supply.[43]

Chandler calculates that a successful army, which had won a battle in mid-campaign, most probably had a 'maximum operational range' of 300–350 miles.[44] Logistics are the life-blood of war, and have always been so, but they cannot command the use that is made of them. Larger armies are not necessarily better armies at fighting, even when they are well enough supplied and capably transported. Marlborough's army and the logistical rules that were all but mandatory for it were no secret, but what he would choose to do with it—Flanders, the Lower Rhine, the Upper Rhine, or southern Germany—often was a surprise to the Marshals of France.

For another example. Owing in substantial part to incompetence the order of battle of RAF Fighter Command was less known to the Luftwaffe than it should have been, but even if German Intelligence had not been the irony that it was in 1940, what German defence planners most needed to know was how the RAF would defend its homeland. Capability offers clues and some evidence about political, strategic and operational intentions, but those fre-quently can only be guesses resting upon shaky assumptions. The defence planner would like to know, but in advance cannot; what the Germans will do with their High Seas Fleet; how the Soviet Union will or might seek to gain political leverage as a consequence of its achievement of approximate parity in strategic nuclear forces; what benefits Iran will anticipate securing as the reward for achieving status as a nuclear-weapon state (NWS). This kind of political and strategic knowledge illustrates why 'so what?' has to be the dominant question guiding strategic enquiry. Rather crude, certainly blunt, and apt to shock the unwary though it is, the strategist's 'so what' question both commands attention and mandates a strategic answer. For politicians, civilian officials, and soldiers to whom strategic reasoning is alien, even if they employ the strategy word liberally as a talisman, this question serves as an intellectually brutal reminder of the nature of their responsibilities to the national security.

False Gods

This book suggests an approach to prudent defence planning that is crafted to provide education in aid of practice. Defence planners have of course to be alert to their contemporary context, because that is the only authoritative source for the provision of assets in the future. The problem that cannot be answered with certain accuracy is the one inherent in our temporal situation. While we will know more tomorrow, that knowledge will only be about the today of tomorrow. The challenge for defence planning is to cope as well as possible with the uncertainties that must always remain such. The fact that tomorrow never comes is a certainty of nature that should not be hard to understand. Often in their practice defence planners nevertheless forget that the blessing of knowledge provided by the passing of time is balanced by the irresistible fact that the felt need to anticipate the course of future history has not been answered satisfactorily by movement in the calendar. The practical challenge to defence planning is to understand how to proceed in the face of uncertainty.

The choice of historical experience as the essential fuel for a tolerably prudent theory of defence planning is not exactly a heroic one. The reason is that there is literally no alternative to education in history for the preparation of contemporary defence planners. Unfortunately, Objective Historians are at least as rare as Omniscient Observers, which means that an argument in praise of historical education has to be prefaced by important caveats. The claim for the utility of history should be understood as being promoted strictly *faute de mieux*. If there were a major source of educational material for defence planning superior to considerable familiarity with history, that agreeable fact would have been readily recognizable long before now. Unsurprisingly, there are serious difficulties with resort to history as a source of wisdom; they are identified and examined closely in the next chapter. However, critics of an historical approach to the understanding of contemporary challenges for defence planning should not be permitted to forget that historical data is the only kind from which the evidence for theory as explanation can be formulated. The practical choice is not between history or something else, because the something else is zero. It is right to be fearful of defence planning conducted on the basis of poor historical understanding. But even sound history becomes something else when it is misapplied in dubious analogy. A historical approach to strategic education for defence planners is advanced explicitly here in good part because it is an existential reality. Regardless of the detail of their personal education, defence planners are the products of their context of time, place, and cultures, all of which provide a past that has meaning to, and encourages particular understanding of, the individual's view of the future. When an official speaks foolishly of the foreseeable future; although he is attempting to gaze forward down the great stream of time, he is doing so with attitudes and opinions gained from the past, both near and distant. The official observer of the future is not outside of time, but rather speaks from today, whenever that is, to a future that can only be imagined. This is not to be lamented and cannot be corrected, because it simply is the way things are and have to be.

We plan for the future by programming for it as best we are able, which in practical terms means that we should conduct defence preparation in a manner likely to prove adaptable to circumstances that cannot be predicted in detail today, and may not even be capable of anticipation as a possibility. There is a sense in which defence planning has to accommodate at least the concepts of 'thinking the unthinkable' and knowing the unknowable.[45] Although one cannot literally think the unthinkable or know the unknowable, one can and should recognize these rather frightening categories of thoughts. Surprise will be what it is, surprising, but by definition ignorance of detail need not be ignorance of future possibility. It is ironic not contradictory to claim that one can be prepared to be surprised.

It is both possible and necessary to be prepared for a future that we do not and cannot know. The challenge to be met is the need to be able to cope tolerably well with a security context for which one cannot plan in detail at all reliably. Because it is always possible that we will fail to prepare well for our future defence, the gold standard should perhaps be devalued to silver and identified with preparation that simply would cope, albeit not well. It is the ever possible likelihood of serious error in defence preparation that obliges recognition of the value of insurance. Prudently conducted, defence planners need a strategy that includes hedges against unanticipated menace.[46] Because every war is unique, each provides a learning experience both special only to itself as well as common to the nature of the activity at all times and in all places; the 'climate of war' is not distinctive among different cases.[47] In the twentieth century, both Britain and the United States coped adequately with the consequences of their pre-war deficiencies in defence planning for the surprising challenges that the political and strategic contexts of the 1910s and 1940s threw at them. Thanks to national geographies with their strategic permissiveness of some serious error, air power, sea power, and a large continental ally provided the insurance that proved necessary. Those were not strictly hedges against weakness in national land power, though, given their dependency upon historical contingency and cooperative German and Japanese strategic error, it would be hard to overstate the importance of chance in Clausewitz's 'climate of war'. For a long war it might be acceptable to tolerate defence planning only to a metaphorical semi-precious standard rather than gold or silver, were it not for the troubling uncertainty as to the adequacy of merely coping as the appropriate benchmark for the good enough. Had Hitler been only modestly more strategically competent, it is plausible to argue that Britain with a new Prime Minister (not Winston S. Churchill) would have made peace with Germany in summer 1940, and that the Soviet Union would have collapsed definitively in 1941.

The British nuclear deterrent force comprising four nuclear powered bal- listic missile-firing submarines (SSBNs) is a good exemplar of national defence planning against no known or even currently credible anticipated strategic necessity, but rather in provision of the ultimate hedge against the worst that might happen to Britain's external security environment in the future. There are several major and a few lesser arguments that support continuing British ownership of duly modernized SSBNs, but by far the most potent, strategically appreciated, is the one claiming strategic value analogous to that of the Royal Navy and the Air Force in summer 1940. At that time of high peril Britons could think with excellent reason, 'thank god we have the Royal Navy'. Happily, they had no less serious reason to be thankful for the pre-war defence planning that created Air Chief Marshal Sir Hugh Dowding's RAF Fighter Command. It is far more difficult for Britain to hedge with nuclear weapons against the unknowable future today than it was able similarly to bank credit for future national security in the 1930s. At that time the mission was to prepare air defence against an uncertain, but assuredly not unanticipated, threat from across the North Sea, if not the Channel, as events in the spring of 1940 were to realize as an appalling actuality.

Many countries have proved unable to pursue an adequate hedging strategy in their defence preparation, even when their leaders recognized or at least suspected the need. No matter how reasonable the argument is recognized to be in favour of hedging options against unexpected catastrophe, as often as not the notional hedges remain only that, notional. The domestic and external contexts for defence planning in peacetime may not be permissive of 'last resort', desperate but still feasible, choices. Not infrequently the reasons why catastrophe looms are the same reasons why it cannot be evaded. For a polity to reduce the danger of its being unable to evade and escape from threat that effectively entails survival, it is necessary for it to function grand strategically. A narrow military approach to defence planning is likely to prove a lethal failing. No matter how sophisticated the methodology employed, the pursuit of quantifiably scientific certainty in preparation for future defence is chimerical and therefore must be folly. Nonetheless, all is not lost because science provides neither a method with direct utility as an aid to strategic judgement, nor any guarantee of tactical success by means of technology that will deliver victory. Fortunately, such disappointment in the potency of the false gods of science and technology does not mean that prudent defence planning and advantage in fighting power have to be benefits secured strictly by chance.

Defence Planning is About Politics

Neither rigorous strategic logic nor expert defence analysis can trump human error, though they might help and ought not to be disdained. As Clausewitz insisted, war is about politics; it must follow that so also is defence planning.[48] The entire enterprise of war and preparation for its conduct or avoidance is political. In common with war, the whole meaning of defence planning is political. Politics is systemically inalienably human; it is about influence, or relative power. Syllogistically expressed, because defence planning is a human endeavour to attend adequately to the future political condition of relative power, so must the planning be understood in terms of politics and its nature. It is worth accepting some risk of overstatement and undue reductionism in emphasizing the political dimension to strategy and its defence planning. Dedicated military specialists conducting military studies often pay only minimal attention to the political implications of their analyses. The strategist's 'so what' question indicates a necessary path of speculation and judgement that must lead to the anticipation of desired political consequences and implications. Warfare is not politics, but it is about politics.[49] To neglect or deny the co-habitation of strategy and policy with its politics, analogically would be akin to making tactical decisions about military behaviour without serious regard for their operational (level) implications, or to design military operations in the absence of strategic sense. This is not to confuse policy with strategy, but it is important to appreciate the conceptual space between political ends and strategic ways. Nevertheless, the 'unequal dialogue' that should be continuous and institutionalized in an orderly process between civilian policy-makers and military planners and executive commanders, addresses concerns that overlap noticeably and unavoidably.[50]

The idea of grand strategy that has been revived both in government and by scholars of recent years, serves to drive home to resistant minds the true unity of politics and its military tools. This combination is not discretionary, but rather merits insistence upon its definitional truthfulness. Grand strategy, a term not employed by Clausewitz with his focus upon the military conduct of war, belongs in strategy's general theory as a collective concept that accommodates the military dimension. My preferred definition is the following:

> Grand strategy is the direction and use of any or all of the assets of a security community, including its military instrument, for the purposes of policy as decided by politics.[51]

Grand strategy can and should be understood to be about 'the calculated relationship of means to large ends', as John Lewis Gaddis rightly argues, but the size of political ends need bear little relation to the size and strategic weight of the security community.[52] The scope for discretion in political and strategic choice can vary widely between communities, but it is likely to prove misleading if one tries to argue that large political ends potentially are feasible only for the weightiest of polities. Williamson Murray for once is not persuasive when he seeks to insist conclusively as follows:

> Yet, grand strategy is a matter involving great states and great states alone. No small states and few medium-sized states possess the possibility of crafting a grand strategy. For the most part, their circumstances condemn them to suffer what Athenian negotiators suggested to their Melian counterparts in 416 BC about the nature of international relations.[53]

This sounds plausible, but on close examination it is found not to be so. It is a mistake to assign grand strategy as the actual or potential possession only of a particular class of polity. Grand strategy certainly is a big idea, but there is no very good reason why that restricts its manifestation only to large national homes. In theory, grand strategy is open to any and every size of state political player. It is an idea important for this study because it insists upon the extra-military context for the military content to defence planning. It may well be true to claim that smaller polities have fewer options for grand strategic choice than do greater polities, but this is neither clearly a dominant (most cases) historical truth, nor can it be sustained logically. Notwithstanding their relative modesty of assets, the lesser state players in the game of nations (e.g. the two Koreas, the two Vietnams, East Germany, and Cuba in the Cold War) demonstrated that latter-day Athenians disdain the policy agendas, preferences, and choices of relative minnow states at their peril.[54] Defence planning is the practice of military strategy in grand strategy, and is conducted in a thoroughly political process—which is scarcely surprising or unfortunate, given that politics is what this behaviour is all about.

NOTES

1. Morton H. Halperin, *Bureaucratic Politics and Foreign Policy* (Washington, DC: The Brookings Institution, 1974), explains the paradigm.
2. At this time of writing the United States is accelerating the pace of its practical and theoretical retreat from the swamp of COIN responsibilities in which it had

floundered through much of the 2000s. Even the limited success so painfully achieved eventually in Iraq has come to be seen as rather less brilliant an achievement than briefly was believed. David Petraeus and Stanley McChrystal were the American military commanders hailed for a short while as the best and the brightest of their generation, men well enough tuned to the needs of 'complex warfare'. It is strangely not wholly unfitting that these leaders had their glittering careers terminated abruptly in some dishonour, albeit principally of their own making, in the same timeframe that recorded the latest episodes of American disillusion with COIN. Fred Kaplan, 'The End of the Age of Petraeus: The Rise and Fall of Counterinsurgency', *Foreign Affairs*, 92 (January–February 2013), 75–90. Much as Kaplan should be read as a well informed and increasingly popular American view that is post-Iraq and almost post-Afghanistan in flavour, so Morton H. Halperin, *Limited War in the Nuclear Age* (New York: John Wiley, 1963), ch. 3, 'The Korean War', reflected eloquently the most expert view of then recent warfare in the contemporary inter-war context between Korea and Vietnam. That context was stated unmistakeably in the book's title. Recent experience of war and the general strategic context colour even expert analyses that are forward-looking. We write from today, whether or not we accept that experience as a model for a tolerable future.

3. Carl von Clausewitz, *On War*, tr. Michael Howard and Peter Paret (1832–4; Princeton, NJ: Princeton University Press, 1976), 76.

4. The literature on the nature and persistence of war is extensive, but typically not deep in insight. Lonely exceptions include a brilliant very short work by Christopher Coker, *Can War be Eliminated?* (Cambridge: Polity Press, 2013), and the conceptually and physically formidable book by Azar Gat, *War in Human Civilization* (Oxford: Oxford University Press, 2006). Scholarly debate on the causes of war has foundered for a century on the rocks of an unmanageable wealth of diverse historical data that might be evidence for theory, and the limitations on understanding imposed, but often under recognized, by moral impulse. To date, neither history nor social science has cracked the code that periodically orders us to war. Gat and Coker's work are better places than most to begin to understand the depth and complexity of the problem, but it is plausible to suggest that the 'why we fight' question is an example of methodological error. In practice we do not wage war, rather do we wage particular wars for distinctive reasons. But compelling though the argument can seem to deconstruct the forensic question, it remains troubling to find high explanatory value in Thucydides' formula of 'fear, honour, and interest'. These potent terms appear to belong inalienably to the nature of our species. Thucydides, *The Landmark Thucydides: A Comprehensive Guide to The Peloponnesian War*, ed. Robert B. Strassler, rev. tr. Richard Crawley (ca. 400 BC; New York: Free Press, 1996), 43.

5. Judy Pearsall and Bill Trumble, eds., *Oxford English Reference Dictionary*, rev. 2nd edn. (Oxford: Oxford University Press, 2002), 1297. For superior explanation of the requirements of theory, see Harold R. Winton, 'An Imperfect Jewel: Military Theory and the Military Profession', *The Journal of Strategic Studies*, 34 (December 2011), esp. 854–7.

6. E. S. Quade and W. I. Boucher, eds., *Systems Analysis and Policy Planning: Applications in Defense* (New York: American Elsevier Publishing Company, 1968), remains a work of exceptional value, see especially the 'Introduction' and 'Summary' by Quade, 1–19, 418–29. This instructive work was a product of the RAND Corporation. In addition to the contributions in Quade and Boucher's book, helpful insight on the origins and early airing at RAND of what became the organization's signature defence analytical methods and approaches, is provided in James Digby, 'Contributions of RAND to Strategy in the 1950s', in Andrew W. Marshall, J. S. Martin, and Henry Rowen, eds., *On Not Confusing Ourselves: Essays on National Security Strategy in Honor of Albert and Roberta Wohlstetter* (Boulder, CO: Westview Press, 1991), 17–29. The short chapter by Andrew W. Marshall in this book, 'Strategy as a Profession for Future Generations', is a neglected classic that merits close reading. I discuss in some detail the major issues pertaining to the role of defence analysis in defence planning in Chapter 5 below.

7. Clausewitz, *On War*, 140.

8. See Michael Howard, *The Continental Commitment: The Dilemma of British Defence Policy in the Era of the Two World Wars* (London: Temple Smith, 1972); and David French, *The British Way in Warfare, 1688–2000* (London: Unwin Hyman, 1990).

9. It is noticeable that today scholars are rediscovering the ancient truth about strategy that it must rest upon a sustainable domestic political consensus if it is to have merit in action abroad. In living memory this enduring truth about the domestic political context for defence planning and strategy was painfully redis-covered in the United States in the early 1970s, and then again in the late 2000s. A sound historical grasp would have pre-empted any need to rediscover what should be common self-knowledge in a democracy. The necessity of a permissive domestic political context as a foundation for military commitment to warfare abroad, is amply illustrated by the domestic troubles that plagued the Duke of Marlborough in several states in the Coalition that provided his army. See David Chandler, *Marlborough as Military Commander* (London: B. T. Batsford, 1973).

10. Stephen Bungay, *The Most Dangerous Enemy: A History of the Battle of Britain* (London: Aurum Press, 2001), is the most persuasive study extant.

11. Williamson Murray, 'The Battle of Britain: The Nazis Stopped (1940)', in James Lacey and Murray, eds., *Moment of Battle: The Twenty Clashes That Changed the World* (New York: Bantam Books, 2013), pp. 292–317, tells the story economically and reliably.

12. The connections between the course of air warfare in 1940 and the pre-war years of defence preparation in the 1930s, is emphasized in Colin S. Gray, 'Dowding and the British Strategy of Air Defence, 1936–40', forthcoming; i.d., 'Clipping the Eagle's Wings: Explaining Failure and Success in the Battle of Britain, 1940', *Infinity Journal*, Special Edn. (October 2012), 5–11.

13. The geographical and geopolitical dimension to strategy is explored in Colin S. Gray, *Perspectives on Strategy* (Oxford: Oxford University Press, 2013), ch. 4.

14. See the discussion of the dimensions of strategy in Colin S. Gray, *Modern Strategy* (Oxford: Oxford University Press, 1999), ch. 1.

15. I have proposed such an approach briefly in Colin S. Gray, 'Strategic Thoughts for Defence Planners', *Survival*, 52 (June–July 2010), 159–78.

16. Williamson Murray, 'Thoughts on Grand Strategy', in Murray, Richard Hart Sinnreich, and James Lacey, eds., *The Shaping of Grand Strategy: Policy, Diplomacy, and War* (Cambridge: Cambridge University Press, 2011), 33.

17. Clausewitz, *On War*, 605.

18. See the Introduction: Defence Planning, a Mission About Consequences, fn. 3.

19. See Colin S. Gray, 'The Strategist as Hero', *Joint Force Quarterly*, 62 (3rd Quarter, July 2011), 37–45.

20. Harry R. Yarger, *Strategy and the National Security Professional: Strategic Thinking and Strategy Formulation in the 21st Century* (Westport, CT: Praeger Security International, 2008).

21. Yarger 2008, 51.

22. Yarger 2008, 52 (emphasis in the original).

23. Charles Krulak, 'The Strategic Corporal: Leadership in the Three–Block War', *Marines Magazine*, 28 (May 1999), 28–34.

24. I am grateful to Antulio J. Echevarria II, for the metaphorical conception of weight for strategic effect. He has written that 'all events in war have weight; even the least can have disproportionate effects'. 'Dynamic Inter-Dimensionality: A Revolution in Military Theory', *Joint Force Quarterly*, 15 (spring 1997), 36. This simple plausible claim has profound implications for the theory and practice of strategy.

25. I have developed this argument with particular reference to the wars and warfare of the 2000s in my *Categorical Confusion? The Strategic Implications of Recognizing Challenges either as Irregular or Traditional* (Carlisle, PA: Strategic Studies Institute, February 2012), and 'Concept Failure? COIN, Counterinsurgency, and Strategic Theory', *Prism*, 3 (June 2012), 17–32. An innovative venture into the contested terrain shared by politics and war is the important study by Emile Simpson that combines first-hand experience with sophisticated, if controversial, theory in his intellectually exciting book, *War from the Ground Up: Twenty–First-Century Combat as Politics* (London: C. Hurst, 2012).

26. On grand strategy see: Paul Kennedy, ed., *Grand Strategies in War and Peace* (New Haven, CT: Yale University Press, 1991); Charles Hill, *Grand Strategies: Literature, Statecraft, and World Order* (New Haven, CT: Yale University Press, 2010); and Murray, Sinnreich, and Lacey, eds., *The Shaping of Grand Strategy*.

27. Murray, 'Thoughts on Grand Strategy', 4.

28. Not all expert commentators on national defence and related matters are impressed either by the challenge of the strategy function or the responses summoned to meet it. The American former soldier and current scholar and controversialist, Andrew J. Bacevich, would have us believe that 'Dempsey's map [General Martin E. Dempsey, Chairman of the US Joint Chiefs of Staff, who was contemplating a very large map of the world] hints at the dirty secret that members of the fraternity of strategists, civilian and military alike, are loath to acknowledge. The formulation of strategy begins by assuming away complexity, reducing reality to a convenient caricature. Strategic analysis is almost by definition dumbed down analysis. To conjure up solutions, you start by simplifying the problem. 'America's Strategic Stupidity', *The Spectator* (London) (12 January 2013), 15. This is a significant criticism, even though it rests upon a serious misunderstanding of its subject. The reduction to which Bacevich refers is essential for the making of strategy, anywhere and at any time. However, imprudent

caricature is a danger born of expediency as well as necessity to which defence planners can be prone.

29. Clausewitz alerts us to this phenomenon when he writes as follows: 'So long as no acceptable theory, no intelligent analysis of the conduct of war exists, routine methods will tend to take over at the highest levels', *On War,* 154.

30. See Arden Bucholz, *Moltke, Schlieffen, and Prussian War Planning* (Providence, RI: Berg Publishers, 1991); David T. Zabecki, ed., *Chief of Staff: The Principal Officers Behind History's Great Commanders,* Vol. 1, *Napoleonic Wars to World War I,* Vol. 2, *World War II to Korea and Vietnam* (Annapolis, MD: Naval Institute Press, 2008); and for useful historical contextuality, Martin Van Creveld, *Command in War* (Cambridge, MA: Harvard University Press, 1985).

31. Gray, *The Strategy Bridge,* 75–6.

32. Superior treatment of the strategic necessity for logistical sense is to be found in Martin Van Creveld, *Supplying War: Logistics from Wallenstein to Patton* (Cambridge: Cambridge University Press, 1977), and Thomas M. Kane, *Military Logistics and Strategic Performance* (London: Frank Cass, 2001).

33. See Dennis E. Showalter, *Railroads and Rifles: Soldiers, Technology, and the Unification of Germany* (Hamden, CT: Archon Books, 1986); Keir A. Lieber, *War and the Engineers: The Primacy of Politics over Technology* (Ithaca, NY: Cornell University Press, 2005), ch. 4; and for a broader, geopolitical and geostrategic view, T. G. Otte and Keith Neilson, eds., *Railways and International Politics: Paths of Empire, 1848–1945* (Abingdon: Routledge, 2006).

34. H. R. McMaster, 'Learning from Contemporary Conflicts to Prepare for Future War', in Richmond M. Lloyd, ed., *William B. Ruger Chair of National Security Economics Papers, No. 3, Defense Strategy Air Forces: Setting Future Directions* (Newport, RI: Naval War College, November 2007), 71.

35. See Paul Kennedy, ed., *The War Plans of the Great Powers, 1880–1914* (London: George Allen and Unwin, 1979); and Richard F. Hamilton and Holger H. Herwig, eds., *War Planning 1914* (Cambridge: Cambridge University Press, 2010).

36. Holger H. Herwig, 'Conclusion' in Hamilton and Herwig, eds., *War Planning 1914,* 231.

37. See the masterly examination of the rival mobilization plans and advances to battle in Hew Strachan, *The First World War Volume 1: To Arms* (Oxford: Oxford University Press, 2011), ch. 3. For a recent heavy blast in the scholars' dispute about the nature of 'the Schlieffen Plan', see Terence Zuber, *The Real German War Plan, 1904–1914* (Stroud: The History Press, 2011).

38. Simpson, *War from the Ground Up,* is an outstanding discussion.

39. See Robert M. Citino, *The German Way of War: From the Thirty Years War to the Third Reich* (Lawrence, KS: University Press of Kansas, 2005).

40. Winston S. Churchill, *Marlborough: His Life and Times,* Book 2 (1933–8; London: George G. Harrap, 1947), 99.

41. Alain C. Enthoven and K. Wayne Smith, *How Much Is Enough? Shaping the Defense Program, 1961–1969* (1970; Santa Monica, CA: RAND, 2005), this is a period-piece classic expressing the concerns and methodological self-confidence of cutting-edge defence analysis in the 1960s. In addition, it explains a kind of defence analysis that is still alive and well, for both good and ill. Issues of methodology in defence analysis are discussed in later chapters below.

42. Adoption of the ring bayonet in place of the plug bayonet was an exception to the general stability in design of armaments. Marlborough's army was converted wholesale to the ring socket system which enabled well-disciplined infantry both to fire their flintlock muskets when the bayonet was attached, and dispense with deployment of specialist pikemen to protect them. The new bayonet was invented in approximately 1687. When combined with the flintlock that replaced the heavier old matchlock musket, the new bayonet helped greatly to convert infantry into a military tool able to manoeuvre for advantage and perhaps decision. See the description of the change in the late seventeenth and very early eighteenth centuries in David Chandler, *The Art of Warfare in the Age of Marlborough* (London: B. T. Batsford, 1976).

43. Chandler, 1976, 19–20.

44. Chandler, 1976, 20.

45. I am grateful to Herman Kahn for the paradoxical idea of 'thinking the unthinkable'. Kahn, *Thinking the Unthinkable* (New York: Avon Books, 1962).

46. Nathan Freier, *Known Unknowns: Unconventional 'Strategic Shocks' in Defense Strategy Development* (Carlisle, PA: Strategic Studies Institute, US Army War College, November 2008), provides useful reminder of the range and extent of possible surprise for the defence planner.

47. Clausewitz, *On War*, 104, defines the climate as being constructed of 'danger, exertion, uncertainty, and chance'.

48. Clausewitz, *On War*, 81.

49. This is not to deny that the necessities of war can be so damaging to the usual superiority of civilian political authority over a polity's military instrument that Clausewitzian logic is reversed, and politics in practice serves warfare rather than vice versa. Indeed, one can be bolder still and argue that politics comes to serve war, while the condition of war in practice really serves the conduct of warfare. The relationship between war and warfare is not explained, or even pursued very intelligently, in the extant literature. It is commonplace to observe, *en passant*, that 'there is more to war than warfare', but this important distinction usually is not investigated: *mea culpa*, though in large company. My brief effort to explain this important distinction was in *Fighting Talk: Forty Maxims on War, Peace, and Strategy* (Westport, CT: Praeger Security International, 2007), 32–5.

50. See Eliot A. Cohen, *Supreme Command: Soldiers, Statesmen, and Leadership in Wartime* (New York: Free Press, 2002), ch. 7.

51. Gray, *The Strategy Bridge*, 262.

52. John Lewis Gaddis, 'What Is Grand Strategy?' lecture delivered at the conference on 'American Grand Strategy after the War', sponsored by the Triangle Institute for Security Studies and the Duke University Program in American Grand Strategy, 26 February 2009, 7.

53. Murray, 'Thoughts on Grand Strategy', 1.

54. This is a persuasive argument of major importance in John Lewis Gaddis, *The Cold War* (London: Allen Lane, 2005).

2

A Strategic Approach

CONTEXTS: STRATEGIC, POLITICAL, HISTORICAL

People cannot simply be trained to function competently as defence planners. The most important questions that defence planning requires to be answered can only be met by minds educated to exercise sound judgement in the face of challenges that are unique in exact character, even though they are persisting in nature. This is why colleges of higher professional military education attempt the impossible should they aspire to train strategists. What they can do, however, is educate in and for strategy, and hope that that education, when thickened by calories of sound experience, will suffice to enable effective but prudent strategic judgement.[1] Outstanding strategic judgement of the class plainly intended by Carl von Clausewitz in his discussion of genius and its expression in an apparently instinctual *coup d'oeil*, is extremely rare.[2] Armies cannot produce trained strategists for higher level duty on the contested ground where politics and war meet—on and about the strategy bridge, to put the point metaphorically. However, strategic genius of an all but immaculate kind is not usually required. That said, the historical record does suggest that even strategic competence can be hard to find. The principal reason for this poverty is nothing more sinister than the awesome difficulties that typically harass and therefore impede strategic performance. Strategy is exceptionally difficult to do well, and as a consequence many, possibly most, people who attempt to do it do not perform well.[3]

This book argues of necessity for a strategic approach to defence planning, alas not usually considering happy situations, friendly to national discretion. The reason to favour integrated logic of the essential formula of strategy lies in its default circumstance of an absence of competitive alternatives. A similar argument commands respect with reference to historical evidence as a basis for defence planning decisions that by their nature must lean beyond our cartography into the foreign land of the future. It is no great challenge to locate and explain the reasons why knowledge and method, no matter how rigorous, cannot reveal that which is literally unknowable. However, working understanding of the future context for defence planning good enough to warrant

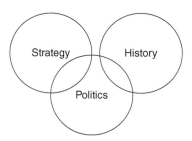

Figure 2.1 Three Contexts for Defence Planning

ascription as prudent should be attainable, even if only minimally so. The pertinent challenge is to identify an approach to defence planning that is both respectful of that which is unknowable, regardless of the claimed brilliance in the quality of methodology in the crystal balls currently on offer by supposed experts, but is not fatally intimidated by unavoidable ignorance. To that end it is necessary to specify an approach to the subject that is constructive rather than despairing. What follows immediately are the most important pieces of pre-theory that, understood inclusively, comprise a strategic approach for coping with the difficulties of the subject. When defined broadly, defence planning can be approached and understood most usefully in the light that is shed by three principal concepts employed to function in cooperation: these are strategy, politics, history, with each functioning as context for the others.

Figure 2.1, a Venn diagram, illustrates geometrically the argument of this book. Although one could claim master status for politics as the most important engine generating the effort for defence planning, such conceptual (or functional) coronation is not suitably enlightening as a navigational guide. The problem with any hierarchical choice for precedence, is that such an approach risks, if it does not surrender pre-emptively by methodological fiat, understanding of the true inclusivity of the whole subject of defence planning. This study is not interested in specifying an idealized elementary model of defence planning ('DP101' this is not). There are no innocently pure 'independent variables' standing alone in this analysis. Each significant concept depends on the others, and defence planning is the compounded product of all three great interdependent variables. Defence planning only makes sense when it is regarded contextually, and the most important contexts are those that lend themselves to decidedly porous categorization as strategic, political, and historical.

Notwithstanding the functional interdependencies among matters strategic, political, historical, and contextual, it is the concept, theory, and practice of strategy that must be accorded the leading organizing role in this enquiry. Pole position is merited by strategy because of the inclusivity of its logical structure and the high forensic value for analysis of that structure. Order and meaning is given to the mission of defence planning and its ever changing menu of possible specific tasks, by the theory of strategy. That theory is unique in its ability to explain what is done, why it is done, and why it can be done well or poorly. Neither politics nor history have quite comparable merit for the purpose of this book. Both are agreeably inclusive, but they are so to a fault. Defence planning is indeed highly, necessarily, and permanently political, in that the choices made reflect the relative influence of contributors to the process of governance. However, to adopt a strictly political approach to the understanding of defence planning imperils fitting comprehension of the dangers unique to this particular form of human social behaviour. While defence planning for future security is and has to be thoroughly political, it is well to recall the sense in Eliot Cohen's insistence upon the need for an unequal civil-military dialogue.[4] The concept, structure, and practice of strategy, to repeat, are pervasively political. Nonetheless, it is essential to remember that they are not politics.[5] Although in a vital sense defence planning and defence practice is a large compound variable dependent upon politics, it is scarcely less important to recognize the authority of the theory and practice of strategy. That which is perceived as being politically desirable may be strategically thoroughly impracticable.

The glory of the most basic elements, the categorical building blocks, in the structure of the theory of strategy, lies in the insistence upon a balancing of political wishes with effecting means, and the ways in which they would be employed. Appreciation of the pervasive potency of politics points to a source of discipline on defence planners that is beyond the narrower confines of the 'grammar' of military expertise and anxiety.[6] But that political discipline provided by policy guidance is empty of strategic merit until, or unless, it engages closely and respectfully with the logic of strategy. Defence planning should be conducted on and across the 'strategy bridge'.[7] With its insistence upon a good enough fit among politically derived (and often changeable) ends, the ways selected to achieve the ends, and the military and other means to be employed, the whole house of strategy is constructed in such a way that the necessary discipline of politics itself is disciplined by the constraints of practice.[8]

The political context that in a vital sense must govern all defence planning comprises the permanent competition for power of decision over community choices concerning future security. This competition is an enduring process, notwithstanding the evolution, and occasional revolution, that changes its characteristics in most polities. The human social condition is always a political one. The implications and ramifications of this point are so deep and inclusive that as a result they can escape proper scrutiny. Clausewitz argues that there is logic to policy, but also there is a grammar to war.[9] There are many constraints on the endeavours of strategists to perform well enough in defence planning, not all of which are political by reasonable definition. The hopes and anxieties that help fuel the political process within which defence planning is done, do not command entirely the subject matter of relevance to defence.

It is prudent to assess generously the relative influence of political judgement and pressure, not least because politics alone provides meaning to the enterprise of defence planning. Policy goals are the ends crafted not only in a political process, but also that must have political significance. One cannot sensibly demote politics from the leading role in defence planning. That said, it is necessary to expand somewhat on Clausewitz's insistence that war has its own grammar, though certainly not its own policy logic. Central to the problem set that the Prussian sought to unwrap and explain, was the inconvenient fact that politics and warfare are activities with different natures. A challenge in statecraft is to employ effectively the threat or use of violence for desired political consequences. The subject is coercion. The menace of fatal non-linearity is all but inherent in this endeavour to convert violence, or force, into desired political effect. Whether or not soldiers understand that their use of force as would-be coercive behaviour is about politics, it is near certain that the violence inflicted and suffered will tend to demote appreciation of other matters (that is to say, politics).[10] More force may trigger more resistance than political compliance. Deterrence cannot be reduced to calculations of (pseudo-) scientifically quantifiable credible menace.[11] Rationality and reason are different concepts that complicate the problems for strategists. The politics of defence planning and the practice of strategy not infrequently are influenced decisively by feelings, even impulses, which may well be unreasonable but will be rational given people's attempts to match their wishes with ways and means of action. Before the time when the consequences of the impulsive action are convincingly demonstrated by events, it may be quite too challenging to distinguish between intuitively sound understanding, under-educated guesswork, and sheer luck. Much as history, unlike historians, teaches nothing, so there is no magical political process able to ensure competence in strategic judgement. That process must decide the content of defence planning, but it is method only. Politics determines who and what succeeds in the endless struggle for relative power, not the policy and strategy consequences of winning and losing the competition. Policy ends are fuel for political strife and require political legitimation. Politics rules, but itself can provide only a vital enablement of policy thought and deed that inherently is neutral on matters of judgement on the context of defence planning.

In much the same way that politics is apt fatally to be unduly and inappropriately pervasive and even commanding as the lead idea in a theory and explanation of defence planning, so also does history have to be rejected for the leading role. It can be difficult to resist allotting the leading star role in this enquiry either to politics or history, because each in its vital way is critically important in unique and necessary ways to our understanding. Historical experience, both personal—in minor key—and as translated and transmitted by historians—in major key—is the only repository of data relevant to efforts in defence planning for future security. It would be difficult to exaggerate the relative significance of history for this enquiry, one might think. After all, given that today is ephemeral with its causal meaning for consequences unknown, and that the future can offer zero information, what else is there other than history? The problem was stated with characteristic vigour, rigour, and clarity by Michael Howard in his Inaugural Lecture as Regius Professor of Modern History at Oxford University in March 1981. Professor Howard offered considerable discouragement to those who insist that one needs to look back in order to look forward prudently. He warned that

> It is safer to start with the assumption that history, whatever its value in educating the judgement, teaches no 'lessons', and the professional historians will be as sceptical of those who claim that it does as professional doctors are of their colleagues who peddle patent medicines guaranteeing instant cures. The past is infinitely various, an inexhaustible storehouse of events from which we can prove anything or its contrary.[12]

Howard drives home his argument with these uncompromising words:

> In short, historians may claim to teach lessons, and often they teach very wisely. But 'history' as such does not. The trouble is that there is no such thing as 'history'. History is what historians write, and historians are part of the process they are writing about.[13]

My purpose here is neither to criticize politics and politicians, nor history and historians, rather is it to argue that despite their great importance, politics and history do not make the grade for conceptual leader in this study.

Rationality and Reason

The reductively simple structure of the strategic function, comprises only three foundational and interdependent elements: ends, ways, and means. Because it is my central proposition to argue that strategy can and should provide the conceptual framework within which defence planning is debated, conducted, and expressed in executive action, it is important to confront the human nature that must shape and drive strategic endeavour. The human nature, with its all but infinite varieties of character, is of course inalienable from the strategy function. This rather banal argument is not at all controversial, but perhaps strangely its logical and historically well-enough evidenced implications have deep meaning for defence planning. It is tempting to analyse defence planning as being a quintessentially rational process. One can locate errors in judgement usually after the fact, but not untypically the errors will be both explicable and probably even excusable because of the limited information that was available at the time. The contingency category of unpatterned, in effect stochastic, events that happen with little if any advance warning, is not a challenge that politicians and officials often are inclined either to worry about unduly, or to spend scarce resources preparing against. An acute problem consequential upon promiscuous unself-critical use of apparently convenient concepts, is that vital assumptions and important nuance tend to be retired from active personal service as a result of too easy a familiarity of terms.

Defence planning should be a rational project, meaning that it plans to acquire and sustain (military) means for the contingent purpose of employing them in ways that advance the political ends chosen as policy. *Quod erat demonstrandum*: the logical interdependence of the whole endeavour is neat and apparently incontestable, at least in nakedly austere reductive theory. However, closer examination of the key concepts in the context of historical experience reveals that, notwithstanding its functional utility, the formula of ends, ways, and means as the intellectual basis upon which a healthy diet of defence provision can rest, is far from trouble-free. In the context of this book, it is sensible to define rational behaviour as that which seeks purposefully to match ends, ways, and means. So far so good, not to say obvious and banal. Further thought reveals the disturbing proposition that there is no Hidden Hand for rational defence planning, working systemically behind the scenes to ensure that polities only attempt what is achievable. It can be distressing to appreciate that a country may well function in a strategically rational manner, yet behave in a way that the verdict of strategic history demonstrates unarguably to have been fatally contrary to reason. But exactly whose reason should we be talking about? It is apparently ironic, possibly even contradictory, to observe that polities can behave rationally in purposefully supporting their policy with means that they believe will be adequate for the bank, though to conclusions that show the whole enterprise to have been contrary to the reason whose fallaciousness was revealed by failure in practice.

Because of the complexity of the strategic realm it is not possible to define rational defence planning only as the planning that future events and non-events (thinking of nuclear deterrence to date) seems to show to have been successful. It is possible to make the wrong choices quite rationally. Apparently superior defence analytical method, employing an ample supply of metric treatment of what is believed to be knowable as usable data for evidence, is entirely compatible with strategic and political catastrophe. How is this possible? Can one plan rationally the strategic course of action to a conclusion that is policy failure by any plausible definition? The abundance of historical examples of abysmal policy failure despite tolerable rationality on defence planning is an episodically persisting reality that is fundamental to the challenge addressed in this study. It is possible to behave rationally, yet to fail politically because the course of subsequent events is so disappointing that plainly one was unreasonable. The rationality of the match between political ends and enabling strategic ways and tactical means, cannot be determined by Omniscient and Objective Strategists, because there are none such. Highly competent professionals, civilian and military, can make lethal errors of policy choice that render the rationality of their defence planning irrelevant.

Because strategy is an art and not a science that rests upon truths that can be verified by replication in tests in any local context, the political judgement that produces policy ends always is potentially the most fatal of traps for those who take undeserved comfort from the evidence of apparently rational process. The problem is that it is all too possible simultaneously to be both rational yet unreasonable. In many cases, it is only when an expeditionary adventure fails that it is fairly obvious that one had been unreasonable in one's well-meaning and purposefully rational conduct. If you believe that your chosen ways and available means are capable of securing the objectives of your policy, then you cannot plausibly be accused of irrational behaviour. When some of the more egregiously unsuccessful examples of modern strategy are considered empathetically, it is evident that wherever gross strategic error lay, it was not in the process of defence planning. To be unreasonable is not necessarily to be irrational. The reasoning behind and in rational defence planning will in probably arguable demonstrable fact be revealed as having been unreasonable because it rested upon false assumptions. More often than not the false assumptions were sovereign in policy practice because they shaped and drove the goals of strategy. This is more than marginally alarming to the cause of rational defence planning, given that it claims, I believe incontestably, that that planning cannot be safeguarded against folly by logical fit among the three basic elements that define and frame the whole house of strategy. It is the strategy bridge between the interdependent realms of politics and military (inter alia) instrument that is most critical to prudence in defence planning. Bluntly stated, national security is and has to be hostage to the wisdom in policy choice that derives from a political process. And the policy that is chosen by political process is wholly at risk to the peril that attends false assumptions.

The permanent fact that there can be no empirical verification of assumptions about the future means that there is a fundamental source of indiscipline caused by the unavailability of evidence, to which defence planning in all polities is ever liable. In practice, most polities, most of the time, police themselves in political processes that are not overly tolerant of bold conceptions that contemporary political opinion judges to be seriously implausible. But, it is well to remember that both the Third Reich in the early 1940s, and the United States in the 2000s, pursued strategically rational paths that led to different qualities of rational failure because their strategy bridges were constructed on the basis of fatally flawed assumptions. What Hitler attempted in Russia stood a reasonable prospect of succeeding, had his beliefs about the enemy been much more accurate than events proved them to be. With some apology for the like categorization, American policy in Vietnam in the 1960s and then in Iraq and Afghanistan, were reasonable enough, if only their assumptions about believed local friends and local foes had been much more accurate. One may incline to believe that better intelligence should be a vital contributor to more reasonable strategic performance. However, scepticism is advisable, because political wishes about preferred policy ends are easily capable of encouraging the authoritative reign of supportive, indeed legitim-izing, assumptions that in retrospect are understood to have been unsound.

The British politicians and civil servants who performed so poorly in the 1930s in their direction of national defence, albeit in ways compatible with development of a world-leading air defence system, were not irrational men. The problem was that their policy goals were forged and pursued on the basis of false assumptions. It was inconceivable to many responsible and apparently well informed people at the time that Adolf Hitler would seriously risk, let alone desire, war, given the awful recent and first-hand memories of their generation and its understandable fears for the future.[14] Uncritical familiarity with, and deployment of, the term 'rational' often seems to paralyze advisable scepticism. Even when there is strong evidence of rationality in the strategic framework binding ends, ways, and means coherently together, the non-trivial issue of external strategic integrity intrudes in two respects.

First, is the external security context accurately defined? Defence planning cannot be self-referential, after all. While, second, even if the outside world is understood and characterized plausibly in ways that appear to be appropriate, are reasonable political goals set and adapted for the national effort? It is important to understand that there is and can be nothing in a national defence planning process inherently able to ensure prudent calibration of the product of that process for coping with security peril. There is no political wisdom for policy in the defence planning process unless a strategy bridge requires, encourages, and enables its timely provision. Whether or not a rational process also is reasonable, and as a consequence likely to succeed, is a vital matter dependent upon the quality of individual politicians as policy makers and the political and strategic advice that they receive and choose to influence the quality of their choices.

The historical record ever lends itself to contestable interpretation and reinterpretation by historians. However, the evidence for success or failure in the greater wars of modern times is clear enough in the consequences of each episode. As usually is the case, consequences are far less arguable than are the causes of victory or defeat, judiciously assayed and rank-ordered in claimed relative significance. The principal reason why strategy should be regarded as the most important of concepts for understanding and explain-ing defence planning, is because it alone can provide the necessary inclusivity of diverse relevant subjects. Strategy provides the discipline of clear enough categorization of behaviours that are distinctive in nature. Also, when employed properly, the theory of strategy encourages understanding of the interdepend-encies that are able to generate the compounded reality of a well-functioning defence planning process. Lest this discussion of theory should mislead or confuse for reasons of its apparent complexity, Figure 2.2 is offered in explanation of what needs to be clear about the theory.

A robust theory of defence planning capable of serving the serious practical demands of government has to recognize those realities of political life that harass and may frustrate orderly method. It should be obvious from the bare outline of the subject represented diagrammatically in Figure 2.2, that the inherent unity of national defence planning as a function that is performed in different ways can, ironically perhaps, be lethally impaired by notable weakness in any of its interdependent parts. Furthermore, examination of great-power performance in the greater wars of the past three centuries, suggests strongly that we should be modest in our ambitions to improve the quality of defence planning that matters most to us. The beginning of wisdom has to be recognition of the major constraints under which all defence planners must suffer everywhere and at all time: the impossibility of knowing reliably what is unknowable about the context for security in the future; the impossibility of acquiring and recognizing certain knowledge pertaining to adversary choices (even if his situation should be predictable, which it will not be); the certainty of error in some of our choices over policy, strategy, and (individual and collective) tactics; the certainty of surprise in the future, including a few wholly unanticipated contingencies;[15] the certainty of surprise over some of the consequences of developments that are not in themselves entirely unanticipated. The list could be longer, but the substantial categories of harassing and frustrating mysteries will serve to register well enough the argument about constraints on strategic performance.

Even when a government means well, plans carefully and apparently competently, the country's security context may deteriorate catastrophically. This book strives to explain that defence planning has to be organized and conducted in the fullest possible appreciation of the limitations under which it has no option other than to function. More to the point and to be constructive, the urgent need is to locate the precepts of prudence that should serve well enough to help guide the fault-liable human executive agents in charge of providing for future security.

To cite a distinctly human challenge systemic to the adequacy of defence planning, world politics is conducted by policymakers in different polities who may or may not be rational in the technical sense. Even if they do relate their goals tidily to their available means and feasible ways, in some cases there is likely to be no discipline policing their strategic behaviour other than the feedback in the consequences of their action. The problem is not so much a world alarmingly beset by irrational leaders, but rather one wherein leaders will roguishly calculate, more likely decide intuitively, to behave in ways that many foreigners may judge to be unacceptably unreasonable. History appears to lend itself to being used to show that in actuality both reason and unreason govern the content of thought that is formally quite rational. What is more, the necessarily subjective nature of reasonableness in argument can be easy to misunderstand. If we decline sensibly to track backwards in our historical understanding from effects to most probable and rank-ordered causes, we find ourselves in the disturbing terrain of uncertainty. There are serious persuasive reasons to disdain the counterfactuality of 'what if . . .' pseudo-history, but with admitted reluctance I confess that counterfactuality does have utility in reminding us that many examples of behaviour and claimed misbehaviour in statecraft and strategy are classified on evidence that is not fully reliable. Machiavelli's 'fortuna', and Clausewitz's 'chance', have to be treated with the respect that they merit.[16] If this stochastic quality is disdained, one may well persuade oneself that outcomes in strategic history more often than not simply reflect the imbalance in resources that competitors prove by events they can bring to the conflicts of their day: QED yet again! The trouble is that usually one can locate persuasive reasons why the course of events that was the unique past might have been different.

It is characteristic of scholarship to find that for which it seeks. Unfortunately for historical empathy it is difficult to seek the causes of events, and even more so of non-events, when we know with certainty the main features of what did occur. When one is certain that war broke out in Europe in 1914 and again in 1939, it is challenging, to say the least, to express confidence in the argument that particular hypothetical alternative events in the earliest 1910s or the 1930s would have led to less awful consequences. We want to believe that defence planning is conducted for a substantially rational and reasonable world political and strategic context. But, if we accept the awesome diversity in the historical reality of politics and strategy, then we need to conduct ourselves in a manner that is uncomfortably, if reluctantly, tolerant of uncertainties great and small. On close and honest re-examination, we discover that many judgements, not only of the common and 'received' variety, reflect nothing much more substantial than the verdict shown in and by a single course of events. The actual unique past was achieved by a process of interdependent influences that is so richly inclusive as to cause one to question the assumptions of rationality and reason that are iconic, if not totemic.

Even if the strategic world were strictly rational and eminently reasonable, one needs to recognize that there are huge fragilities obscured by these concepts of power. There is no omniscient judge on what is rational and reasonable for defence planning. Moreover, the policing of that matter is left in the authoritative but—to us today—conceptually unsatisfactory hands of future events. The strategist sadly is obliged, *faute de mieux*, to cope with and for a prospective future that will not reliably reward his rationality and reasonableness. Defence planning is a true 'wicked' problem set; one for which even the superior looking options may well prove grossly inadequate.

Surviving in the Badlands: The Strategy House of Ends, Ways, Means—and the Enemy

From the time of Herodotus in the fifth century BC, to NATO's protracted traumatic experience in Afghanistan nearly twenty-five centuries later, understanding of the enemy on his own terms has been recognized as close to essential for the effective, certainly for the efficient, practice of strategy. This sensible sounding, unarguably prudent nugget of ancient wisdom might be the key to good order in defence planning, were it not for the inconvenient problems that its mantra-like invocation can serve to obscure. Even when the enemy of tomorrow seems plainly to be predictable with high confidence, understanding of him is apt to err for reasons that cannot usually be disarmed by attainable knowledge on our part. Recent debate by Western scholars about the value of cultural understanding of actual and potential enemies has yet to be concluded. Current opinion among debaters favours a compromise position between those who aspire seriously to deploy cultural knowledge as a vital aid in the prediction of the behaviour of Others, and those who regard such knowledge more as educational understanding than as providing reliable predictive guidance on future enemy action.[17] The reason for opening discussion of this topic here is because the great, if abstract, formula of strategy conveyable economically as ends, ways, and means, needs to be appreciated as one which, when applied in historical practice, can only make sense when contextualized with reference to an enemy or enemies. For reason most basically of geography, it is usual for polities to have their more stressful political and strategic relations with other polities close at hand. Civilizational commonalities frequently provide no fully reliable grounds for cooperative relations. Everywhere and always, strategy is an adversarial project.

It is possible to pretend that there is no necessity for a principal foe to be identified and adopted formally or informally as such. Often, indeed, polities appear genuinely to forget that strategy must have value in adversarial terms, whether or not those terms are appreciated long in advance of time of active need. The theory of defence planning for national security requires contextualization with reference to risks, threats, and dangers that may need to be countered. The first category in the whole formula of strategy, policy ends, rightly are assumed to be goals and their purposes that either will, or might well, be opposed by 'Others'. An inescapable challenge to prudence in strategy-making is the fact that the quality of our own strategy depends substantially upon its closeness of supportive fit with the quality of our policy ends. Notwithstanding some methodological obsessions among social scientists, it should be needless to say that there are no truly independent variables identifiably in sight with the aid of scholarship. But the challenge to prudent defence planning is the confusion of an often chaotic reality. Although peaceful interdependence probably is the norm in the great stream of time that is the past we interpret as history, it is not at all reliably predictable.

Indeed, even when a temporally trackable and relatively simple bilateral interstate competition is considered, the measure and exact character of interdependence between the contestants is distinctly arguable. The Soviet–American nuclear arms race certainly featured much interdependence of rival programmes. However, the internal dynamics of the competition had powerful, in some respects superordinate, influence on the arming behaviour directed abroad as latent menace. One can argue that in the political, strategic, and technical-tactical interdependencies that characterized the arms competitive systems, each superpower competitor deserved to be regarded in good part as a variable independent of influence by its foreign rival. Each country competed in its own ways and for its own reasons of strategy. Interdependence was a defining reality of the competition, but the American assumptions and assertions about allegedly lock-stepped mechanistic action-reaction in rival weaponry, were over-simple and unsafe in a scholarly sense.[18]

The discussion immediately above illustrates the problems that heavily reductive theory has difficulty evading. A polity conducts defence planning only because it is assumed, really unarguably, that the world of the future either will be or could be a dangerous place. It is not possible for the chosen strategy (or strategies) to function if it is denied usable policy ends for defence planners to attempt to accomplish. By metaphorical analogy, they would be attempting to make bricks without straw. Clausewitz insists famously that '[t]he political object—the original motive for the war—will thus determine both the military objective to be reached and the amount of effort it requires'.[19] With particular respect to defence planning in peacetime, this advice would appear to mean be prepared to meet whatever political demands are placed upon you, whenever that might be in the future. I exaggerate for the clarity of economy, but it is undeniable that such political guidance could have no navigational value. The ways and the means cannot complement each other in order to effect purposeful strategic tasks, if there are no politically charged goals translatable into strategy ends. Policy ends are not eternal. Defence planners have to design strategy (as strategies) that both supports a national policy that is liable to shift, and is able to cope well enough with foreign opposition. This explanation affirms a contextual reality for defence planning that always contains both a domestic political authority ever likely to shift modestly or even radically in the guidance it provides, and a basket of foreign perils that is inherently dynamic. As if this were not challenging enough, in addition there is the certainty of major and minor contingent events that could vary widely in character on the dependent-independent scale. Suffice it for now to register the points that both the necessarily politically desired ends of policy, and the strategic ways in which available (military, inter alia) means are chosen to advance them, are made and revised endlessly in the process of governance. Defence planning is a permanent and therefore always an incomplete project. What needs emphasis is the dynamism in and of every piece of the national security puzzle. There are no final moves, which assumes optimistically that a great (i.e., nuclear) war is not probable in this century. The inherent fragility of this assumption is obvious.

Williamson Murray has written claiming that 'it is more important to make correct decisions at the political and strategic level than it is at the operational and tactical level. Mistakes in operations and tactics can be corrected, but political and strategic mistakes live forever'.[20] The challenge to a polity as a national security community for its defence planning in peacetime is to know how to avoid the worst of mistakes referred to by Murray. Adroit management of the process of defence planning cannot avoid the authority of the super-ordinate fact that policy ends ultimately have meaning not so much for the orderly guidance of the domestic realities of national defence, but rather for the influencing of the polity's largely foreign security context. The ends of security policy are not 'given' in much detail, in good part because security dangers, both the mature and the possible, inherently are dynamic. The defence planner prudently has to assume, perhaps hope would be a better descriptor, that the dangers relevant to his mission fall largely in the category of dependent, rather than independent, variables—meaning that his efforts reasonably may be anticipated as likely to influence potential enemies desirably. It is important to bear Murray's point constantly in mind. While it is vital to make sound decisions about how to fight, it is of much greater moment to decide whether or not to fight, and with whom. Obviously, the scope for political discretion varies widely. But, in the current era which is understood probably correctly enough as being one permissive of historically exceptional discretion over 'wars of choice, rather than necessity', it is not hard to see why Murray's claim of paramountcy for political and strategic decision is important.

The enduring logical structure of the strategy function is expressed in the categorical triad of ends, ways, and means, but as with all general theory, application to particular cases is a task beyond its purpose and competence. Critical review of defence planning in historical practice reveals unsurprisingly that high competence by planners has been the exception rather than the rule.[21] There are good reasons why this has been so, not all of which indicate readily avoidable error.[22] If defence planning as an expression of strategy was easy to do well, strategic history would not be littered so generously with examples of strategic failure. Although usually it is necessary that there be both winners and losers in strategic competition, superior command performance for and then with a dominating strategic effect is by no means unarguably the typical story even in cases of achievement of undoubted success overall. The general theory of strategy tells defence planners that theirs is the task of effecting and sustaining a hugely troubled, perhaps unstable, marriage among three parties or categories with clearly distinctive natures. No matter how well coordinated and how agreeably and necessarily comple-mentary ends, ways, and means can appear in a pleasingly parsimonious

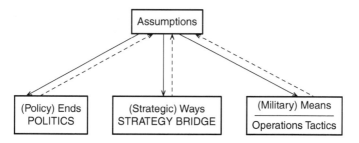

1. Assumptions shape beliefs and influence behaviour at every level, and they tend to endure.

2. Each activity (politics, strategy, tactics) is contextual for the others.

Figure 2.2 Strategy and Defence Planning: Basics

PowerPoint™ presentation, the reality of practice easily demonstrates that fission not fusion commonly is the actuality.

The general theory of strategy could hardly be clearer or easier to understand.

The strategy function is explained reductively in Figure 2.2 with great austerity as ends, ways, and means (and the oft neglected assumptions), does require high level official judgement to be aware of the identity and categorical differences between the strategy pieces. Also, it is necessary for strategy-makers as defence planners to recognize that those most responsible for action in each of the three categories have foci and a rank ordering of priorities distinctive to their particular category of immediate concerns, even though their different levels of behaviour (strategic, operational, and tactical) must fuse to achieve delivery of strategic effect.[23] Hierarchical representation of ends, ways, and means translates closely enough into purpose, method, and instrument. In principle, there is no doubt that the politics of policy ends is the engine that powers the gestalt of strategy for national security, but in practice the great admirable simplicities of general theory are revealed readily to be potentially misleading examples of over simplicity. The reductive austerity with which the basic structure of defence planning needs to be understood is likely to mislead the unwary, notwithstanding its virtue for general education. These examples of dysfunctionality illustrate the problems that the standard formula of ends, ways, and means is apt to provide:

1. *Policy ends* expressive of political choices and preferences are decided with too little regard for the ways and means needed for their realization. This is a common de facto anti-strategic malady. The first two years of the American Civil War for the Union side, and the First and Second World Wars for the German part, provide particular plain historical examples of political wishes functionally disconnected from practical and prudent contemplation of strategic method and instrument.

2. *Strategic ways* may be adopted because policy guidance is weak or even absent. When a polity's leaders turn the political key for their soldiers to go and fight, those warriors will want to wage the kind of warfare that privileges what they believe are their particular strengths. Military beliefs about best current practice is called doctrine, and sometimes style. The German proclivity for sweeping operational manoeuvre intended to outflank and possibly encircle the enemy, expressed and revealed what can be identified as akin to a national template for swift decisive victory in Continental warfare.[24] The decidedly mixed historical record of success and failure with this German way in land warfare (for examples: 1870, 1914, 1918, 1940, and 1941), raised operational method to a position of relative influence over strategy that usually—excepting 1870—ultimately proved fatal. Germans succeeded in demonstrating with admirable clarity that there is far more to war than the operational level of its warfare.[25]

3. *Military means* effect rather than affect strategy and policy. In many, indeed probably in most, wars the military instrument achieves an unhealthy measure of practical control over the political and strategic guidance that should precede and make sense of its endeavours. This inversion of sense, logic, and even ethics, is the product of the nature of the competitive violence that is combat. No real matter what belligerents believe, or once believed, their war to be about, the institution of combat has a dynamic that always threatens to side-line the reasons that should be policy and the politics behind it. Directly stated, warfare can dominate the war whose subordinate enabling expression it should be. War is a duel, as Clausewitz avers, but it is a duel ever liable to become self-referential.[26] The extreme violence and chaos of warfare can have the effect of relegating policy and its politics, as well as would-be strategic direction, to a waiting area pending resolution competitively in battle. Because policy and strategy must be expressed in and by tactical behaviour, the concerns and net performance of that behaviour may well become the real contemporary driver of national belligerent effort, substantially in place of policy and strategy. Warfare must have strategic and political meaning, but that necessary, ubiquitous, and eternal fact need not in practice assign a subordinate role to tactics and operations. This malady has been termed pejoratively the 'tacticization of strategy'.[27] Neatly compelling though this idea may be, it is likely to mislead and confuse, rather than enlighten. The reason is that strategy cannot be tacticized and it is a serious error to express that conception in a way that indicates its feasibility. If tactics are effectively commanding behaviour, then strategy must be absent. There is no tactical variant of strategy; they are distinctive phenomena.

4. *Assumptions* are made and held about each of the three categories—ends, ways, and means—and about how each does or should be able to relate to the others.[28] While it is essential for strategy to appreciate the vital nature of the relations of interdependence that should bind the three categories as enablers

of the mission of national security, defence planning has always been extraordinarily vulnerable to potential errors in assumptions. By definition, defence planning is conducted for safe passage through the *terra incognita* of the future. When this mission is unwrapped, the all but self-evident truth about dependence on assumptions is readily revealed as comprising a number of challenges to understanding that compound quite alarmingly. To be specific, the defence planner cannot know for certain how effective his planned armed forces will prove to be in the future. He needs to, but cannot reliably know: how the tactical-technical grammar of war will change (evolution, revolution, or both); how the relations among different kinds of military capability will alter; when, where, and how enemies will have to be met and thwarted—and who they will be; and how well or poorly our defence planning choices will perform in combat against the choices made by our enemies. Futurological net assessment of conflict requires the making of assumptions for every component vital to the analysis. It ought to be true to argue that the ends, ways, and means that need to be assumed about competition, crisis, and war in the future is an exercise in educated guesswork. Of course a great deal is known generically about the future, especially the near future, but there is sufficient dynamism and retrospectively detectable non-linearity in the course of history for the education from experience, which is all that is available, to be recognized easily as perilously fragile.

The 'badlands' in, or perhaps that are, strategic history cannot be traversed safely without educational assistance from strategy's general theory, and possibly not even with it. However, a firm grasp of its elemental categorical structure at least can serve a vital policing duty. Unfortunately, general theory per se cannot meet particular cases of interpretive necessity. In principle, recognition of the basic structure of strategy should advance the prospects for pragmatic success with statecraft for national security.[29] But, if recognition of the general theory is truly the beginning of, and great enabler for, prudent statecraft and strategy, it is at most only that. Wisdom may not advance beyond a promising early appearance, and concepts that should enable are often not found in practice to be sufficiently fit for the purpose chosen by the political authority of the day. The theory of strategy and of international politics is well decorated with words of power; heavy-duty concepts and propositions that, alas, failed to achieve traction when and where they might have made a large benign difference to the course of events. The contextuality of historical time, place, and circumstance, governs the practical merit of ideas. For an obvious example, appeasement is a most useful, and indeed prudent, concept to translate into policy, always provided the potential adversary of the day is not unappeasable. Similarly, deterrence is an indispensable concept for the guidance of policymakers and of warriors, but they need to understand that not all adversaries are deterrable, at least not every day, in all circumstances and for the indefinite future.[30]

Contingent Mysteries

Had I been writing this book late in 1950, it is not implausible that I would have anticipated, perhaps more daringly predicted, that atomic bombs would most likely be employed in future conflict wherein one or more belligerent was nuclear armed. If we fast-forward thirty-plus years from the darkest days of the Korean War to the early 1980s, reluctant acceptance of the strong probability of future nuclear use in war had been replaced by an abundance of anxiety about nuclear peril, notwithstanding the decades of multidimensional prophylaxis devoted to the matter. Nuclear related anxiety was entirely appropriate to 1950 and, say, 1983, to select a year not entirely at random. Nuclear related fear for the future was rational and reasonable in 1950 and 1983, and each of these two illustrative years can be deployed to cast useful light on the critically important subject of contingency central to this study; it is a principal fuel for uncertainty.

With regard to the strategic contexts of the two years, in 1950 the Soviet Union had no usably deployable atomic weapons, while in 1983 the context was one of mutual nuclear plenty. The specific events of 1950 and 1983 were not predictable; they could not have been forecast or anticipated with noteworthy assurance. The dangers of nuclear war fuelled in real-time by the course of the war in Korea in 1950, with the massive scale of Chinese intervention late in the year, and the implications, grasped principally in retrospect in the West, of the Soviet reaction to NATO's Able Archer nuclear release exercise in November 1983, made sense contextually that was only of very limited real-time value for national security.[31] The task of the defence planner is so to prepare his polity prudentially that it is able to cope well enough with dangerous developments or happenings in the future—contingencies, as they are called. Such contingencies are not specifically predictable and neither can they be anticipated and forecast with confidence. Social science is very much in the business of trying to produce usable prediction-quality theory. It is unarguable that effects must have causes, just as they must have consequences. However, this logically and empirically impeccable compound claim is not quite the open door for understanding of the future, or even of the past, though that is a lesser challenge, that it may appear to credulous social-scientific optimists.[32] The problem is that a dread event—for example, the decision to begin World War III—cannot reliably be predicted on the basis of confidently anticipatable mono-causality, manageable in the adversarial relationships of statecraft and strategy.

If one focuses as the master challenge to be met on the problem of ensuring that the adversary polity should never be able to decide rationally to go to nuclear war, it may seem on the 'evidence' of non-war as if one has performed brilliantly as a defence planner. The awful and awesome catastrophic contingency of a nuclear war appears capable of being met by preventive management of the necessary and sufficient cause of the fatal happening. As a policy science, modern strategic studies sought to be capable of inventing prediction-quality answers to the decisive questions for policy in crisis-time action. The aspiration has been to generate recommendations for policy, strategy, and military posture that in the nuclear case discussed here would be robust against shocks and lesser surprises for the indefinite future. This was gold-standard policy science indeed! If the Cold War could have been guaranteed to remain cold because that happy condition could be assured by a metrically testable and therefore reliably knowable condition of mutual assured destruction, the defence planners of East and West would have been able to rest high confidence in the extreme unlikelihood of a World War III. Such a catastrophe could not literally be an impossibility, because deterrence was presumed prudently to require the presence of nuclear strike forces sufficiently surviv-able to be launched in retaliation to a surprise nuclear attack. The assumed mono-causality of this logic was breath-taking. The reductionist theory of the technological peace explained, in effect, that a great East–West conflict would not—not could not, to be fair—happen, provided the long-range nuclear armed forces of both sides were sufficiently survivable as to be capable of assuring the destruction of the other superpower. It followed logically that, if adequate survivability was highly probable, crisis stability would be the benign result. Missile exchange arithmetic enabled one to calculate how many weap-ons to deploy, in synergistically complementary basing modes, given their various but distinctive vulnerabilities. Vulnerability calculations were key to the course of much expert defence analytical controversy, and that controversy fuelled intense debate about the technical terms of arms control agreement.[33] But, the intense arguments in the 1970s, with all too rare exceptions, failed to engage with the fundamental strategist's question—so what?

There were excellent reasons in the 1970s and later, why it was prudently reasonable to assume that US defence planning should not be relaxed about the balance, or highly arguable but anticipated (by some), imbalance in strategic nuclear forces. That said, it was not reasonable to believe that the most momentous of decisions for war or peace were sensibly reducible to a net assessment of the calculated military advantage in a nuclear 'exchange'. It was not plausible to anticipate a Soviet willingness to chance their arm at a disarming first strike. Nonetheless, it was prudent for American defence planners so to direct US performance in the strategic forces' competition that Soviet strategists should be unable to deliver a 'victory is probable', let alone 'victory is (near) certain', briefing to desperate and highly stressed political leaders. This argument illustrates how a sensible concern—to deny the Soviet Union even a modestly credible first strike capability—can achieve what one could call explanatory creep.

Contingency always has context. A nuclear attack intended to disarm would be an awful contingency, and very likely one that neither would nor possibly could be anticipated. It is a challenge to the defence planner to know, not merely guess, what particular contingencies would mean for national security. Even more of a challenge than that posed by the need to comprehend consequences, is that pertaining to the anticipation of possible causes and their effects. One superpower or the other most probably would win a great nuclear war on calculable military-technical points, should there be the technical means and political motives to conduct such a net assessment. It is probably inevitable, and it may even be desirable, though I admit to being sceptical, that such speculative calculations should be made. But, what is not at all desirable, and indeed may be dangerous, is if the military metrics of combat are permitted to creep into pre-eminence as a believed sufficient cause of decisions for war in contexts that provide or approximate necessary conditions. Anticipation of decisive military advantage if war is initiated sooner rather than later was a factor which helps explain the exceptional historical significance of 1914 and 1939, and the military bar that political-strategic confidence needs to jump has been raised significantly by the nuclear condition. However, statecraft and its defence planning is not reliably reducible to strategic, let alone narrowly military, net assessment. One should expect that policymakers are more likely to choose war when they are persuaded that success is very likely. But, also it would seem to be the case that states do not usually fight just because their leaders believe they will win. War and the strategic issues thereto pertaining are about politics.

Defence planning cannot aspire to deliver an objective national security as a reward for its prudent calculation by net assessment of threat management. It would be unwise for a social scientist to claim that particular highly undesirable contingencies would be impossible. Regarded accurately as a creative art that may benefit modestly from some social science, strategy must allow for exceptions to what are well evidenced as sound precepts for relevant behaviour. Willingness to recognize the unanticipatable contingency, notwithstanding its possible affront to our notions of rationality and reason, characterizes a superior strategic sense founded upon respect for the contextuality of happenings.

Perils to national security do not emerge from nothing and manifest from nowhere. Even if a decision is made to fight now, apparently on the basis of belief that victory today is highly probable, monocausal exploration usually is as poor in revelation of why war occurred in (1914, 1939, or 2003 inter alia), as may appear compelling in highly reductive social science.[34] The root problem, which really is a condition, for understanding the challenge of defence planning is the all too rich and diverse contextuality of historical events. The history of debate about force planning and programming in defence planning in many countries, shows clearly a measure of explanatory creep attaching to unduly simple net assessment.[35] Indeed, sometimes the assessment is not very persuasively net. Iconic, 'magic' numbers come to be invested with potency of meaning for national security that they do not merit. Of course, the bureaucratic and other dimensions to the politics of national security, oblige contending advocates to seek such authority as they can find or invent conveniently in praise of numbers for military capabilities that tend to increase in dignity with the maturity of age and familiarity. This is not to demean, let alone scorn, the numbers that express much of defence planning. However, it is to suggest that defence planning understood inclusively is the field of grand strategy, not only military strategy. Moreover, it is to claim that defence planning thus regarded and approached, cannot be handled with strategic sense if monocausality in effect characterizes the authoritative assumptions with respect to the dangers of future war.[36] The fundamental reason is because the course of history is moved along by too many diverse influences that shape the context for thought and behaviour.

Events necessarily can derive meaning only from their context, they are not the genuinely stochastic happenings of some independent variable, presumably a capricious deity entertaining himself. It has to follow that specific military metrics, no matter how competently net assessable, (and how could one be sure, short of experience in the adversarial happenings in the field of actual battle space?) cannot alone, or nearly so, be invested with more than modest meaning. The defence planning challenge of seeking to plan against unwanted contingency in some time(s) in the future, cannot be met in the main by providing adequately so as to cope well enough only with a principal menace. In addition, the defence planner cannot assume that it is possible to make robust provisions even for a range of perils envisaged with a liberal tolerance of possibilities well beyond the pale of contemporary expert endorsement as high probabilities.

Defence planning has to be understood as an effort to work around what reasonably can be characterized as a formidable barrier to rational behaviour. Specifically, it is a challenge of heroic proportions to prepare for circumstances that either are unknowable, or at best can only be appreciated as possibilities. The fact that the particular contingencies of most interest to defence planners cannot be known reliably in advance, is more than a minor problem for rational planning. However, due recognition of the authority of context raises questions about the planning project that are more daunting still. Among the enduring problems with contingencies are the facts not only that they occur in history as happenings that were unexpected and therefore surprising, but also that the causes necessary to produce effects as contingencies probably are enshrouded in the mystery of a future context that is not foreseeable with any confidence. When we consider the complexity of possible causal relations and the consequent uncertainties that pertain to the understanding of political and strategic behaviour, the scale and quality of the challenge to prudent defence planning is clarified. There can be no evading the difficulties posed by persisting facts for defence planners. First, they cannot know today with actionable certainty which surprising contingencies will happen tomorrow.

Second, they do not know reliably what the relevant future whole context for national security will be. Third, despite episodically energetic scholarly assault, the cause, or causes, of war remain in truth a mystery. The problem of war causation continues to excite understandable interest and alarm, but it persists in resisting analysis for reduction to a simple solution or solutions. This is not a book undertaken for the mission impossible of helping resolve the issue of war conceived as a problem; rather is it seeking to identify ways to cope with dire events that require understanding as possibilities so enabled by context that in effect they are a condition. The sharpest end of this argument for this enquiry has to be the war-prone condition that is contextual for national security and hence for its defence planning. The structure of challenge of the contingency challenge to defence planners is identified and explained in the Box below.

It is rational, and it can be reasonable for politicians to believe that their polity is not condemned simply to be a passive victim or beneficiary of the whims of capricious deities or some unalterable Iron Law of politics. Instead, typically they behave as if their polity's future security can be influenced by the prudence of their efforts in defence planning. The future may be unknowable, but politicians need to believe, or at least appear to believe, that the community is capable of improving its future security by wise grand-strategic choices bearing directly and indirectly on national security in the future. One does not have to endorse the thoroughly unsound belief that the polity's future security

---

Defence Planning, Context, and Contingency

Defence planning strives to achieve some understanding of future political and strategic context, because that context produces the contingencies with which defence planning must attempt to cope.

But, context is a compounded concept that is not so tamed by theory that with sufficiently careful study its dangers can be well enough understood, treated, and even preventively defanged.

Even a secure analytical grip on (future!) context and its diverse working parts cannot much help with the need for wisdom in prediction, because crises do not have to follow a linear course, with events occurring in mechanistic obedience to some (non-existent) Law of Political-Strategic Interaction.

If we seek to connect defence planning as purposeful theory and behaviour with wars won or avoided, as the case may be, there is no evading the challenge posed by irreducible ignorance about the causal chain that can lead to conflict (won or lost). We do not know the structure of the future security context which must be the source of possible future contingencies, but even if we did, we could not know in reliably useful detail why one contingent happening rather than others will occur.

All of this argument demands that we treat the certainty of contingency in the context of chance, in practice meaning that although nothing can happen without cause, that causation is not usefully predictable.

context is predictable with assurance, in order to be able to claim, sincerely if substantially hopefully, that the future can be influenced in favour of a benign character as a result of forethought, foresight, and forward planning today. An appropriately sceptical reaction to that claim would be surprise that such confidence could attend defence planning intended to advance security in a context that is unknown. In that undateable context unanticipated contingencies will be triggered, some few among which could pose serious dangers for us, but with regard to which we do not and cannot identify which menaces might mature into major threats. Restated, the defence planner is required in effect to perform contingency planning for unknown and unknowable contingencies.

It is more than mildly challenging to be both respectful of scholars' efforts to develop prudent plans for public policy with social science, yet suitably sceptical about quests for certain knowledge that may be sound as rational theory but are profoundly inappropriate for the generation of would-be prediction quality advice. There is much that politicians and their defence planners need to know about the future, but that does not mean that it is knowable. The challenge is not so much to improve reliable knowledge about the security contingencies that will be triggered from and mature in a future context. Rather is the need for understanding of how best to cope with the uncertainty. The reality of our security condition, indeed the inalienable human context for all defence planning, is a temporal situation where the future is coming whether we are ready or not. Defence planning conducted in ignorance and therefore necessarily significantly by guesswork, is simply the way things are and must remain. Efforts to pierce the veil cast by time over a future that always begins immediately but can never arrive, are both futile and apt to be dangerous in the illusions they can fuel. However, all is not hopeless, provided one elects to seek help carefully from human experience in the past, for the purpose of preparing prudently for the future.

Strategic Sense

The defence planner is fortunate in the educational value of the well evidenced and long tested theory that can and should be mobilized to assist in understanding this subject. The strategic approach to defence planning, notwithstanding the problems addressed in this book, is not only a superior choice, also it happens to be the only appropriate one. To explain, the defence planner can turn with high confidence to two masterworks. The judgement he will find in the general theory of strategy penned with great subtlety in most of its essentials by Carl von Clausewitz, and in the theory of statecraft and war that is there to be mined from the history of the Peloponnesian War written by Thucydides, are the necessary bedrocks for education.[37] These are neither to be regarded as sacred texts nor as books that are flawless, but they are timeless in their grasp of the enduring features of their subject. Defence planning for national security should draw heavily upon Thucydides writings very late in the fifth century BC, and Clausewitz's work from the late 1810s through the 1820s. The two authors are potently complementary. Thucydides explains inclusively the connections between war and the politics of statecraft with particular reference to what today is termed grand strategy. Clausewitz analyses forensically the nature of war, its functioning as an instrument of policy directed by strategy and waged in combat with tactics. Few subjects are blessed with bequests from the past as worthy of intellectual dominance as is Strategic Studies in its debts to these classic Athenian and Prussian authors. This means that a study today of the apparently enduring challenges facing defence planners for national security, has excellent reason to be confident they can address the hopefully lengthy remainder of the twenty-first century educated by reliable theory that is as ancient as it is modern. Our contemporary problems of national defence are challenges within categories that can be understood in noteworthy part by these works that are classic in the full meaning of that much overused and abused concept. Minimalist sound definition requires that something may be considered a candidate for classic status if it has stood the test of changing fashions over a long period of time.[38]

I hypothesize that defence planning should be approached as a strategic mission, and that its conduct needs to be regarded as strategic performance. Always provided one accepts and adopts a suitably inclusive understanding of strategy, it is safe enough to proceed and treat the problems of defence planning for national security in some detail. The theory of strategy educates would-be strategists as to the identity of the interdependent building of the subject blocks and the relations among them; but it cannot aspire to train the minds of its aspirant practitioners: it educates, but does not train—doctrine it is not. The strategically educated defence planner will know from the theory he has grasped the nature(s) of the basic enduring elements of his professional task, but he cannot know in advance the particular choices about variable character(s) that should be made. It has to be recognized that because strategic command performance is an art and not a science, even well-educated strategic minds may fail because of a deficiency of imagination as well as because an adversary's strategists were as good or better. Those enemy strategists may have benefited from contingency leaning in their favour for no better reason than unmerited good fortune.

This chapter has argued that strategy is the most appropriate way with which to approach defence planning; there are no alternative approaches that deserve consideration as fully worthy competitors. However, that bold claim is sustainable under critical fire only if it is sufficiently inclusive and rigorous in its comprehension of strategy. To meet adequately both reasonable and some possible unreasonable objections to my argument in favour of strategy as preferred conceptual organizer and guide, my understanding of the theory that explains strategy is exposed in outline in the box below.

The General Theory of Strategy

Nature and character of strategy

1. Grand strategy is the direction and use made of any or all of the assets of a security community, including its military instrument, for the purposes of policy as decided by politics.
2. Military strategy is the direction and use made of force and the threat of force for the purposes of policy as decided by politics.
3. Strategy is the only bridge built and held to connect policy purposefully with the military and other instruments of power and influence.
4. Strategy serves politics instrumentally by generating net strategic effect.
5. Strategy is adversarial; it functions in both peace and war, and it always seeks a measure of control over enemies (and often over allies and neutrals, also).
6. Strategy usually requires deception, very frequently is ironic, and occasionally is paradoxical.
7. Strategy is pervasively human.
8. The meaning and character of strategies are driven, though not dictated and wholly determined, by their contexts, all of which are constantly in play and can realistically be understood to constitute just one compound super-context.
9. Strategy has a permanent nature, while strategies (usually plans, formal or informal, expressing contingent operational intentions) have a variable character, driven but not mandated by their unique and changing contexts, the needs of which are expressed in the decisions of individuals and institutions.

Making strategy

10. Strategy typically is made in a process of dialogue and negotiation.
11. Strategy is a value charged zone of ideas and behaviour.
12. Historically specific strategies often are driven, and always are shaped, by culture and personality, while strategy in general theory is not.

Executing strategy

13. The strategy bridge must be held by competent strategists.
14. Strategy is more difficult to devise and execute than are policy, operations, and tactics: friction of all kinds comprise phenomena inseparable from the making and execution of strategies.
15. The structure of the strategy function is best explained as comprising political ends, chosen ways, and enabling means (especially, but not exclusively, military) and the whole endeavour is informed, shaped, and may even be driven by the reigning assumptions, both those that are recognized and those that are not.
16. Strategy can be expressed in strategies that are: direct or indirect; sequential or cumulative; attritional or manoeuvrist-annihilating; persisting or raiding (more or less expeditionary); or a complex combination of these alternatives.

17. All strategies are shaped by their particular geographical contexts, but strategy itself is not.
18. Strategy is an unchanging, indeed unchangeable, human activity in thought and behaviour, set in a variably dynamic technological context.
19. Unlike strategy, all strategies are temporal
20. Strategy is logistical.
21. Strategic theory is the fundamental source of military doctrine, while doctrine is a notable enabler of, and guide for, strategies.

Consequences of strategy
22. All military behaviour is tactical in execution, but must have operational and strategic effect, intended and otherwise.

This theory, chosen here to be presented in 22 dicta, can educate defence planners about all the more important dimensions of their subject, while it avoids making judgements that need to be made in practice strictly to fit contemporary or undisputed future purposes and conditions.

The overarching concept of a strategy bridge facilitates conceptual grasp of the full implications of matters strategic. The theory and practice of strategy encompass the whole subject of defence planning. Strategic ways chosen to employ tactical means for policy ends selected by a permanently political process is the all but pulsating dynamic reality of the subject here. Just as politics and its policy never really sleep, neither does the practice of strategy about and in defence planning. It is not often poetry in motion, but it is an historical story with permanent narrative process. The obvious commonsense, as well as the physics, in the statement that the future can never come, has powerful meaning for the practice of defence planning that too frequently escapes prudent contemporary understanding.

Study of the defence planning function for national security can usefully be characterized in notable, though not sole, part as examination of the challenge of attempting to cope with 'known unknowns', and yet more problematically, with 'unknown unknowns'. This is not to forget the sense in some residual anxiety over the accuracy claimed for beliefs and actions that tend to be dismissed categorically as 'known knowns'. An obvious problem with this last mentioned category is that it points erroneously to matters asserted as truth, when often they only belong in the arena of assumptions. When assumptions are shared widely by people confident in their approximate accuracy, they are unlikely to attract much sceptical, let alone severely critical, attention. The scope for the making of false assumptions about topics potentially important for national security, necessarily helps drive its practice. We try to do what we must as competently as we are able, despite our undeniable limitations of knowledge and understanding. The defence planning challenge is essentially to seek to understand how best we can cope with the need for prudent thought and behaviour regarding a permanently future condition for which currently 'known knowns' are both in desperately short supply, and even when supplied should not be fully trusted. President Ronald Reagan was prudent when he said of arms control agreements, 'trust, but verify!' The principal enduring difficulty is that whereas trust is an ever seductive quality to endorse, verification of evidence relevant to its justification tends to be available only in retrospect, if then—by which time it will cease to be of much interest, save to the proceedings of trials about alleged War Crimes.

NOTES

1. See Colin S. Gray, *Schools for Strategy: Teaching Strategy for 21st Century Conflict* (Carlisle, PA: Strategic Studies Institute, U.S. Army War College, November 2009).
2. Carl von Clausewitz, *On War*, trans. Michael Howard and Peter Paret (1832–4; Princeton, NJ: Princeton University Press, 1976), 100–103.
3. I have been considerably relieved to find that Williamson Murray shares my low opinion of the strategic competence to be found in the human estate, past, present, and future. In his *Military Adaptation in War: With Fear of Change* (Cambridge: Cambridge University Press, 2011), 7, Murray argues that 'incompetence, rather than competence, lies at the heart of man's character'. This sad judgement should be read in the context of Murray's earlier claim in *War, Strategy and Military Effectiveness* (Cambridge: Cambridge University Press, 2009), 98, that '[i]n the end, competence in strategy and policy is the most important component in the success or failure in the conduct of war over the past 400 years'. Given the extraordinary difficulties that can harass strategists at work, it is scarcely surprising that so few of them have merited even candidate-genius status.
4. See Eliot A. Cohen, *Supreme Command: Soldiers, Statesmen, and Leadership in Wartime* (New York: Free Press, 2002).
5. The unarguable proposition that war and strategy are about politics, should not be allowed to seduce people into believing that war and its warfare is politics. An outstanding book that is in some peril of compounding categories unduly, is Emile Simpson, *War from the Ground Up: Twenty-First-Century Combat on Politics* (London: C. Hurst, 2013). It is possible that I am an unduly conservative Clausewitzian, but I am uncomfortable risking the appearance of fusing war and its warfare with politics.
6. I apologize to the memory of Clausewitz for my borrowing, if not outright expropriation, of his wonderful and usefully somewhat contestable concept of the 'grammar' of war. *On War*, 605.
7. Colin S. Gray, *The Strategy Bridge: Theory for Practice* (Oxford: Oxford University Press, 2010).

8. I am grateful to T. E. Lawrence for his analogy by metaphor in his definition and description of 'the whole house of war'. *Seven Pillars of Wisdom: A Triumph* (New York: Anchor Books, 1991), 191. My debt to Lawrence was substantial in my *Perspectives on Strategy* (Oxford: Oxford University Press, 2013), ch. 6.

9. Clausewitz, *On War*, 605.

10. See Simpson, *War from the Ground Up.*

11. A requirement for credibility as a condition necessary for successful deterrence is a prudent assumption, but one needs to be aware that all studies of the theory and practice of deterrence are shot through with potentially lethal uncertainties that could derive from human personality and contingency. Deterrence, including nuclear deterrence, is not and cannot be a science. There is no testable, which is to say scientific, certainty what will be required for deterrence which assuredly can be provided by a particular kind and quality of military posture. The fact that debate about (nuclear) deterrence is attended by, or perhaps one should say decorated with, numbers should not confuse us. The core of this important feature of our subject is human choice, and that effectively is always more or less discretionary. People can choose to do foolish things that are irrational and unreasonable. It is a troubling thought that deterrence is very much a human subject as well as, and indeed sometimes even instead of, being a political one. Whether or not intended deterrence functions well enough must be a politically meaningful question, but the individual human element can be critically significant. The literature on the theory and practice of deterrence is enormous, but the following few items are exceptionally heuristically helpful: Herman Kahn, *Thinking About the Unthinkable* (New York: Horizon Press, 1962); Keith B. Payne, *Deterrence in the Second Nuclear Age* (Lexington, KY: University Press of Kentucky, 1996); and Lawrence Freedman, *Deterrence* (Cambridge: Polity Press, 2004).

12. Michael Howard, *The Lessons of History* (New Haven, CT: Yale University Press, 1991), 11.

13. Howard, 1991.

14. For what amounts to a civilizational temperature reading, possibly a general health check, see Richard Overy, *The Morbid Age: Britain and the Crisis of Civilization, 1919–1939* (London: Allen Lane, 2009). The historical context is explained magnificently in meticulous diplomatic detail in Zara Steiner, *The Triumph of the Dark: European International History, 1933–1939* (Oxford: Oxford University Press, 2011).

15. These contingencies are commonly identified as Black Swans. Events that were wholly unanticipated, yet deeply consequential, have come to be so labelled. This rare but potentially catastrophic phenomenon is described and explained, perhaps over-explained, in the insightful and exciting book by Nassim Nicholas Taleb, *The Black Swan: The Impact of the Highly Improbable* (New York: Random House, 2007). The Black Swan is a brilliant conception of high merit, but its practical value for defence planning is rather limited. Nonetheless, just acceptance of the legitimacy of the notion of strategic history being interrupted and disrupted by entirely unanticipated but deeply consequential happenings, can be important. Such recognition helps legitimize the principle of prudence in preparation against

the possibility of great surprises that could occur notably unheralded, and might function as true strategic shocks.

16. On fortuna see Niccolo Machiavelli, *The Prince*, trans. Peter Bondanella and Mark Muna (1532: Oxford: Oxford University Press, 1998), ch. xxv; Sebastian de Grazia, *Machiavelli in Hell* (New York: Vintage Books, 1994), 202–15; Philip Bobbitt, *The Garments of Court and Palace: Machiavelli and the World that He Made* (New York: Grove Press, 2013), chs. 5–6; and Corrado Vivanti, *Niccolo Machiavelli: An Intellectual Biography* (Princeton, NJ: Princeton University Press, 2013). On chance, see Clausewitz, *On War*, 85–6; Katherine L. Hearbig, 'Chance and Uncertainty in *On War*', in Michael Handel, ed., *Clausewitz and Modern Strategy* (London: Frank Cass, 1986), 95–116; and Thomas Waldman, *War, Clausewitz and the Trinity* (Farnham: Ashgate, 2013), ch. 5.

17. The contested ground between culturalists and anti-culturalists is explored and examined in Colin S. Gray, *Perspectives on Strategy* (Oxford: Oxford University Press, 2013), ch. 3.

18. Theories of arms-race dynamics were very much in season in the mid–1960s and through the 1970s. However, the history of the Soviet–American strategic arms competition did not provide convincing empirical proof of tight arms interaction. Eventually, strategic history moved on from a global context dominated by the great Soviet–American Cold War, and scholars also moved on as times changed and as a consequence so did fashionable concerns valuable for career advancement. Barry Buzan and Eric Herring, *The Arms Dynamic in World Politics* (Boulder, CO: Lynne Reiner Publishers, 1998), makes a worthy effort to unlock the mysteries of what they termed the 'arms dynamic', but my own view has long been one dominated by scepticism about alleged patterns of tightly interactive competitive behaviour over armaments. See my book, *House of Cards: Why Arms Control Must Fail* (Ithaca, NY: Cornell University Press, 1992), esp. ch. 2, 'Weapons and War'. More than twenty years on from publication of this book, I have not been obliged by argument and evidence to change its negative conclusions about the worth of theory on the value of arms control, or on the plausibility of speculation about the dynamics of arms racing. I will admit that I may be hard to convince.

19. Clausewitz, *On War*, 81.

20. Murray, *War, Strategy, and Military Effectiveness*, 98.

21. Murray, 2009, ch. 6, 'History and Strategic Planning: From Rome to 1945'. Also of considerable interest is Mark Jacobsen, Robert Levine, and William Schwabe, *Contingency Plans for War in Western Europe, 1920–1940*. Report from The RAND Strategy Assessment Center, R–3281–NA (Santa Monica, CA: RAND, June 1985). The context of rather warlike peace that was still the condition of the Cold War at the time of composition of this interesting study, meant that the authors very plainly were in somewhat historical analogous mode, as between the consequences of incompetence and ill fortune in the inter-war decades, and their contemporary temporal location in the mid-1980s.

22. It is worth noting that historians continue to debate the question of whether or not the Great War of 1914–1918 was avoidable and should have been avoided. This conflict that was triggered by the political consequences that followed from the

assassination in Sarajevo on 28 June 1914 of the heir to the Austro–Hungarian throne and his wife, cost the lives of more than 9 million soldiers and probably approximately 17 million, military and civilian, overall. The course of history is abundantly contingent, but it is eminently plausible to argue that this war was the most significant event-episode in the course of the twentieth century. A recent outstanding study of the immediate provenance and proximate causes of the war is Christopher Clark, *The Sleepwalkers: How Europe Went to War in 1914* (London: Allen Lane, 2012).

23. Edward N. Luttwak, *Strategy: The Logic of War and Peace*, rev. edn. (Cambridge, MA: Harvard University Press, 2001), ch. 15, is the most cogent development extant of argument about essential disharmony among strategy's different levels of behaviour.

24. For strategy, or its absence, in the American Civil War, see Williamson Murray, 'The American Civil War', in John Andreas Olsen and Colin S. Gray, eds., *The Practice of Strategy: From Alexander to the Present* (Oxford: Oxford University Press, 2011), 199–218; and Donald Stoker, *The Grand Design: Strategy in the U.S. Civil War* (Oxford: Oxford University Press, 2010). Strange to say, perhaps, the abundance of studies of the two world wars of the twentieth century do not include at present truly dominating texts on strategy in those conflicts. Nearly everyone who writes about these very great wars has something to say about the strategies chosen and pursued, but that 'something' typically is not much privileged in authors' attention. Strategic commentary, often perfunctory, pervades this rich literature, but to date it has not appeared in a form comparable in quality to operational, tactical, technical, social, and indeed moral treatments. With reference to the last category, see Michael Burleigh's outstanding book, *Moral Combat: A History of World War II* (London: Harper Press, 2010). Probably the work that is most convincing in its sustained attention to strategic matters remains R. J. Overy, *Why the Allies Won* (London: Jonathon Cape, 1995), which is very persuasive, and may well largely be correct.

25. See Robert M. Citino: *Quest for Decisive Victory: From Stalemate to Blitzkrieg in Europe, 1899–1940* (Lawrence, KS: University of Kansas Press, 2002); and *The German Way of War: From the Thirty Years' War to the Third Reich* (Lawrence, KS: University of Kansas Press, 2005).

26. Clausewitz, *On War*, 75.

27. See Michael I. Handel, *Masters of War: Classical Strategic Thought*, 3rd edn. (London: Frank Cass, 2001), 353–63, for an explanation of the 'Tacticization of Strategy'. This is an important subject, as US and British astrategic misconduct in Iraq and Afghanistan has attested clearly in the 2000s. The relationship between strategy and tactics is in urgent need of disciplined theoretical attention, if misconception and its practical ill consequences are to be arrested and revised in future military operations.

28. Although most defence professionals accept readily enough the claim that assumptions are extremely important, this subject is one that is grossly under-theorized. T. X. Hammes, 'Assumptions—A Fatal Oversight', *Infinity Journal*, 1 (Winter 2010), 4–6, is an exceptionally valuable reminder of this intellectual poverty.

29. This belief was basic to my writing of *The Strategy Bridge*. I recognize that it had to rely upon more assumptive material about its potential educational value for the future than was desirable.

30. There is continuing merit in Fred Charles Ikle: 'Can Nuclear Deterrence Last Out the Century?' *Foreign Affairs*, 51 (January 1973), 267–85; and 'Nuclear Strategy: Can There Be a Happy Ending?' *Foreign Affairs*, 63 (Spring 1985), 810–26. Time has expired on Ikle's question in the first article cited, but unfortunately the question still enjoys a half-life that is noteworthy.

31. On the 1983 war scare see Dimitry (Dima) Adamsky, 'The 1983 Nuclear Crisis— Lessons for Deterrence Theory and Practice', *The Journal of Strategic Studies*, 36 (February 2013), 4, 4–41; and Steven J. Cimbala, 'Interpreting Nuclear History: Lessons Retro—and Prospectively', unpub. Paper, July 2013. The Adamsky article is interesting, but overreaches on the evidence it presents; Cimbala's analysis is more balanced.

32. I did not plagiarize Ken Booth knowingly when I wrote this rather pejorative comment about 'credulous social-scientific optimists', but I wish to acknowledge that back in the late 1970s he had written scathingly about 'the missionary zeal of social science optimism', so I cannot be reliably certain of the independence of my phrasing on the subject. See Booth, *Strategy and Ethnocentrism* (London: Croom Helm, 1979), 138.

33. I admit to some personal participation in the nuclear debate, for example: Colin S. Gray, 'War Fighting for Deterrence', *The Journal of Strategic Studies*, 7 (March 1984), 5–28; and 'ICBMs and Deterrence: The Controversy Over Prompt Launch', *The Journal of Strategic Studies*, 10 (September 1987), 285–309.

34. Social science strives with methodological rigour for a clarity of explanation by necessarily reductive theory. It can be impeded, if not embarrassed in its control of undesirable detail by recognition of a cast-list of candidate causal variables that is unmanageably generous. Good examples of high historical granularity of detail include: Clark, *Sleepwalkers*; and Donald Cameron Watt, *How War Came: The Immediate Origins of the Second World War, 1938–1939* (New York: Pantheon Books, 1989). However, a few historians do transcend the 'stovepipes' of preferred disciplinary method, as for example does R. J. Overy, with his magnificent *Why the Allies Won*, which balances in virtue his first-rate capsule study, *1939: Countdown to War* (Allen Lane: London, 2009).

35. On net assessment as method see: A. W. Marshall, 'A Program to Improve Analytic Methods related to Strategic Forces', *Policy Sciences*, 15 (1982), 47–50; Stephen Peter Rosen, 'Net Assessment as an Analytical Concept', in Andrew W. Marshall, J. J. Martin, and Henry S. Rowen, eds., *On Not Confusing Ourselves: Essays on National Security Strategy in Honor of Albert and Roberta Wohlstetter* (Boulder, CO: Westview Press, 1991), 283–301; and 'The Impact of the Office of Net Assessment on the American Military in the Matter of the Revolution in Military Affairs', *The Journal of Strategic Studies*, 33 (August 2010), 469–82.

36. See Keith B. Payne, *The Great American Gamble: The Theory and Practice of Deterrence from Cold War to the Twenty-First Century* (Fairfax, VA: National Institute Press, 2008).

37. Clausewitz, *On War*; Thucydides, *The Landmark Thucydides: A Comprehensive Guide to the Peloponnesian War*, ed. Robert B. Strassler, rev. trans. Richard Crawley (*c*.400 BC; New York: Free Press, 1996). The most useful analytical appreciations of these classics are, respectively for the two giants of strategic thinking: Antulio J. Echevarria II, *Clausewitz and Contemporary War* (Oxford: Oxford University Press, 2007); and Athanassios G. Platias and Constantinos Koliopoulos, *Thucydides on Strategy: Athenian and Spartan Grand Strategies in the Peloponnesian War and Their Relevance Today* (Athens: Eurasia Publications, 2006).

38. This author is friendly to the traditional view that books should only be considered as candidates for classic status if they are at least 100 years old. In my personal short-list of classics on strategy I breached the '100-year rule' with respect to 5 of my 10 classic authors. For a spirituous analogy of principle, whisky is regarded authentically only to be such if it is at least 8 years old (and preferably older!).

3

Historical Context

(1) The Great Stream of Time

PROVENANCE, LEGACY, CONSEQUENCES

Just as everything that bears upon defence planning must occur in physical geography and will be the result of human thought and behaviour, so also everything must happen in time. In their path breaking 1986 book, *Thinking in Time: The Uses of History for Decision Makers*, Richard E. Neustadt and Ernest R. May, grappled productively with a challenge central to this study.[1] They wrote persuasively about the value for understanding that follows from the concept of time viewed as a never ending stream. I argue here that there is no golden key, no magical analytical method or amazing new, or even old, technology that can foresee the future in detail. However, a combination of historical contextualization and the appreciation of unending motion in time, should improve the odds on achievement of adequacy in prudent anticipation. This chapter and the next explore and examine the promise of a heavily, though not exclusively, historical approach to the problems faced by defence planners.

Reluctant though many social scientists may be to recognize it, the focus of this chapter is not discretionary for this enquiry. It would be agreeable were I able to present the argument here only as one competitive with some variably attractive alternatives. Not infrequently, a major problem with expansive concepts is that their limitations are apt to be as obvious and pressing as they are misleading. For example, as potential aids to understanding for policymakers and officials, culture and geography simply are too easy to employ and abuse.[2] With reference to the challenges for defence planning, history similarly prospectively offers so much assistance to understanding that it is hard to sort the gold from the base metal in the ever contestable record of experience. Unfortunately, though, there is literally no choice other than to strive to comprehend how we should try to learn from history. The beginning of possible wisdom is adoption of a suitable approach to the subject.

Specifically, it must be strictly recognized as necessary, if regrettable, that experience is the sole source of evidence to support education in preparation for the conduct of defence planning. Because we can have no experience in and from the future, the past and our experience of it has to comprise the sum total of experiential resources available to help us cope with whatever is to come. Given as unarguable that the future itself can contribute nothing to our endeavours to manage and control it, the intellectual and material sovereignty both of the existential unique past, and of our often contested understanding of it, means that efforts to plan for the future have to be thoroughly indebted to what is chosen speculatively from history.

No matter how ingeniously one seeks to escape temporal imprisonment, there is no way in which one can gain useful knowledge about the future from the future. Since the future always begins right now and is ever moving, one would be well advised to eschew internet or other search for a crystal ball. Fortunately, the physical constraint that limits us strictly to the present, since we cannot change the past and the future is always only notional, can be somewhat reduced in its ability to harm our performance in planning prudently for the future. The potential of ignorance to be a cause of damage can be lessened by an approach to understanding that is temporally inclusive and holistic. We should approach time with the understanding that the subject is, has been, and always will be, a continuously moving stream of phenomena. Unsurprisingly, the stream metaphor has implications vitally important to the defence planner. Although this ought to be recognized easily as all but self-evidently true, the way in which we categorize neatly in a trinity happenings that are past, present, and to yet come in the unbounded future, hampers appreciation of dependencies that are essential to understanding of the whole. Although ignorance in the particular about the future is strictly unchangeable, this persisting truth is more than marginally undermined by the concepts offered as the title to this section; provenance, legacy, and consequences. Once one accepts the working proposition that the future has to be the product of the present (where else can it come from?), while in its turn the present can stem only from the past, useful light is shed for historical understanding. Even when choices for the future made creatively with imagination are intended in good part as rejection of previous ideas and behaviour, the connection of past and future, mediated and executed by the ever dynamic present, is decidedly alive and well. Whether or not decision makers reject the past, they and their decisional products with subsequent consequences are deeply in debt to that past.

The provenance for the present day provides all of the assets and liabilities that appear, in current thought and behaviour, and the evanescent present will make the similarly mobile future. Provenance has positive and negative legacy value for today, and today is always contributing to make tomorrow. Consequentially, the future is always the compounded product of the past, processed as to its meaning for the future by today. This is not a deterministic approach to understanding, at least it is not so in a reliably predictable manner. A social scientific approach to history is ever prone to capture by an overly reductionist, even monocausal, explanatory urge misdirected by unsuitably rigid methodology. Cause and effect is not a simple mechanism of action and reaction that readily yields revelation of its secrets to the discipline of the rigorous scholar. When a very great event appears to lend itself conveniently to simple causal explanation—as in 'Hitler's war' for a familiar case—one should realize that even the near indisputably principal causal factor, the seemingly demonic führer, required no small amount of contextual assistance in order to achieve the eponymous infamy claimed for him.[3]

If historical experience is approached as evidence of thought and behaviour that is both continuous and also relentless in its temporal downstream consequentiality, then one can identify the past, necessarily presented as typically competing histories, as evidence to employ in our attempts to cope well enough with the future. Admittedly, such creative mining of the past in order to help the present influence the future is not a reliable high road to security and advantage, but, it is the only road extant.

By Extrapolation to Anticipation?

The two concepts that title this section capture much of the intellectual activity relevant to defence planning. Most of the content reflected by that planning is an attempt to anticipate future need. The determination of that need requires development and production, one cannot say discovery, of an anticipated security context. That rather grand, perhaps pretentious, compound context has several major contributing sub-contexts. For example, if defence planners decide or are instructed to lean their imagination forward thirty years, the broad contextual question might take the form, 'what will the world be like in the early 2040s?' But, in order to give the enquiry more focus and bite, in effect one will need to challenge, actually to evade, physics. One would need to target the future contexts currently believed likely to have significant bearing on national security thirty years on from today. While many (sub-) contexts assuredly will have some relevance for defence planning in the 2040s, it should not be unduly controversial to choose the political and the military-technical as the ones most likely to reward futurological speculation today. If contemporary defence planners guess prudently about the dominant relations of power in the period of future global politics chosen as the current focus of medium-term interest, they will enhance the prospects for future security. If in addition they succeed in guessing well enough about the future 'grammar' of war, in its warfare, they will deserve the thanks of fellow citizens and the just rewards of a handsome pension and a peaceful older age.[4] Of course, strategic history is propelled by many factors other than politics and the character of warfare, but nonetheless, those two large baskets of uncertain phenomena have the potential to dominate the strategist's terrain.

The argument above is not intended to be severely reductionist, even though it may appear so. Following the logic already advanced in support of a strategic approach to the challenge of defence planning, it is agreeable to register the important claim that strategy can and should be understood with an inclusivity that licenses its adoption as the most suitable framework for all aspects of this enquiry. The subject here is the way in which one approaches future strategic history. Strategy's general theory acknowledges and respects many aspects of human life that are not most typically associated closely with matters strategic, but which nonetheless do or may have strategic significance. That general theory, for example, includes readiness to appreciate such factors as the human, the moral, the geographical, and the temporal, none of which in their natures essentially are strategic; if by strategic one chooses to focus relatively narrowly upon the element of force in history.[5]

Defence planning should recognize the potential pertinence of factors that are as richly diverse as they can be either perilously interdependent with other factors or even scarily truly independent; the asteroid hazard, for example.[6] It is only sensible to accommodate as much of the unknown future as feasible, in as simple an architecture of theory as possible. It is necessary to give prominence to what the evidence available suggests should be regarded as most important. Also one must make suitable allowance for the potential effect of surprise. It is ironic that we can be confident in our certainty about surprise in the future. In other words, we know that some events, both singly and, more commonly in malign or benign combinations, will not be expected and may not even be anticipated as possible. Appreciation of the persisting reality of this irony is helpful, even though it may not appear so. If one is somewhat ready to be confronted with challenges for which one is sure to be unready in many respects of detail, at least there is some reason to hope that the likelihood of thoroughly inappropriate responses triggered by faulty problem diagnosis should have been reduced in advance.

It is necessary to clarify just what is meant here by history. Much as my definition of defence planning is highly inclusive, so also is my preferred understanding of history. Because of the discretionary human processing required for defence planning, the relevance of the past is much less than one might suppose. The past needs explaining by the present before it can be claimed as a source for lessons or other advice, positive and negative. This rather obvious, if pedantic, point, has potent implications for defence planning. The future cannot be examined on its own terms, because it does not now have any such. If, for example, we choose to assume an international order twenty or thirty years hence as being one organized in many respects as expressing a bilateral superpower balance between the United States and China, with each pole attracting a satellite cluster of security dependants, that would be a view from now which says more about today than it could about a modestly distant tomorrow. Indeed there would be some agreeable truth in the unwelcome vision, but it would be truth about today far more than it could possibly be about tomorrow. There is no escape from temporal discipline. We are what we are and where we are, and we can think what we think only with the resources available to us now. Necessarily, fictional 'tomorrows' always are, or were then, made today, whenever today briefly happens to be. It would be tempting simply to surrender in recognition of the discipline of time, indeed of the laws of nature, and simply eschew endeavour to know the evidently unknowable. For two pressing and mercifully interdependent reasons I choose to resist that temptation.

First, unarguably, though also unhelpfully, we must recognize that defence planning has to be movement ordered for the dark, concerning which the light necessary for prudent guidance cannot be provided reliably.[7] The reason that defence planning has to be done is because we cannot avoid the future. Ready or not, we will be in tomorrow's 'today'. The alternative to defence planning would be not to conduct such an on-going exercise, but the future security context that will be ours cannot be evaded. Given that many polities should be able at least to influence, if not necessarily shape significantly and preferentially, their future security context, it is all but self-evident why purposeful defence planning is not an activity lacking would-be prudent futurists. For most polities, the defence planning function sensibly is not regarded as discretionary. Even if one is not optimistic about one's national ability to nudge international security relations in a relatively benign direction, there should be no convincing argument for an attitude of true passivity. Whether or not you believe that the quality of future national security can be much influenced by national endeavour, there is a political and indeed a moral obligation on governments to make the attempt. The fact that scholars could argue with good reason that too little either is known or knowable about the future to warrant a particular attempt to make provision for and about it, is simply beside the ever transient temporal point. Ready or not, knowledgeable or not, the future will be the today of tomorrow.

Second, and possibly much more helpful, is a suspicion that the argument aired here may be unduly pessimistic because it rests upon an implicit assumption that could be somewhat wrong. It is a substantial error to be rigid in the clarity of one's temporal distinctions between the past, the present, and prospectively the future, that is the whole of history. Both scholarship and commonsense tell us that human thought and behaviour, no matter how creative, can only be the product outcome of today's assets, which have to have been inherited from yesterday. There must be causal connection from the past to the future. So much for the good news. The bad news is that the course of our past even when filtered and interpreted as our history, is inherently, as well as variably, uncertain. This is the case notwithstanding the fact that it is (or was) there in the past somewhere uniquely existential and fit for the generally contestable explanations that are recognized as history. Because the future is made of the past, that past might be understood in ways that could offer some guidance for planning for the future. The caveats necessary to add to this dangerous thought are almost forbiddingly awesome. The master objection that appears in variants of the refrain claiming that 'history does not repeat itself, only historians do that', is almost always true, indeed necessarily so, in matters of detail at least.[8] That powerful and all too valid caveat duly registered, one should not be over impressed with its explanatory reach or depth. The baffled defence planner as would-be futurist need not despair. Frustration caused by the impossibility of obtaining objective facts about the future is certainly a condition beyond cure, but it is not one entirely beyond useful alleviation. Historian Nicholas Rodger indicates some reason for hope, albeit one that invites only modest celebration. In Rodger's words:

> Since history is impossible to escape and bad history is difficult to avoid, the historian has at least the essential function of distinguishing the two, of warning against bad history and false analogy. Historians may have no special qualifications to predict the future, but at least they can check the misuse of the past. For strategists and policy makers, however, this may not be enough. I know from experience that people can be very annoyed with historians who insist how much better qualified they are than anyone else to avoid the dangers of predicting the future by false analogy with the past but then refuse to risk their reputations by making any predictions at all. The historian must always be intensely conscious that history never repeats itself exactly; historical parallels are never really parallel, and the 'lessons of history' are at best general warnings, not specific instructions. It has been well said that 'history never repeats itself, but sometimes it rhymes'. Historians cannot help noticing resemblances between the present day and the periods they study, and these may at least suggest pitfalls to avoid and possibilities to exploit.[9]

If Rodger's cautious endorsement of the proposition that historians should be able to perform some variant of what Sir Walter Bagehot judged to be the three rights of the British monarch—to be consulted for advice, to encourage, and to warn—is taken at least a half step further, one can see possible particular merit in the recasting of the function of theory by Harold Winton.[10] The latter allows that theory must define, categorize, explain, and connect for its field of focus. But, in addition, he insists that theory can, and by plain implication should attempt to, lean forward into what currently is beyond reach as empirical knowledge. In Winton's words:

> Finally, theory anticipates. The choice of verb is deliberate. In the physical realm theory predicts. Isaac Newton's theory of gravitation and Johannes Kepler's laws of planetary motion, combined with systematic hypothesis testing, allowed

Urbain Jean Le Verrier and John Couch Adams independently to predict the location of Neptune in 1845. But action and reaction in the human arena are much less certain, and here we must be content with a less definitive standard. Anticipation, however, can be almost as useful as prediction.[11]

Winton proceeds to cite Marshall Mikhail Tukhachevsky and other Soviet officers who, in the early 1930s, anticipated the potential of armoured forces in future 'deep battle' to penetrate and unhinge an adversary's army at an operational level for lethal strategic effect.[12] What Winton is arguing is that while theory should not endeavour to predict what will happen, it is reasonable to expect it to be capable of anticipating some developments in the future. The term that describes such anticipation is extrapolation. Great caution is required when one extrapolates from the current and (believed to be) known, in order to claim to anticipate what is empirically unknown. But that is only a caveat; it need not be a lethal blow. What can be lethal, however, would be extrapolation out of the context of future strategic history. How and why does that history move? Even if we should guess correctly as to the potential in the development of a particular technology, or the popularity of specific ideas, the strategist's main question still demands answer—so what? It follows that we need to establish what matters most, and why, in past strategic history, if we are to seek usefully for prudent guidance concerning the future. In particular it is necessary to examine both a major trouble with historical analogy as a possible magical key for the defence planner, and also the feasibility of recasting analogy so as to render it more useful to defence planners.

Perilous Analogy, Dangerous Anachronism?

Argument by analogy, especially assertion with colourful analogical illustration, is so commonplace as not to be at all remarkable. It is not hard to understand why this should be so. To use analogy is to enlist the aid of the familiar to help explain the relatively unfamiliar. But, frequently in debate analogy is employed without scholarly discipline and in brutally reductionist form. Common cultural knowledge allows, indeed encourages, debate with shorthand eponymous reference to behaviour. Particular proper nouns and sometimes their adjectives are deployed in order to convey economically a meaning or implication that has the political power to harm or support the person, thought, or activity under discussion. For prominent examples, reference *en passant* to 'Hitler', 'Byzantine', 'Kafkaesque', 'Napoleonic' (if the speaker is British), 'Teutonic', are all epithetical uses of exceptionally reductionist analogy. Typically, the use of such epithetical reductionism as these is assumed to relieve the speaker or writer of the wearisome duty of making a case for the chosen analogy. The very familiarity of the culturally common analogy often has a deceitful purpose, in that it is hoped by its user to lend persuasiveness to claims concerning a much less well known event, person, or condition that is beyond confident contemporary understanding. However, there is a non-trivial problem if the event in question is unquestionably non-existential. What can happen is that historical analogy is employed allegedly to shed light on some future possibility. This often warrants characterization as the poorly known in attempted support of the unknowable.

In his invaluable book, *Historians' Fallacies*, David Hackett Fischer explains why evidential deficiency can be lethal to the attempted use of analogy in futurist argument. Before we strive to proceed further with examination of the promise that may or should lie in the past and present as some guide to prudent preparation for the future, it is necessary to take Fischer's stricture against impossible analogy fully on board. He argues as follows:

> The *fallacy of prediction by analogy* occurs when analogy is used to anticipate future events—as it often is, in the absence of anything better. The trouble with futurist analogies is not that they might be wrong, but rather that they must be utterly untestable and inconclusive. The problem is not that there is a probability of error within them, but that there is an indeterminacy of probability. It is not possible to distinguish a true historical analogy from a false one without an empirical test of its inference. As long as one of those parts remains in the future, the analogy is untestable.[13]

Unfortunately, historical analogy cannot be employed as an aid to understanding for defence planners because, unarguably, analogy claims the pertinence of comparison, whereas the future is so non-existential as to defy empirical testing. It is quite a challenge to our imaginative genius to endeavour to explain important aspects of some future possibility in terms say, of, 1914, 1938–9, or 1962. Even if we believe we have a good grip in retrospect on understanding the dynamics of the events of those years, how can we know what it was about them that should have educational merit for us looking forward, when we cannot know what the analogy ought to teach? As appreciation of the adversarial quality of the duel should be inalienable from study of strategy, so also must it be recognized that two episodes are needed if one is going to analogize.[14] There is no satisfactory means of escape from the logic mandated by the laws of nature. Because the future has not happened, one cannot help explain necessarily hypothetical events in it by means of insightful inference from historical analogy.

While granting readily that there is and cannot be a methodology that sufficiently skilled defence analysts are able to employ in order to fast-forward their knowledge miraculously into the future, all is not lost. If, instead of attempting to predict the future, we are willing to be satisfied with some ability only to anticipate it, we could, possibly should, be on a path to knowledge for understanding, and to theory for more effective practice in strategy. Moreover, one discovers that the strategist's favourite question, 'so what?' has a most useful sceptically exclamatory timbre. If one declines to be unduly discouraged and depressed by the scale and quality of the challenge to the defence planning function posed by ignorance of the future, some life rafts of method, though not lifeboats, can be spotted and employed. Accepting considerable risk of scholarly disapproval, I suggest that there is high value to be found in making and daring to employ the logic of what amounts to grand analogy: the proposition that a quality of compelling understanding that has practical utility for defence planning can be secured from careful study of the past. Hackett's lethal objection to futurological prediction resting upon claimed analogy is simply evaded by means of the assumption that time, the strategic history in our human past, has revealed categorical continuities in strategic thought and behaviour. It follows, if one is persuaded of the plausibility of this proposition, that it should be meaningful for defence planning to anticipate a future that resembles the past. Closely analogous details of time, place, circumstance and so forth, will be lacking between the past and episodes of strategic history yet to occur, but 'so what?' The 'so what' question flags the need for flexibility and adaptiveness in a defence planning process that can never be informed with complete reliability about the context for action in the future. The primary need is for a prudent careful acceptance of the integrity of the idea of the whole great stream of time understandable as strategic history. Defence planners should understand their roles and functions as contemporary agents for thought and behaviour that in their most essential features have not altered over time.

The argument advanced above is a light year removed from the assertion that nothing changes. Furthermore, my argument does not amount to a claim that the pesky details of change over time are unimportant. Rather do I suggest that defence planning can and should be educated by appreciation of what tends to work well enough and what does not, insofar as our access to historical knowledge for understanding permits. What is endorsed here is not much by way of a methodology, reliably usable only by super-skilled social scientists, and still less is it a crystal ball that reveals what needs to be known. Instead, what I suggest is that a hybrid activity that combines historical scholarship and a social-scientific appetite for theory should be capable of providing defence planners with useful guidance.[15] Such educational guidance from strategic historians cannot guarantee that prudent choices will be made, let alone that friction and accident will not blight the future. The general theory of strategy that applies to the whole subject of this study insists that chance and friction are ineradicable from strategic history—past, present, and future.

My belief that the past, present, and future of human strategic experience is essentially a unity may be regarded by readers as either a contradiction or an irony. I claim that despite the myriad changes in many potentially relevant matters, strategic history is a continuum in time appreciated as an unending stream. Changes in the character of strategic history typically are as unarguable as they prove undemanding of revolutionary alteration in their subject's nature. There is sharp contrast between the episodically momentous changes in many features of the past, and the readily identifiable continuities.

It should be possible to avoid the killer objection to analogically founded prediction, or even anticipation, by declining to seek probable truth in claimed analogy, save in one admittedly arguable large respect. Guidance should be sought from an understanding of strategic history which requires or invites recognition as persisting context for strategic thought and behaviour. The logic in Fischer's claim concerning the 'fallacy of prediction by analogy' still holds, but the argument is that strategic history should be considered as comprising grand analogy for a strategic future that always has to be missing much knowable detail. To claim that the past is the future should not warrant labelling as analogy by assertion. Happily, the reason is empirically testable. What one is claiming is that strategic history reveals an unchanging nature. If this claim is deemed plausible, notwithstanding some understandable residual doubts, the implications are profound. Most especially are they authoritative for some of the dilemmas over the challenge in finding methodology suitable for use in the education of defence planners. The approach recommended here for adoption does not direct effort intended to achieve reliable knowledge of the future, because that must be mission impossible. Instead, defence planners should be educated on the general understanding that strategic history all but begs to be recognized and used carefully as possibly relevant evidence concerning generically persisting matters of politics and strategy.[16] In order to prepare prudently for the future we need to look back to the past. We should do so both because there is no practicable alternative, and also because strategic history is a rich vein to be mined heavily, even though it contains much detail that is only background for the purpose central to this discussion. History essentially can and should be regarded as a unity. As a second-order truth this unity is created and sustained by the permanence of politics in and about the human social condition, while this enduring dominance by political process has to be accepted as a lasting product of the human condition itself—and this human condition has to be regarded as permanent.[17] This argument critically does not rest upon assumptions. There is no need to make assumptions about human political thought and behaviour bearing upon the question of security; instead there is verifiable empirical knowledge, and therefore reason to believe also that we have reliable understanding of the essentials about our future strategic history.

The grand analogy that the past and present provide for the future must be short of specific detail that may well prove critically important. It is sensible, however, to pose directly a question that tends to escape notice and therefore attention and serious attempt at answer, because it seems too modest in ambition. Specifically, what level of knowledge of the future do would-be prudent defence planners strictly need to have in order to be somewhat confident that their efforts will prove good enough? Empirical uncertainty pertains to most if not all specifics concerning the time, place, and circumstance of strategic happenings in the future, but that is a general truth ever liable to conduct a negative empirical audit over the plans and programmes aided with the use of any methodology.

The methodological conundrums that attend analogy should be reduced drastically by adoption of the approach advocated here. We should seek both more and less as evidence from the potential that is historical experience. On the one hand, little value should attach to particular claimed analogies, because the past serves up evidence, usually contested, of thought and behaviour of every variety. Argument by asserted analogy will never be short of ammunition, even though we can be confident that much of it will be defective. On the other hand, considerable merit can and should be found in historical phenomena that appear persuasively to appear and reappear frequently in discernible patterns. One of the virtues of a respect for patterns is that one is not thereby unduly inclined to detect close similarities in particular example under scrutiny.

While one needs to be alert to the possibility of surprising developments that may require some national strategic response, it is well to remember that geopolitics, human behaviour and its politics, and the Thucydidean triptych of statecraft that privileges fear, honour, and interest, combine to provide powerful armament for strategic anticipation. Although times certainly do change, defence planners alert to the enduring merit in Thucydides' judgement should not miss much that could be anticipated, even if not predicted. Revolutions in grand strategic choice and therefore orientation do occur, but they are rare because inevitably polities approach their future on the basis of what they have either chosen, or have been obliged by *force majeure*, to accept as their most relevant grand strategic context. Even when the context alters radically as a consequence of technology, for example the maturing of potential menace from the air, that danger is not usually unheralded or shockingly sudden. The German air threat to Britain in 1940 was the third such effort at coercion of this kind, numbers one and two were met and defeated in the First World War. English and British strategic anxiety about menaces rooted in continental Europe can be traced back more than two millennia. The circumstances have always been unique in detail, but the challenge set has been generically stable in its geopolitical and geostrategic circumstance of geography. For a contemporary example of detection of pattern in national strategic behaviour, it is pertinent to quote the following negative judgement of Colonel Gian Gentile on his country's persistence of grand strategic error with counterinsurgency:

[h]earts-and-minds counterinsurgency carried out by an occupying power in a foreign land doesn't work, unless it is a multigenerational effort. It didn't work as touted in Malaya, Vietnam, or Iraq. Yet the narrative has become so hardened and dominant that folks continue to believe that progress can be made in Afghanistan because a better general has ridden onto the scene and his army is doing something different.

What is important for my examination of defence planning is not the question of the sense or otherwise in the British and particularly the American behaviours to which Gentile refers, but rather the apparent fact of national strategic behaviour that has become habitual and therefore, arguably perhaps, cultural.[18]

Social scientific, even some scientific, theory tolerates occasional exception. Using history in attempting to understand the future ceases to be mission impossible, provided one is respectful of the variety of historical experience, and—no less important—one is sensible about feasibility and necessity with regard to defence planning. Realism about the latter helps greatly to rescue historical enquiry from the danger posed by impractical demands for assistance from those obliged to attempt to peer forward in time.

In order to render historical analogy useful to defence planners, one needs to approach a past ready for view at different levels. At the level of tactical agency, each historical episode had its own specific course, with the detail of deeds, misdeeds, accidents, and the rest, seriously influenced by period, place, and circumstance. The deeper historians delve into the who, what, when and how—and even the why, faithful to the time—the more unique each case must appear to have been. Given that all historical episodes worthy of note had rich uniqueness, it is plain to see why the possibility of analogy is so imperial as to be all but useless. Everything, so it would appear, has been done or at least attempted somewhere by someone. When one then reminds would-be perpetrators of the sins analogical with respect to futurology, the case for analogy would seem to collapse beyond rescue. Defence planners have to cope with an absence of certain knowledge about specific detail, most essentially because such knowledge is not obtainable. Historical analogy cannot provide it, but that negative judgement should be contextualized by the appreciation that no other methodology can foresee, anticipate, compute, and calculate to produce reliable specific knowledge about particular future events. Useful understanding of what is likely to occur in the future should be obtainable if one considers history as probably evincing patterns in human security behaviour. Such patterns will appear to obtain, when and if they do, to behaviour identifiable generically by contextual character. All human behaviour has context for meaning, and from which it draws fuel for thought and action. The intellectual foundation for this approach to history as a resource for statecraft and defence planning was stated inimitably by Thucydides.

The absence of romance in my history will, I fear, detract somewhat from its interest; but if it be judged useful by those inquirers who desire an exact knowledge of the past as an aid to the understanding of the future, which in the course of human things must resemble if it does not reflect it, I shall be content. In fine, I have written my work, not as an essay which is to win the applause of the moment, but as a possession for all time.[19]

Translators differ over choice of words and latitude in expression to convey meaning clearly for their time, but there is little room for doubt as to Thucydides' reasoning on the prospectively enduring authority of his text. He tells us that he is writing a classic work, in the least controversial meaning of that descriptor, because it should prove to be 'a possession for all time'. He is able to write, he hopes, for all time because the future 'course of human things must resemble [the past] if it does not reflect it...' It is my contention that assistance for defence planning can be derived from the grand analogy that is strategic history. Thucydides' history was confined to the period 431–411 BC, but we have the benefit of a past, necessarily future to Thucydides, that flowed on for nearly 2,500 years. By logical inference, his claim is for analogy, but we do have substantial grounds for assuming that sufficient time has passed for the views in his history to have been well tested empirically. If Thucydides' *History of the Peloponnesian War* is the necessary aid to education in statecraft for which George C. Marshall was moved to argue in 1947, it is plausible to assume in that regard that it should be no less applicable to the twenty-first century.

The perils of anachronism that lurk in all argument with some content from historical analogy, should simply be accepted because they cannot be avoided with complete reliability. It will have to suffice to be aware of the problem and to seek to avoid it, though even good intentions require a caveat or two. For a leading example, the actuality of the great stream of time lends a somewhat problematic quality to historical judgement that is not clearly avoidable. Our inalienably contemporary condition casts a shadow of suspicion over the quality of all our historical assessments. For example, we cannot avoid approaching understanding of the crisis of summer 1914 and its immediate provenance with the attitudes of today, duly informed by knowledge of what followed from 1914 until our present day. There is a sense in which the existential past has gone, while its recovery is only ever partial because the retrieval operation is executed by people who cannot help but reflect significant features of the present in their representation of the past. This may make for better history, though one can rarely be sure of that. When we seek to make sense of history, what we mean, usually under acknowledged by ourselves and by our students and other readers, is that we intend to make better sense of, for example, the events of 1914, than has been made before. When we claim a more accurate understanding of historical events than appears to have been extant at the time, we ought to be right because we are blessed with some comprehension of the consequences of their contemporary happenings. But, understanding of the causes of the human behaviour that generated the consequences of which we believe we can be certain, can tempt us into profoundly ahistorical country. The reading of the course of history backwards, from effects to well-, if not certainly, attested, causes, should be an invaluable aid to understanding, save for two considerations. First, there is an apparent inexorability in the cause-and-effect nexus of such well-informed history, which is always liable to such capture that it suppresses the imagination unhealthily. The possibly critically important human element of discretion, of choice, is at risk of improper suppression by selected facts as the single path followed from apparent causation to results. Second, because the contemporary thought and behaviour could not be blessed by such knowledge (foreknowledge to their authors), we are near certain to be more or less unempathetic to the decision-makers and their decision-making of their time.[20]

This text endorses the proposition that while the past should be preserved insofar as possible in its own integrity with meaning in and for its own time, interest in it in the context of our contemporary needs for prudent defence planning should not be embarrassed unduly about arguably possible anachronism. I do not mean to claim that social scientists should be ignorant of, or indifferent to, temporal historical integrity. But, as a possible aid to contemporary defence planners our primary concerns regarding Thucydides on Athens and Sparta in the fifth century BC, Josephus on Jewish–Roman relations in the first century AD, or Gerald of Wales on containing Welsh rebels and insurgents in the twelfth century, bear upon their possible and probable meaning for us today.[21] This meaning needs to be extracted as best we can interpret these texts with reference to our needs as we see them now. To write thus, despite its grounds for offence to those who insist upon our seeking knowledge of the past that has integrity in past terms, is not to be indifferent to that integrity. But, it is to insist that valuable though antiquarianism certainly is, it cannot be allowed to be a concern for defence planners now. Although it is important that historians should strive to understand, say, Roman behaviour on its own terms insofar as that is possible, it is even more important for our contemporary defence planners that Roman choices and their probable consequences be understood and interpreted for their possible enduring meaning. We are interested in that meaning for today and tomorrow, regardless of its currency in Roman times.

The use of history endorsed here is one that rests firmly upon empirically derived theory that is mature and, despite some appearances to the contrary, truly is respectful of truth in strategic historical experience. Although defence planning in a sense has to be a plunge into the unknown, it is also a heroic venture that should rest upon the empirical theory derived from millennia that explains about, and allows for some anticipation of, the future, in the context of statecraft and its strategy. It could be argued that the relevance of Thucydidean theory and the general theory of strategy to the future must only be a matter of assumption. That is technically temporally correct, of course, but it is not merely an interesting hypothesis. My master claim, assumption if you insist, is that the future will resemble the past, though not at all reliably in detail. My other, necessary, claim is that sufficient is knowable today about the context of future strategic history for defence planners to place much confidence in what they can learn from history. This does assume that the history consulted will be carefully regarded with due appreciation of the choice for discretion exercised, and with respect for the episodic practical authority of contingency that was not always reasonably anticipatable. Surprise happened, and will happen again.

Learning from History

If it is plausible to argue that the history of most interest here can be considered the product of a great stream of time, there should be scant reason for disdaining the possibility that careful study of the past and the present ought to be capable of shedding useful light on the future.[22] Indeed, it would be unreasonable to suggest to the contrary. If past, present, and future can be approached on the assumption that they refer to the same idea of time, only in different phases, it would be difficult to argue persuasively that there is likely to be very meaningful discontinuities among phenomena in the temporal phases. At least that should be almost self-evidently true if the evidence for dominant continuities is sufficiently compelling. It so happens that we are able to approach the future with high confidence in our generic anticipation of it, because we do know with much assurance what the future will hold for us, at least we do when we seek to identify with broad brushstrokes of comprehension. It is understandable why defence planners should be troubled deeply by uncertainties about the future, but it would be far less understandable were they to find those uncertainties disabling of their ability to perform their duty and plan prudently for the future. The reason is that although the future is unknown and unknowable in specific detail, it is far from obscure at a level vitally useful for prudent defence planning. The dishes that the kitchen of future strategic history will serve up for the pleasure or pain of polities will be unique in detail, but the ingredients that made them are very well known, as indeed even are the habits and preferences of major chefs with known strategic cultural affiliation. Thought of the novelty of much of the detail of our future security can be exciting both of anxiety and hope. But due appreciation of what strategic history should be allowed to say to us as usable theory for anticipation of the future, should be regarded as an essential partial offset to the unavoidable ignorance of futurism. Scholars sceptical of the value of history in the education of defence planners might reflect with profit upon two statements made cryptically by John Lewis Gaddis:

> We know the future only by the past we project into it. History, in this sense is all we have.
>   and
> We're bound to learn from the past whether or not we make the effort, since it's the only data base we have . . . [23]

It is a reasonable assumption that future strategic history will resemble the past and present. Because it rests upon the evidence of 2,500 years, this is not a recklessly bold claim. Argument by allegedly supportive, but really only illustrative, analogy inherently is fragile when it asserts important similarities between single events or even episodes. However, when one claims, as here, that the entirety of strategic history, across time, geography, culture, polities, and technologies, offers a convincing level of similarity of human thought and behaviour, one is advancing analogical argument that should be respected for its weight of supporting empirical evidence. It is my thesis that strategic history to date has shown major continuities across time, place, and culture. It is only sensible to anticipate that future strategic history will resemble its past and, for us, present, because the reasons for the nature of past and present are not anticipated as likely to change radically. Biology and sociology compel the politics of anxiety about, and struggle for, security. There is extant no plausible basis known to this strategist for assuming that that political engine will effect transformational change in future strategic history. A persisting truth with deep relevance for defence planning is that the more detailed a prediction, the more likely it is to be incorrect: its potential utility must stand rigorously in proportion to the confidence that can reasonably be placed in it.

The defence planner is not in need of historical knowledge for its own sake, no matter how deeply it may enlighten with understanding of other times and places. That sentence is likely to give offence to professional historians who may believe that it reveals a social scientist's contempt for the vital context-uality of all historical knowledge, as well as for the cultural assumptions then authoritative. It is my contention that defence planning needs to be informed by the understanding that should result from a close alliance of historians and social scientists. I argue for the central significance of strategy as the mode of thought that best fits this subject. If we apply the basic triadic template of strategy to the possible mobilization of historical understanding for the advantage of prudent defence planning, the logic of appropriate argument, as well as important caveats, are revealed readily.

With respect to any particular proposal for a military operation, the defence planner is in need of specific contextual understanding. The tide-table for particular beaches in Normandy literally is of vital significance, as are near real-time weather forecasts. Generalizations about amphibious operations and plucky soldiers with the will to win in a just cause, emphatically should not suffice in providing adequate assurance of probable success.[24] Indeed, the promotion of hope poorly concealed as a basis for strategic decision, is thoroughly inappropriate. The information from examination of which useful knowledge for relevant understanding might be derived, does not rest necessarily electronically or on the printed page. Defence planning is not assisted at all by some reified History conceived as a mythical agent, or even much by the histories written by professional historians, unless the latter are clear in appreciating the kind of assistance their labours need to be designed to provide. However, expertise on particular places, periods, and happenings, is apt to be largely that and little else. It is commonplace to see book jacket 'puffs' that both praise a work of historical scholarship for its apparent profundity, and then cap such possibly appropriate praise by advising that our political leaders would be much assisted in their political leading if they were so wise as to invest the time into being educated by the work in question. Such 'puffery' not infrequently mirrors historians' brief claims for ontological virtue in the conclusions they draw. The objection to such professions of alleged benefit is neither that they are inherently false, nor that they are advanced merely meretriciously. The problem typically seems to be no more, nor less, than cultural. By and large, historians and social scientists are members of distinctive scholarly tribes. Their purposes, and therefore their methods, differ, because of the differences in their respective scholarly projects. Trans-cultural thought and behaviour certainly are possible, but they are not well represented among those interested in strategic matters.

There is necessity for contemporary strategic studies to seek and find assistance from the contemporary guardians of military or, better still, strategic, history.[25] In my experience over several decades I have found an unhelpful mutuality of professional disdain to be both deeply felt and quite widespread. Social scientists are wont to dismiss historians as largely irrelevant to contemporary problem-solving because allegedly they are wedded unduly to mere narrative detail, and are professionally ill-disposed to the production of theory that might have useful bearing on current and future security conditions. For their part, historians are wont to find abysmal historical ignorance among (social scientific) students of contemporary strategy, and to be almost reflexively dismissive of efforts by those strategists to reach back into history in the hope of finding helpful inspiration and perhaps guidance.[26]

There are a few honourable exceptions to the guardians of scholarly option-purity of discipline as just described, but tribal exclusivity remains unhealthily prevalent. The result is a sad situation where potential mutuality of benefit for understanding is sacrificed on the altar of a misconceived professional purity. Historians tend to be frightened to generalize beyond the near reach encompassing their narrow patch of foreign land in the past, while social scientists are nervous of making much historical reference for the broad purpose of seeking analogous wisdom. Contrary to appearances, perhaps, I recognize that historians have some good reason to be suspicious of bold generalization and entertaining, if dubious, analogy. Similarly, the poor education in history that is almost standard among students of strategic studies today, means that they would be unlikely to analogize wisely, were they so ill-advised as to venture into such perilous terrain as that of the seriously past.

Cross-disciplinary effort more often than not invites, and probably merits, the charge of anachronism. A century's worth of Hollywood's misrepresentation of Republican and Imperial Rome provides ample entertainingly amusing illustration of what is meant by the potent concept of anachronism. Our contemporary thought is presented in fancy dress, albeit usually without the helicopters—though one reviewer of the 2000 movie, *Gladiator*, was so moved by the apparent modernity of the Roman way of combined-arms battle in the opening sequence, that he was moved to comment that helicopters would not have seemed unduly out of place. Notwithstanding the rather defensive disclaim by social scientists for the alleged fixation upon 'mere narrative' on the part of historians, they can find some solace in the evidence of fellow historians looking back with possible benefit to the past from the present. For example, in his magisterial account of the coming of the First World War, historian Christopher Clark attested to the possible value in employing analogy. Somewhat unusually to say the least, he finds merit in understanding of the present for improved understanding of the past. A principal difficulty with this refreshing approach is that it has to assume a quality of comprehension of the very recent and present day that is likely to prove fragile. Clark explains his appreciation of analogy as follows:

> And yet what must strike any twenty-first century reader who follows the course of the summer crisis of 1914 is its raw modernity. It began with a squad of suicide bombers and a cavalcade of automobiles. Behind the outrage at Sarajevo was an avowedly terrorist organization with a cult of sacrifice, death and revenge; but this organization was extra-territorial, without a clear geographical or political location; it was scattered in cells across political borders, it was unaccountable, its links to any sovereign government were oblique, hidden and certainly very difficult to discern from outside the organization. Indeed, one could even say that July 1914 is less remote from us—less illegible—now than it was in the 1980s. Since the end of the Cold War, a system of global bipolar stability has made way for a more complex and unpredictable array of forces, including declining empires and rising powers—a state of affairs that invites comparison with the Europe of 1914. These shifts in perspective prompt us to rethink this story of how war came to Europe. Accepting the challenge does not mean embracing a vulgar presentism that remakes the past to meet the needs of the present, but rather acknowledging those features of the past of which our changed vantage point can afford us a clearer view.[27]

Clark is worth quoting because he has offered with optimum clarity an example of an historian finding high value in recent unpleasantness for better understanding of a significant event in European history. One should add that, for good or ill, most of our understanding of the post-Cold War troubles in the Balkans stems from people who were more vulgarly presentist and somewhat social-scientific, than they were professional historian. There is merit in Clark's openness to inspiration from the present for improved comprehension of the past. But, there is an obvious fragility in the argument just quoted. Specifically, professionally fashionable lines of enquiry and interpretation are always likely to prove transitory. Quite radical challenges even to the apparent certainties of past and most contemporary historians inevitably appear. Historians do not earn their reputations by arguing, in effect, 'me too', on major topics. For a relatively recent example of radical challenge to orthodox historical understanding, one can cite Terence Zuber's exciting dissent from the thoroughly settled belief that there was a suitably eponymous 'Schlieffen Plan', drafted by the then German Chief of the General Staff in 1905, and executed in notably amended form with grimly unsatisfactory results in August–September 1914.[28] Zuber failed to capture the high ground of historical (re)interpretation, but he did succeed in compelling his fellow historians to attend more carefully to their treatment of the relationship between the Field Marshal's somewhat fantastic grand design at the time of his leaving office, and the would-be deadly, but fatally flawed, misdeed eleven years later. Although it is encouraging to see evidence of a willingness by an historian to consider the relevance of the near present to the past, the specificity in the analogy, whether from past to present or vice versa, has to be cause for anxiety if not alarm. The value of possible historical evidence for our contemporary defence planning cannot prudently be anchored to argument by particular detailed analogy. Such analogy must be illicit for the future conclusively for the reason explained above: we cannot know just how it will be in the future, so that the past might be able to help analogically with explanation. Because we are unable to anticipate, let alone predict the future in detail, we must eschew the temptation to rummage through historians' arguments in search of nuggets of insight that might be proven by future events to have had analogical value—had we only known for sure in advance just what it would be that would be in need of analogical wisdom.

The kind of knowledge generated by historians tends not to be user-friendly in meeting the needs of defence planners. Those unfortunates are condemned to struggle with the inconvenient implications of the laws of nature that prohibit the detailed knowledge of the future about events that result from human discretion. Since the past and arguably the present are all that can be known in detail, the challenge is to seek a way in which what is known of past and present can be of assistance in preparation for the future. Because of our access to the past in our history(ies) we do know the strategic nature of the future, though we cannot secure reliable knowledge about its exact character. Furthermore, we are unable to be entirely confident as to what to think about the strategic dimension to our future, we have reasonable grounds for confidence in our understanding of how to approach it. If we will discard exaggerated anxieties about the fragility of prediction for a future that has to be unforeseeable in detail, we should be able to make good enough use of what we do know probably well enough that should be closer to the status of relevant knowledge than merely guesswork. Chapter 4 hazards specific answers to the questions posed here quite strictly only at the level of choice appropriate to the most suitable approach to adopt. It is essential to decide how to think about defence planning; from this discussion we can shift into application of the chosen approach. Following the admirable Harold R. Winton yet again, history (interpretations of, stories about) can be used for advantage to defence planning if we employ theory with discipline to define the field to be studied; categorize phenomena within the field of study; explain what has been studied; connect the field of study to other related fields; and even anticipate what is yet to come.[29]

The defence planner cannot sensibly look to history as an aid to anticipation of the future in specific detail of time, place, and circumstance, but that immutable inconvenience does not mean that little of value is known about what is to come. It is important to register the implications of the abundantly evidenced facts that the defence planning function has always been thoroughly human, pervasively political, and comprehensively explicable in terms of the general theory of strategy. It is logically compelling to see high merit in the worth of historical experience, provided we do not insist on hunting for an unobtainable specificity. The challenge is to use wisely what we believe we know, while refusing to be diverted into blind alleys in pursuit of unknowable detail. Furthermore, the mission here is to help educate defence planners in how to think about their tasks in the present, not to suggest what they should think. Answers to the latter question can only be provided following study of the specific topics in their anticipated future context. That said, there are subjects and topics that can be anticipated as requiring strategic decision for which extensive historical experience is available for careful use. There are a few such subjects that lend themselves to relatively confident judgements for the future, despite their unknowable detail. For two examples of this category of usually confident specific anticipation, one could cite the realms of counterinsurgency conducted abroad, and arms control and disarmament. Unsurprisingly, strong political and moral feelings tend to energize debate on these two contemporary subjects. The argument here is that there is the empirical evidence from many years of effort concerning these two issue-areas, sufficiently compelling as experience to enable us to make decisions in regard to their likely strategic utility in the future, unusually confident that we can anticipate their prospective record with accuracy. Evidence for success or failure in such issue-areas as these is now available from an impressive time span, and lends itself to highly plausible explanation by the theory that we employ for strategic navigational assistance.[30] When strategic behaviours of close categorical type persist in generating similar effects and consequences, there is persuasive reason to treat categorical conclusions about such past behaviour and its consequences as having predictive utility for the future. The methodological boldness in that argument requires a hop, rather than a leap of faith.

Surprise, Shock, and Contingency

By definition, surprise is unexpected, but whether or not it proves shocking for security is another matter, one that is determined by the quality of defence planning. Shock effect, commonly and for good obvious reason, is the product of surprise. There is need to be careful in using particular words of power, among which shock merits a prominent place. However, we need to be careful lest a familiar concept of convenience that does have a plain enough principal meaning, is permitted a descriptive reach that overextends its explanatory value. The concept of strategic shock has attracted the attention of futurists of recent years, but it is far from certain that this exciting idea has been contextualized adequately. It is necessary to cast some sceptical light on this still fashionable concern.

As Winton argues, theory requires careful definition of the most relevant key terms.[31] In the context of this examination of the defence planning function, what is a strategic shock? Eminent futurists claim that 'strategic shocks change the nature of "the game" itself'.[32] The problems with this unqualified claim are that it is neither a general truth for strategic history, nor is its explanatory reach as extensive as plainly is implied. If a strategic shock is understood strictly to mean a sudden surprise event that has implications and consequences of a revolutionary nature, then the concept has considerable utility. It claims that there is a category of surprise that has exceptionally severe implications and possible consequences. Plainly, the concept of 'strategic shock' is one that could, and probably should, occasion nightmares for strategic planners. But because of concept creep and a fuzziness born of porosity between conceptual categories, strategic surprise and strategic shock are apt to be allowed a degree of interface that results in unpoliced merger. It is necessary to observe that not all strategic surprises are really very shocking, and that not all strategic shocks escape adequate management eventually by their potential victims: the temporal dimension to strategy enjoys close to pole position in relative importance for defence planning. One cannot plan to be surprised, let alone shocked, but it is feasible so to plan for national security that surprise, even when shocking, is not so damaging in its consequences that recovery from harm suddenly suffered is fatally impeded.

Strategic history provides evidence of surprises with shocking implications. The Trinity A-bomb test in Alamogordo, closely followed by the one-plane, one-bomb, atomic strikes on Hiroshima and Nagasaki, must approximate reliable illustration of what is meant by strategic shock. However, the revolutionary changes in warfare and arguably in statecraft triggered even by this almost exemplary strategic shock, had shocking implications and consequences that were neither technically extant nor fully comprehended before the early to mid–1950s at a minimum, and possibly even by the mid–1960s.[33] Even the most obviously strategically shocking event(s) of the twentieth century took time to mature. It is a matter of historical record that both the agent of this particular strategic shock, the United States, and the disadvantaged Soviet adversary, coped well enough with the undoubtedly great happening(s).[34] This unarguable fact has large implications for the attitude and approach most appropriate for adoption towards surprise and shocks in the future by strategic planners.

Unfortunately, the futurist already quoted who claimed that 'strategic shocks change the nature of "the game" itself' was mainly in error. Moreover, the high quality of this inaccuracy is so important that the substantial measure of sense in the claim is hard to rescue from the debris in the scholarly crash. As usual, it is not possible to promote understanding or even meaningful debate without first defining terms. Because this exercise must allow some room for cognitive discretion and personal taste one cannot assert that my personal preferences in definition are correct. However, one can be unambiguous, even if controversial. When a scholar defines 'strategic shocks' as those that 'change the nature of the game', it is plausible to understand that as meaning revolutionary change. Of the five meanings allowed to revolution in the *Oxford English Reference Dictionary*, the one most suitable in focus for my purpose here is 'any fundamental change or reversal of conditions'.[35] This may seem to be mere academic pedantry, but a large question useful to this study has to be in play here. Specifically, have or might surprises that attract characterization as strategic shocks have 'game-changing' implications for national security institutions? Or, should the exciting concept of strategic shock be discarded? The proper context for consideration of argument about this is that of the eternal phenomenon of persisting tension between continuity and discontinuity. Foundational to the argument presented in this study is my belief, only arguably my assumption, that 'the game' of competitive national and international security has not changed fundamentally, notwithstanding the changes, even revolutionary ones, discernible in its altered character over the centuries. Change is not contested here. But, undoubted change in the character of war and peace, and in thought and behaviour about warfare and security, national (et al) and international, has not changed 'the game' of nations fundamentally. The fact that much of timeless value about politics, ethics and strategy continues to be found persuasively in texts from ancient Athens and China, as well as from pre-industrial Prussia, suggests powerfully that the concerns addressed diversely across millennia, are ones that are as classic as are the texts to which I refer.[36]

The nuclear revolution probably has effected a truly major—I am too uneasy about 'fundamental' to employ it—change in the potential character of (some) warfare. But, the possibility, even probability, that nuclear war would be a game ending, not merely changing, event, has not incontestably transformed the game of nations to date. Unarguably, one hopes, the now permanent nuclear context should mean that great war between the greater states ought not to be a live policy option any more. However, deterrence can never be thoroughly reliable, and its achievement is believed widely, if not quite authoritatively, to require a capacity to wage some nuclear warfare if necessity so demands. Defence planners cannot and do not dare assume that the absence of nuclear use in anger for nearly 70 years, is proof that nuclear deterrence is an eternal and ubiquitously reliable condition in the future game of nations. The absence of evidence of nuclear use since 1945 is not proof of its impossibility in the future.[37]

Strategic shocks have occurred, but the severity of the demands that they come to be understood to make, often are met, though not always with prompt creativity. The major blights on and in strategic history have been neither banished nor transformed, except probably for the worse. Strategic surprise triggering strategic shock can energize as well as paralyze and disable. Strategists strive to be problem-solvers, for which vital task they can find educational assistance from the wisdom of classic texts that provide a general theory of strategy.

In a vital sense the communal investment made through defence planning can be regarded as contingency provision. The provision of armed forces of different kinds for the future is more of a contingency fund against a range of possible dangers and opportunities than it can be preparation to meet identifiable future needs. As a general rule such needs will not be locatable with high assurance far in advance of their appearance. Of course, governments are obliged politically to claim that they have good reason for their defence planning choices. But the reality is a condition wherein guesswork can only be improved, not transformed.

NOTES

1. Richard E. Neustadt and Ernest R. May, *Thinking in Time: The Uses of History for Decision-Makers* (New York: Free Press, 1986), esp. ch. 14.
2. The difficulty as well as the value of culture and geography as conceptual tools for understanding strategic matters, are explained in Colin S. Gray, *Perspectives on Strategy* (Oxford: Oxford University Press, 2013), chs. 3–4.

3. It is probably fair to say that deep research of great events tends to make a case for research that would be deeper still. Quite aside from the practical constraints of time and motive that limit historical research, not untypically there is the 'satisficing' criterion which requires only that the explanation, or theory, be judged good enough. In practice, the search for complete and entirely reliable truth is, or would be, a chimera. Scholars of a strongly scientific persuasion understandably find frustrating this impossibility of certainty about historical understanding.

4. Carl von Clausewitz, *On War*, trans. Michael Howard and Peter Paret (1832–4; Princeton, NJ: Princeton University Press, 1976), 605. By way of an educated foray into the unknowable, Martin Rees, *Our Final Century: Will Civilization Survive the Twenty-First Century?* (London: Arrow Books, 2003), is as good a fairly popular expedition as any, and better than most. Notwithstanding his deserved eminence in science, it is an unalterable fact that Sir Martin does not know the answer to the question he poses in his book title, and neither does he know how to find the answer. Truly the impossible is exactly that. The futurological literature is ever lively, because of our insatiable human interest in it, but it is eternally condemned to disappoint. Antulio J. Echevarria II, *Imagining Future War: The West's Technological Revolution and Visions of Wars to Come, 1880–1914* (Westport, CT: Praeger Security International, 2007), offers helpful insight on who tended to be more correct than not, about what, and why. As a general rule it is entirely safe to assume that futurological literature is both thoroughly unreliable and will remain so.

5. See Table 2.2, 'The General Theory of Strategy'.

6. Reasons for worry are well supplied in: Duncan Steel, *Rogue Asteroids and Doomsday Comets: The Search for the Million Megaton Menace That Threatens Life on Earth* (New York: John Wiley and Sons, 1995); and Mark Bucknam and Robert Gold, 'Asteroid Threat? The Problem of Planetary Defence', *Survival*, 50 (October–November 2008), 141–56.

7. Richard Danzig risks understatement of the challenge in his choice of title with *Driving in the Dark: Ten Propositions About Prediction and National Security* (Washington, DC: Center for a New American Security, October 2011), but the analogy nonetheless is valuable as an imperfect indicator of the relevant quality of the challenge.

8. The most enlightening discussion of the alleged 'lessons of history' remains Michael Howard, *The Lessons of History* (New Haven, CT: Yale University Press, 1991), ch. 1.

9. N. A. M. Rodger, 'The Perils of History', The Hattendorf Prize Lecture, *Naval War College Review*, 66 (Winter 2013), 10–11.

10. Walter Bagehot, *The English Constitution* (1867; London: Oxford University Press, 1928), 67. Harold R. Winton, 'An Imperfect Jewel: Military Theory and the Military Profession', *The Journal of Strategic Studies*, 34 (December 2011), 853–77.

11. Winton, 'An Imperfect Jewel', 856.

12. See V. K Triandafillov, *The Nature of the Operations of Modern Armies* (1929; Ilford: Frank Cass, 1994). Also see: Jonathan M. House, *Combined Arms Warfare*

in the Twentieth Century (Lawrence, KS: University Press of Kansas, 2001), 90–6; Christopher Bellamy, *The Evolution of Modern Land Warfare: Theory and Practice* (London: Routledge, 1990), ch. 4; and for a useful study of the Russian strategic historical context, Richard W. Harrison, *The Russian Way of War: Operational Art, 1904–1940* (Lawrence, KS: University Press of Kansas, 2001).

13. David Hackett Fischer, *Historians Fallacies: Toward a Logic of Historical Thought* (New York: Harper and Row, 1970), 257, emphasis in the original.

14. Clausewitz, *On War*, 75.

15. For example, historian John France has written a superbly ambitious yet surprisingly detailed (near) global military history, *Perilous Glory: The Rise of Western Military Power* (New Haven, CT: Yale University Press, 2011), but the book is seriously limited in its value to defence planners because the author either does not appear to know how to exploit his immense historical erudition in order to provide answers to the strategist's pressing questions. To be just, there is no reason why a professional historian should do this, unless he is alert to the potential value of his work for national security in the future.

16. I do not deny that not all historians will agree with my argument. However, not all historians agree with each other, any more than do more or less socially scientific strategists among themselves. It would appear to be the case that almost regardless of their primary disciplinary affiliation, some scholars are more inclined to emphasize continuities in history than are others. For example, such notable historians as Williamson Murray and John France—notwithstanding my comment in n.15—have written in a manner that on balance is friendly to the notion of strategic historical continuity, while Benjamin Isaac and Hew Strachan have stressed discontinuity. This is an important issue, but it is not one permissive of scientific resolution: there is no objective test methodology that could determine beyond argument whether continuity or discontinuity is dominant in strategic history. From the impressive canon of each of the scholars just mentioned see: Murray, *War, Strategy, and Military Effectiveness*; France, *Perilous Glory*; Hew Strachan, 'Strategy in the Twenty–First Century', in Strachan and Sibylle Scheipers, eds., *The Changing Character of War* (Oxford: Oxford University Press, 2011), ch. 27; and Benjamin Isaac, *The Limits of Empire: The Roman Army in the East* (Oxford: Oxford University Press, 1990). In his many writings Michael Howard could be quoted as being allegedly on both sides of this issue of historical continuity or discontinuity. See his books, *Lessons of History*, and *The Causes of Wars and Other Essays* (London: Counterpoint, 1983). In truth, the spread of scholarly opinion on the subject of historical continuity, or not, is a spectrum, and centres on disagreement that cannot be resolved objectively by any method. Moreover, neither end of the continuity-discontinuity spectrum is demonstrably more correct than the other. All scholars recognize the existential historical reality of a mixture of change and continuity. Whether or not one is inclined to employ notionally clear, if not rather abrupt, historical periodicity to categorize temporally, substantially is a matter of personal preference. My dislike of categorization that I deem unduly exclusive, reflect methodologically attitudes and opinions that have matured over many years. For a relatively recent example, see Colin S. Gray, 'Concept Failure? COIN Counterinsurgency, and Strategic Theory', *Prism*, 3 (June 2012), 17–32.

17. Stephen Peter Rosen, *War and Human Nature* (Princeton, NJ: Princeton University Press, 2005), is a bold and rewarding venture into deep biological and psychological waters.

18. Gian Gentile, *Wrong Turn: America's Deadly Embrace of Counterinsurgency* (New York: The New Press, 2013), 128.

19. Thucydides, *The Landmark Thucydides: A Comprehensive Guide to the Peloponnesian War*, ed. Robert B. Strassler, rev. trans. Richard Crawley (*c.* 400 BC; New York: Free Press, 1996), 16.

20. By way of example, it is not unknown for an author knowledgeable about a period to stray over the line demarcating historical contextual integrity, into a highly contestable zone wherein subject and intellectual biographer effect an injudicious merger. A biographer slips into probable anachronism when he writes a book claiming to reveal what the historical subject really meant, but did not quite say with sufficient clarity. The product is a book that may be substantially correct in an important sense, but which nonetheless has to be regarded as 'unsafe', to cite a legal notion from Scottish law. A good example of this possible malpractice is Philip Bobbitt, *The Garments of Court and Palace: Machiavelli and the World That He Made* (New York: Grove Press, 2013). The problem with this book is not so much that it may be misrepresenting Machiavelli, but rather that Bobbitt is unduly present in the argument. It is only prudent to balance Bobbitt with Vivanti, *Niccolo Machiavelli.*

21. Josephus, *The New Complete Works of Josephus* (Grand Rapids, MI: Kregel Publications, 1999); Gerald of Wales (Giraldus Cambrensis), *The Journey Through Wales and the Description of Wales* (London: Penguin, 1978).

22. I am pleased to acknowledge with gratitude the major contribution to my understanding made by Neustadt and May, *Thinking in Time*, and John Lewis Gaddis, *The Landscape of History: How Historians Map the Past* (Oxford: Oxford University Press, 2002).

23. Gaddis, *The Landscape of History*, 3, 8–9.

24. See Paul Kennedy, *Engineers of Victory: The Problem Solvers Who Turned the Tide in the Second World War* (London: Allen Lane, 2013), ch. 4; and Harold A. Winters, *Battling the Elements: Weather and Terrain in the Conduct of War* (Baltimore, MD: Johns Hopkins University Press, 1998), for a valuable examination of the granularity of needed geographical information for strategists.

25. This professional challenge was well flagged and discussed in Bernard Brodie, *War and Politics* (New York: Macmillan, 1973), ch. 10. Three first-rate studies help explain Brodie's professional position, located as he was between and among history, social science, and physical science. See Ken Booth, 'Bernard Brodie', in John Baylis and John Garnett, eds., *Makers of Nuclear Strategy* (New York: St. Martin's Press, 1991), 19–54; Barry H. Steiner, *Bernard Brodie and the Foundations of American Nuclear Strategy* (Lawrence, KS: University Press of Kansas, 1991); and Barry Scott Zellen, *State of Doom: Bernard Brodie, the Bomb, and the Birth of the Bipolar World* (New York: Continuum, 2012).

26. Despite my earnest endeavours over many years, the concept of strategic history has not been adopted widely, as I believe it deserves. The concept is defined in Colin S. Gray, *The Strategy Bridge: Theory for Practice* (Oxford: Oxford University

Press, 2010), 10. Also, the idea could hardly be trashed more prominently than in my *War, Peace and International Relations: An introduction to strategic history*, 2nd edn. (Abingdon: Routledge, 2012). However, company of good quality is not entirely absent, as in Ken Booth, *Strategy and Ethnocentrism* (London: Croom Helm, 1979), 42–4.

27. Christopher Clark, *The Sleepwalkers: How Europe Went to War in 1914* (London: Allen Lane, 2012), xxii–xxviii.

28. For the long orthodox view, see Gerhard Ritter, *The Schlieffen Plan* (London: Oswald Wolf, 1958). The exciting theory that there was no real Schlieffen Plan has been advanced boldly by Terence Zuber. See his *Inventing the Schlieffen Plan: German War Planning, 1871–1914* (Oxford: Oxford University Press, 2002), and *The Real German War Plan, 1904–14* (Stroud: The History Press, 2011). Predictably, Zuber's revolutionary thesis has met well organized resistance, as in Annika Mombauer, 'German War Plans', in Richard F. Hamilton and Holger H. Herwig, eds., *War Planning 1914* (Cambridge: Cambridge University Press, 2010), 48–79. To date it seems to be the case that the Zuber thesis has been defeated, and not only on points.

29. Winton, 'An Imperfect Jewel', 854–6.

30. See Gentile, *Wrong Turn*, and Colin S. Gray, *House of Cards: Why Arms Control Must Fail* (Ithaca, NY: Cornell University Press, 1992). What these two books have in common most essentially is development of a theory which explains why an entire category of thought and behaviour about statecraft and strategy is unsound, and therefore fails when applied in practice. Gentile's argument is that COIN methods applied by foreign forces always fail, while I argue that because arms control is about politics it is always either irrelevant and unneeded or impossible. Because these arguments do not appear to be specific to agents or time, it follows that such reasoning should be sound with respect to the future. It may be needless to say that fundamental arguments such as these tend to meet a lot of opposition. Unsurprisingly, officials and scholars do not like being told that their sincere efforts cannot succeed; that, in effect, they are engaged in mission impossible. Persistence with forms of strategic astrology should be confidently expected as a consequence.

31. Winton, 'An Imperfect Jewel', 854. The need for clear definition should be so obvious as to invite a charge of banality against those, like this author, who seek to insist upon it. Many scholars either fail to appreciate the need for such definition, or cannot be bothered to supply it. Definition is not unlike punctuation in that it is essential for conveyance of exact meaning.

32. Nathan Freier, *Unknown Unknowns: Unconventional 'Strategic Shocks' in Defense Strategy Development* (Carlisle, PA: Strategic Studies Institute, November 2008), 5.

33. See Bernard Brodie, *Strategy in the Missile Age* (Princeton, NJ: Princeton University Press, 1979), ch. 5; and Zellen, *State of Doom*.

34. See Lawrence Freedman, *The Evolution of Nuclear Strategy*, 3rd edn. (Basingstoke: Palgrave Macmillan, 2003).

35. Judy Pearsall and Bill Trumble, eds., *Oxford English Reference Dictionary*, rev. 2nd edn. (Oxford: University Press, 2002), 1234.

36. Namely: Thucydides, *The Landmark Thucydides*; Sun Tzu, *The Art of War*, trans. Samuel B. Griffith (*c.* 490 BC; Oxford: Clarendon Press, 1963); and Clausewitz, *On War*.

37. Those who choose imprudently to take comfort believed to be reliable from the admittedly impressive fact of nuclear non-use since 1945, are recommended to read Nassim Nicholas Taleb, *The Black Swan: The Impact of the Highly Improbable* (New York: Random House, 2010).

4

Historical Context

(2) Patterns for Anticipation

GOING BACKWARDS TO GO FORWARD

Because the future is coming for us, whether or not we are prepared adequately, there can be no evading the challenge addressed here. It simply is a fact that the future is not reliably knowable. Thus far I have laid heavy emphasis upon the certainty of uncertainty. It is necessary to be uncompromising in this emphasis lest one is ensnared into the error of believing that the future is usefully foreseeable in some matters of vital detail. This is a case where it is first essential to destroy before one can build constructively with the necessary value. US Marine Corps basic training is similar in design and purpose. One needs to know what literally is unpredictable and unknowable, in order to avoid foolish quests after a certainty of knowledge that must be impossible to obtain. By discarding the folly of scholarly efforts to make a science of politics and strategy, we open our minds to what we can and should know about the past and present that deserves to be valued for its practical bearing upon security in the future.

Because politics and strategy are arts and not sciences, they are not subject areas fit for scientific examination, able to yield prediction quality results.[1] This argument should be appreciated so readily as to be regrettable that it needs to be made explicit. Nonetheless, as with so much about politics and strategy, apparent absolutes often really are not so. For example, although culture, geography, and technology are not sufficiently potent to fuel a wholly satisfactory theory of strategy, neither must any of them be neglected in a suitably inclusive theory.[2] The future is not predictable in detail, but that does not mean we are condemned to be completely ignorant about it. This is fortunate, since the past and the present is all that is available to us as the source for evidence.

Two ideas that have had a rough passage in this text thus far are analogy and anachronism: both are critically important. The perils of analogy were outlined in Chapter 3; condemned in particular was the idea of analogizing for an unknown and unknowable future. Once we recognize what cannot be known about the future, no matter how exciting the proposed methodology, we should also seek to identify what might be anticipated and why that may be so. 'It is no accident', as Soviet scholars used to say, being dutifully faithful to the idea of a pre-scripted theory of history, that the stream of time shows evidence of great continuities, notwithstanding the evident discontinuities. Williamson Murray claims persuasively that '[h]istory suggests that war is a non-linear phenomenon, which explains why it is so difficult to pre-determine the outcome once the iron dice are rolled'.[3] Unfortunately, 'non-linear' may be held to mean or imply discontinuity, when all that need be meant by it is not in a continuous straight line. One needs also to beware of the reification in the claim that 'history suggests'. Of course, 'history', let alone History, does not exist and cannot possibly suggest anything. History is the product of historians; the past is gone and cannot authentically be retrieved.[4] It is convenient to claim that history obligingly has made a helpful suggestion, but one needs to appreciate that this is not possible. It is probable that Murray's appropriate and innocent characterization of history as being non-linear might mislead the unwary. Rather than press the important point about the common non-linearity of events and their consequences, it is more important to signal the basis for confidence in endeavours to seek knowledge about the future in and from the past. Accepting the risk of theoretical overreach, it is possible to construct an empirically supported theory of future defence planning that rests explicitly on assumptions that are plausible. The use of historical data that may be evidence as a guide to thought about future defence planning, depends upon the following propositions and argument:

- Human nature has been constant in the characteristics it can favour, with the privileged features reflecting local contexts of time, place, and circumstance.

- Human behaviour creates and acts in and upon a political context. Human social existence is unavoidably political.

- All political behaviour is about power, whether directly or indirectly, notwithstanding the wide variety of forms of expression in which it is manifested. Political power is best understood as influence.

- Relative power always plays a role in human relationships.

- All human history is political history, and all political history can be regarded as being in some measure strategic history. The human need for security has mandated the social life that requires political process for tolerable social order.

- The chain of reasoning above leads inexorably to recognition of the concept of strategy ultimately as the intellectual binding necessary for this enquiry.[5]

This claim for the high relevance of past experience as a source of guidance for the future rests upon two vital assumptions. Specifically, I argue that the future will bear recognizable, indeed anticipatable, resemblance to times past and present. There can and should be an empirical basis to arguments about alleged or denied continuities from past to present, but once one seeks to cross that River Styx into the unknown, the future, candidate evidence stops abruptly. Nothing about the future is capable of being verified, it is all a matter of belief, faith, and trust. This is more than a little frightening to those who respect and typically require evidence. Because empirical evidence directly about the future is wholly unobtainable, one is obliged to acknowledge that futurology, including its expression in defence planning, can neither be science, nor can even be regarded as social science, with the latter's typically relaxed approach to certainty of proof for theory worthy of the name. This may or may not be regrettable, but it is a fact. Defence planning has to be an art. I am not tempted to say 'only an art', because the requirements for effective art are in no important respect inferior to those for science.[6]

Argument about historical continuity as contrasted with discontinuity, is obviously critically relevant to the issue of whether or not historical experience has much to provide us by way of education relevant to future defence planning. If one is willing to find possible help in historical experience, that willingness requires belief that time is an endless process wherein past, present, and future have common generic referents. In other words, strategic history is manifested in thoughts, deeds, and situations as different in their character as they are common in their nature, regardless of temporal context. There is an obvious peril of anachronism attached to this approach. Moreover, historians typically and properly are most careful in seeking to grasp the particular detail of thought, deed, material, and circumstance specific to the time and place of their professional focus. My ambition here is to identify aspects of strategic history that are candidates to be evidence of possibly eternal human strategic thought and behaviour. It should not be doubted that a careless word here or there, or a necessary caveat omitted, have the potential to mobilize the professional wrath of historians. Social-scientist barbarians will be located, vilified, and should be punished severely for trespassing on the sacred turf of the past with its integrity ... and so on. Certainly I cannot promise to avoid such blasphemy, but I can promise to be alert to the danger of anachronism and inappropriate historical analogy. But one must insist upon the need to explore the past and present for their possible value concerning the future, if only because there is no other help available. Indeed, once one overcomes or regretfully but determinedly ignores the outrage of some professional gamekeepers of the past, one realizes that in fact there is really nothing at all outrageous about the belief that study of the past should be able to help educate us navigate the future. If this were incorrect, one would be arguing that all the strategic thought and behaviour, the whole, often grim, historical experience, had no relevance for the future. That would be an outrageous, even ludicrous, assertion.

The common objection that 'history does not repeat itself' merits two responses. First, one can respond with the ever useful exclamation, 'so what!' The persisting reality of change is recognized, not conceded. Second, one explains that the maxim is unduly reductive because there appears to be an essential unity to strategic history that is expressed in the repetition of situations and their challenges, if not in the language used at the time to describe and consider them.[7] For us to write today about Romans designing and executing strategy is indeed to be anachronistic. However, Romans and their successors in Byzantium performed strategically, and for very long periods they were notably prudent in their defence planning.[8] It would seem that our contemporary general theory of strategy is good enough to serve as a methodological key adequate to facilitate our ability to make use of historical experience for the anticipation of strategic need in the future. It is not a golden key that translates miraculously the strategic meaning of the past into cautionary tales specifically applicable to future contexts. But in order for history to be a useful source of guidance for defence planning, we do not need to know strictly what to do in detail. The quest after defence planning that would prove prudent, is a hunt only for 'good enough'; not for perfect knowledge.

The Discipline of Strategy

A principal virtue of the concept of strategy is that its structure encourages, requires, and enables the exercise of discipline—intellectual for the theorist, practical for the executive. There is a glorious inclusivity about strategy's conceptual and practical reach that is hard to evade without notice and beyond capture. Anyone unable to understand the strategy concept, must *ipso facto* be unfit to attempt defence planning by any definition of that mission. Undoubtedly, (political) ends, (strategic) ways, and (military) means, plus assumptions, is an extremely reductionist formula to consider as the leading forensic aid in the understanding of historical experience and making prudent preparation for future defence. Ironically, perhaps, the very terseness of the language for this tripartite, possibly quadripartite categorization, contributes inestimably to clarity of meaning. Ends, ways, means, and assumptions are indeed inclusively large ideas, but they are anything but vague. The basic architecture of the strategy function should say nothing specific about the chosen content for each category in any period, but it flags unmistakeably the distinctive purposes of each. Equipped with the logic of the structural connections of the mutual dependencies between ends, ways, and means, any historical period or episode can be examined for its possible meaning for today. One can be thoroughly respectful of historical distinctiveness in matters great and small, and appreciative of cultural differences, yet still consider historically distant, even very alien, happenings in a framework that has integrity across centuries.

Although we cannot know what will happen in the future, we can be confident in our knowledge of what it will be like. There is no pressing reason to believe that the future for defence planning must be substantially different from the past or present. To hazard a bold claim, we know enough about the past and the present in order to know the nature of our future history, notwithstanding the certainty of uncertainty about the character of the future. It is all too easy to feel overwhelmed by what we do not and cannot know about tomorrow, forgetting the powerful reasons that exist for us to be relatively optimistic about our ability to cope with the uncertainty.

With particular respect to defence planning, there is an exceptional need for collaboration between the somewhat rival mind-sets and methodological biases of the historian and the social scientist. On the one hand, attitudes more characteristic of social science are essential, because defence planning has a dominant need of theory for explanation and even, with great care and important caveats, for anticipation. On the other hand, the contextual and particular knowledge of history is wholly essential to provide fuel for the theories of social science. In common with global weather, world history is unknowable in advance by prediction, though some anticipation is just about feasible. Climatology and history are intimately related, but both successfully resist would-be conclusive scientific examination. This point is obvious, but is nonetheless important to recognize as a fundamental constraint upon the subject of this text. There is no way in which a requirement for guesswork can be eliminated from the job description of the defence planner, but there is an important way in which his guesses can be helped by education in relevant knowledge. That knowledge is not to be found in a short-list of favourite historical analogies, not least because of the unanswerable question, 'analogies in the past to what, exactly, in the future?' Particular historical events or episodes cannot be trusted for analogical value, because their very distinctiveness requires an unachievable particularity in anticipated knowledge about the future. What the defence planner seeking useful knowledge needs is the benefit of the leverage given by the social scientist's theory over the historian's detailed knowledge of the past.

To make progress in understanding the help that should be available from across professional boundaries, it is necessary to recognize the sensible limits for defence planning ambition. It is important to appreciate what understanding is, and is not, achievable by disciplined enquiry. Complexity is a problem in understanding both the past and the future. Of course there is a categorical distinction between what has occurred and what has not, but both categories are somewhat compounded in the concept of the great stream of time. In this view, past, present, and future are all history, the only difference is one of existentiality. It can aid appreciation of history to recognize fully that the past is gone and is always in large, if variable, measure irrecoverable. Such recognition can be helpful in understanding that our reliable knowledge of the past is, or may be, in its indeterminacy closer to our grasp of the future than often is assumed. Yet more important for the defence planner is appreciation of those well-known characteristics of our human past and present that prudently can be accepted as navigation aids for future defence planning. Defence planning for the future—near-term, mid-term, and possibly even long-term—can know much of what it needs to know. Such planning should not be regarded substantially as akin to 'driving in the dark', at least not without headlights.[9] The conceptual key that opens the door to understanding the utility of history for the future, is recognition of the essential unity of history, in all of its past, present, and future. Once one is willing to accept the proposition that the future will be like the past, only different in detail, one is then in a position to appreciate the value in historical knowledge of a particular kind. What can be provided is the social scientist's explanation as theory of categories of behaviour from the past and present. Viewed thus, the subject can be explained as follows:

The future will be shaped and driven by:

- Human thought and behaviour.
- Political thought and behaviour.
- Human thought and behaviour in quest of security enabled by (always relative) power understood as influence.
- Human political thought and behaviour in the quest for security, made manifest in performance of the strategy function.

The relevance of historical knowledge and understanding is all but self-evident when one recognizes that the defence planning function for community security has been as enduring in its nature as it has been ever changing in its local character. No-one in the past could know in important detail what the challenges the future would bring. It follows that we should be able to see the future in the past and present, because human historical experience has not revealed any change in its nature. Since we know that Athenians, Romans, and Mongols, inter alia, needed to behave strategically in functional terms, whatever the cultural flavours of the time may have been, we can access and make our sense of their behaviour. It would be anachronistic were we to claim that our contemporary strategic ideas, including the modern concept of strategy, is to be found in all times and places past. But, it is not at all anachronistic to discuss, say, Roman and Byzantine strategic thought and behaviour, when that quality is regarded functionally. It does not matter whether Roman generals spoke in detailed terms that would be recognizable as strategic at the US Army War College today. What does matter, though, is the fact that those generals were obliged to strive to function strategically in ways consistent with our meaning of the term.[10] Such strategic functioning has differed hugely in its referents in detail, but ends, ways, means—and the temporally dominant assumptions, is a formula resilient in its elemental architecture against historical varieties in forms of expression. Framed by the basic triad of strategy, the remainder of this chapter explores and examines what is knowable from the past with some confidence and what therefore should be useful for future defence planning.

History: What Do We Think We Know?

What we do not know about the future may well kill us, but since ignorance of specific detail is a condition of human life that cannot be cured, it must be endured with such imperfect insurance as limited knowledge of dire possibilities allows. It is useful to realize that it is not the mission of the defence planner to make correct choices for a more or less distant security context. 'Getting it right' cannot be the task. Judgements as to the rightness of defence plans will only be possible in historical retrospect, and even then there will be grounds for argument over alleged causes and effects. The past does not lend itself to a scientific method of enquiry about defence planning. Scientific truth, to be such, is testable experimentally and must always be revealed as identical knowledge, regardless of time, place, and circumstance of testing. Despite the earnest but futile endeavours of my fellow social scientists, the truth about the future that may be obtainable from the study of historical experience is not of the kind that Sir Isaac Newton would have respected as scientific.[11] But, given the impossibility of applying science as a key to knowledge of the future, help from another source is possible.

To argue metaphorically with a still useful partial analogy, one can conceive of the function of defence planning as being somewhat akin to that of planning for safe travel by road—albeit road travel absent a quality of driver 'interest' that could render the vehicle a weapon by prior intent. Nearly all communities take road safety more or less seriously. Political authorities everywhere know that accidents will occur, regardless of the rigour with which road safety is addressed. Certain knowledge of some failure in the future does not however suffice to discourage efforts to promote safety. Moreover, societies world-wide tolerate, in effect condone, some failure. Modern societies choose to live with death and injury on their roads rather than strive for an unattainable perfection of safe travel. More than a century of experience with the motor car has taught most societies what tends to work and what does not, by way of rules, regulations, and physical constraints for and on road travel. Our understanding of strategic history is usefully somewhat analogous to the road traffic context in that we are amply armed with expensive and diverse historical experience, and we know the system is abundantly populated with the possibilities of accident. But, the vital part of the analogy is that with respect both to road safety and to strategic behaviour between polities, certainly imperfect knowledge is well worth having. We cannot predict with certainty how, when, where, or why, a particular road accident will occur but nonetheless we find high value in a road-safety system that we know contributes to personal and general public safety. By analogy the strategic history of the past two and a half millennia can yield a level of understanding of what tends to work with respect to politics, statecraft, war, peace, and strategy, and what does not. What the study of history cannot provide is historically transferable particular truth. Scholars can aspire to understand why war occurred in 1914 and 1939, but did not in 1962 or 1983. What those cases cannot be pressed individually to reveal is any certain general truth about war, crisis, and peace, because the circumstances of each were *sui generis*. One may venture generalities about context, personalities, and perceived power relations, but one should not hazard hypotheses that could fail for reason of detail necessarily unique to a particular occasion.

In a scientific age it can be no easy matter to attempt to explain why knowledge and understanding of strategy and its politics is irreducibly limited. Because of the adversarial nature of statecraft and strategy, it is impossible to be certain that one's choices are correct. Emile Simpson develops this thought and takes it to its logical conclusion when he argues as follows:

> Ultimately wars are phenomena which are external to everyone: that is, wars go beyond the boundaries of any individual experience because they are defined by the aggregated activity of a multitude of people. However, what unites individual experiences into 'war' is their association with the clash of organised violence. In this sense, while policy intentions of either side will shape war, war has its own independent existence, formed through reciprocal violent clash.[12]

National security is not a subject that lends itself to unilateral decision, regardless of external events. Context demands that the discipline of external relations be accepted. In short, the fitness for purpose of our statecraft and strategy is by no means determinable at our own discretion. Although the remainder of this chapter explores strategic history in a quest for useful knowledge and understanding, there can be no denying the limits to the attainable. The challenge is to navigate between on one side the rocks of historical uniqueness, and on the other airily banal generalization. History is so richly endowed with strategic practice and malpractice that it can be recycled, spun and PowerPointed™ purportedly to reveal any lessons that are expedient to the believed need of the moment.[13] These sundry perils are accepted here because there is no choice. Human political experience, our understanding of it as history (i.e., contested histories), is all that is available as evidence to provide aid for future defence planning.

The chapter proceeds to historical experience categorized in three clusters of subjects: human nature, politics, and ethics; statecraft and war; and strategy and military power. The concluding section discusses briefly the advantage of learning from the experience of others, across time and cultures.

HUMAN NATURE, POLITICS, AND ETHICS

Whether we are would-be business travellers, historians in other words, or merely foreign tourists studying for pleasure, it is all too easy for the 'Otherness' of the past to impress us unduly. Much as perceived cultural distinctions can depress the ability to recognize common features about humanity, so the 'foreign country' truth about the past may dull the ability to recognize historical continuities and the biological, sociological, and psychological reasons for them. Fundamentally, the past is usable as a variably accessible resource bank of human experience in all situations, simply because it is human. No matter how we conceptualize the past, it is really the past. Bronze and Iron Ages, Steppe and Other Empires, Ages of Gunpowder, ones defined as Nuclear, or labelled allegedly as being owned by Information Technology— the most significant thread common to them all is humanity. In an important sense we are what our technology (inter alia) has allowed us to be, but human agency binds the entire narrative of strategic history. This truth is so obvious that it is frequently under recognized and undervalued.

We can and do make strategic sense unavoidable in our contemporary terms of Athenian and Spartan political and strategic behaviour, even though we recognize in principle, if not always in fact, the differences in mental and material circumstances between then and now. The consequences of victory, stalemate, or defeat, have varied very widely across centuries, but we can strive to allow for that when we consider times past.[14] I am not arguing that the strategic past really is like the strategic present and future, if only we look hard enough beneath the surface of language and artefacts. Rather is my argument the more modest claim that there is sufficient commonality between then, now, and, in anticipation, the future, for history to be mobilizable as an aid to education for future defence planning. My claim for an analogous strategic past is of necessity rather general, but nonetheless it has implications, at least, that are plainly specifically applicable. Candidate conclusions that can be drawn from the historical record most relevant to this first category are now discussed.

Strategic history attests richly to the fundamental fragility of the rational actor model of strategy. The structure of ends, ways, and means, with the whole shaped in every part by assumptions, is logically impeccable. Unfortunately the strategy function is employed necessarily by human beings (and their organizations) who are always more or less flawed. Both theorists and practitioners have difficulty coping with the enduring structural difficulty for the strategy-making and execution process caused by the Other that is the adversary. Ends, ways, and means, and their pertinent assumptions typically suffer much loss of strict rationality when they are applied, as they must be, in strategic conflict. However, even more troubling than the characteristic weakness in treatment of the Other as a realistically dynamic agent, is the apparent fact that the understandable, even anticipatable, logical implications of strategy are lethally vulnerable to the true subjectivity of the rational thought process. It is not as well understood as it needs to be that rationality and reason are entirely capable of an unholy fusion. The problem for strategic anticipation lies not so much in possible irrational adversarial behaviour, as in behaviour that is thoroughly rational, albeit hugely unreasonable to us. The point in need of firm grasp is that rational thought and behaviour only require the purposeful pursuit of particular policy goals by means using ways chosen carefully to secure them. Rationality is not required to pass some test for objective veracity. If a polity behaves in a sincerely, if expediently, instrumental strategic fashion, sufficiently convinced in its assumptions and calculations that its ways and means will advance its political ends usefully, it is behaving rationally. The obvious problem with this appreciation is that there is literally no sanity check on thought and behaviour. It might be objected that when policy goals and available ways and means are massively asymmetrical, the polity in question must, or would, be acting irrationally. Unfortunately this would be as false in theory as it could be deadly as a basis for policy and strategic behaviour in practice. When states misbehave in our estimation irrationally, they may be guilty only of behaviour that appears unreasonable to us.[15]

The importance of this point about rationality and reason would be difficult to exaggerate in its relevance to future defence planning. It is not sufficient only to grasp the adversarial nature of strategy. That is because the situational, cultural, and even the human personal, characteristics of an adversary serve as caveats that should limit the confidence with which future behaviour can be anticipated. The belief common among expert commentators that potential adversaries can be trusted to be faithful in the service of their own interests thus contains a potentially fatal weakness. It cannot and should not be assumed that rationality has an objective commonality of political and strategic content, which is to say common with ours. The dangers in underexamined assumptions about the deterrence of nuclear armed adversaries are particularly obvious. Beliefs about, attitudes towards, and hopes for the future, reside very much in the poorly evidenced realm of assumption country, and that should oblige us to treat the contested concept of culture with serious respect.[16]

The record of strategic history, no matter how it was explained and justified in contemporary concepts and language, demonstrates with abundant grisly evidence that humans have been, and indeed remain, capable of any and every form of coercive behaviour. Quite aside from the eternal and ubiquitous actuality of the harm caused incidentally by the persisting phenomenon of war with its defining violence in warfare, it has been a fact that there are no limits to the harm that we humans are prepared to inflict when perceived necessity and sufficiency marry. We can forget that the 'grammar' of war should be governed by politics, with the logic of policy in its quantity and quality.[17] Often, expert discussion of trends in warfare seem forgetful of the necessary instrumentality of the military instrument.[18] Although warfare does have its own abiding nature, as well as a highly variable character, its future is not a subject sensibly capable of strictly self-referential prognosis. The character of future warfare in both quality and quantity will depend nontrivially upon the weight of political fuel with which it is promoted.[19] Tactically viewed by isolated events, one can show an apparent trend towards ever greater discrimination in the precise use of violence, enabled critically by technology.[20] However, the strategic historical record shows that the scale of warfare and the quantity of harm to people and property are driven primarily by the quantity and quality of the human will to fight in the case at issue. The greater wars of history were not rendered great by their military ways and means, but rather by the political determination that insisted upon their conduct.

This point has a pressing implication for defence planning, in that it suggests powerfully that trends in warfare privileging highly discriminate violence have no reliable meaning as a trend for the future, because they cannot address the real problem. Historical experience reveals that political will, not the art or science of war and warfare, determines the quantity of future war as well as its character(s).[21] The sovereignty of political will over war (and peace)—past, present, and future—is a persisting source of uncertainty for defence planners. Too often, warfare is considered as a technical phenomenon, a variable essentially independent of matters political. This is a serious error.[22]

The historical record of politics as the engine necessary for the generation of war has been so permissive of local variation by time, place, and circumstance, that its generic parentage of conflict can be underappreciated. What matters is not the abundant menu of perceived provocations that can produce conflict and war, but rather simply the common engine of political process that transforms concern into antagonism, which matures into hostility expressed in the competitive violence of war. The defence planner cannot be certain that he needs to be ready to provide military forces for a particular contingency in a few years' time that assuredly will trigger a demand from higher political authority for an action plan. However, he can be confident in his understanding of the relevant political context. Although defence planning most typically is conducted in time of peace—or at least non-major war—its range of concern and its putative reach must encompass circumstances that are far from peaceful. It can be difficult in peacetime to shake organizations into willingness and readiness to confront the extraordinary. A significant value of historical education is the opportunity it affords, even requires, for consideration of the political and strategic challenges presented by highly unusual circumstances. There is need to recognize that strategic behaviour in circumstances believed to include the greatest possible danger to national survival, do occur, albeit mercifully only very rarely. Super-threats do arise and not always on long notice for the convenience of defence planning.[23] The point is not to suggest that defence planning should endorse an ability to meet challenges of the highest order, simply because the historical record demonstrates unarguably that they can occur, but rather that a competently composed historical understanding will recognize the episodic reality of extreme danger. It is in the nature of the political context for human history from which we cannot escape, for there to be a possibility, which relatively rarely is an actuality, of major war. Normal times of non-alarm are systemically unfriendly to, probably not permissive of, the extraordinary measures that in the politics of wartime may scarcely even be controversial.

Honest appreciation of the full implications of the political context for future strategic behaviour, requires anticipation of some extreme instances of perceived necessity. This is not to question the higher authority of a moral standard, nor the need for ethical conduct in its affirmation. But it is to say that the record of strategic history shows that the practice of strategic ethics is governed largely by the variable character of the constant nature of politics. This sovereign variable intervenes between the practice of strategy and the moral values that always require interpretation in ethical application.[24]

Historians are plausible when they claim strategic advantage as a benefit that can flow from moral advantage.[25] But it is yet more plausible to argue that the course of strategic history is not dominated by a moral narrative. Just and therefore good enough national purposes are not usually perceived as such widely abroad, and they may be contested at home also. In need of emphasis here is not so much the variability of the ethical ideas that stem from contending founts of moral standards, but rather the eternal and ubiquitous functioning of political process. In dimension after dimension of strategic planning, once one burrows below the surface of apparent meaning and activity, one finds political behaviour in thought, word, and deed. This is scarcely a stunning revelation, but a great deal of both expert and popular public commentary on matters of importance for defence planning gives the appearance of undue innocence regarding the light (perhaps not always the guiding light) or shadow cast by politics. For example, defence planning must involve technical analysis of forces, their generation and support. Also, the employment of forces certainly must meet authoritative ethical and legal standards. But it does not follow in practice that defence planning primarily is either an exercise in expert defence analysis, or prospectively is design for the application of our moral values and legal rules. Morality and its local ethics, as well as careful technical analysis approximating in many respects in the hopes of some, a 'science' of defence preparation, only contribute to the subject here; they do not define it.[26] If anything can be understood reductively as defining defence preparation, it must be politics, which conceptually is captured appropriately by the essential inclusivity of strategy's ends, as expressed in its classic enduring minimalist formula.

STATECRAFT AND WAR

Defence planning cannot usually be conducted with the calendar marked helpfully with the dates of future crisis and war. Notwithstanding that common hindrance to efficiency, planners in many countries can be confident they need to prepare for a political context that will not be bereft of all danger of war. It should not be forgotten that defence planning entails preparation for war in good part in the hope that such war in the future as may be deterrable, in fact will be deterred. As the Latin tag claimed somewhat contestably, *si vis pacem, para bellum*! This is one of those maxims that contains as much wisdom as folly. Unilateral under-armament, let alone disarmament, can be quite as perilous as the consequences of the over-armament that might fuel a classic security dilemma.[27] The Thucydidean trinity of 'fear, honour, and interest', will be as ready as ever it was in Ancient Greece to provide the necessary and sufficient fuel for future conflict. The human nature that finds political and therefore also strategic behaviour necessary in the eternal search for a tolerable condition of security will never be free from the fear of war. Such anxiety is reasonable, given what one is obliged to recognize as facts of our all too frequently strategic history.

It is not possible to predict wars in the future. The leading reasons why war eludes human grip for control or, *in extremis*, elimination, are because it is in practice too varied in most aspects. Also, improved understanding need not be a sufficiently potent cause of peace.[28] The outbreak of most wars is not meaningfully attributable largely to error and incompetence in statecraft, even though the consequences of war frequently attract that retrospective judgement. Rather is war, though usually not the war that actually happens, often chosen in the classic Clausewitzian manner, intended to be an instrument of politics. Of course, particular historical political and therefore strategic contexts provide distinctive fuel for future conflict. All historical periods yield contexts of perceived or anticipated threats and opportunities relevant to, if not necessarily authoritative over, the defence planning of the period. Defence planning is served with the hypothetical challenges of 'what if...?' scenarios. There is danger of self-capture in scenario choice, but also there would be danger in declining to test security and defence provision against some definite quantities and qualities of current or assumed future menace.[29] Peril to the integrity of defence planning lies in the necessity for choice. This is a 'wicked' problem that does not allow a verifiable correct answer, unless, as here, one is willing to be satisfied with defence planning geared to a standard of 'good enough' when considered in the light of an admittedly contestable prudence.

Two lessons that can be learnt from strategic history are, first, that wars are not specifically predictable, and second, that even the wars that could be anticipated often have a character that was not accurately foreseen. We should learn from strategic history that war is live interactive lethal theatre that cannot be scripted in advance for a predictable course and outcome with the consequences intended by the more successful belligerent.[30] This should be widely understood and unarguable, as it tends to be ignored when war is launched. The relationship between politics and war is not always as straightforward as a speedy reading of Clausewitz may mislead one into believing. If we yield the authority I believe we must and should to his claim that war is a 'true political instrument', one plainly distinctive in its means, there is no real difficulty in allowing that instrument a potential effectiveness achievable by different routes.[31] Given that the most important element in the theory of war is its instrumentality for politics, it is really a secondary matter whether or not that instrumentality is exercised through actual battle.

Politics, meaning the political process that interprets the needs of contested interests and the anxieties thereto pertaining, causes and uses war. With its desiderata locally defined, the statecraft with which security is protected includes the military instrument. Respect for the rich variety of unanticipated events and episodes in the historical record, suggests that strategic choices for the future need to be as inclusive as seems likely to prove compatible with overall strategic effectiveness. A leading lesson of strategic history, and one that heavy attention to the detail of strategic analysis is likely to miss, is the near certain lethality of political and strategic error, as contrasted with mistakes in tactics or logistics and personnel. It would be difficult to exaggerate the relative importance of this lesson from historical experience. If a community fights the wrong war in the wrong way, the entire enterprise, at all levels, even those that had merit, will fail. The American experience of successive failures in Vietnam, Iraq, and Afghanistan is proof of this conclusively attested claim. The truth in the claim helps drive this examination of defence planning towards placing emphasis on politics and strategy, though hopefully not to the short-changing of tactical concerns. As a strategist, the defence planner dare not be uncritical and uncomplaining in accepting passively the political hopes he is given in the guise of policy 'ends'. Those 'ends', the product of an ever dynamic political process, very largely will determine the strategic value of his military means. While those means certainly have to be fit enough for violently competitive purpose, also they need employment for appropriate political purposes in effective ways.

It is only sensible to recognize that incompetence, if not gross folly, is quite a normal quality of life, not excluding politics and strategy.[32] Nonetheless, many and even possibly most of the errors in statecraft, including defence planning, let alone in the conduct of war, are not lacking of excusatory justification for reason of mitigating circumstances. What matters most for this enquiry is not so much that the abundant evidence of error be acknowledged, but rather that it be accepted as normal—perhaps not abnormal is an appropriate nuance— and essentially unavoidable. Indeed, many cases of apparent incompetence reflect nothing more worthy of blame than wrong choices made under con- ditions of great uncertainty in a systemically adversarial and creative context. Statecraft, war, and strategy, are all of them in their natures competitive projects at least partially worthy of analogy to the duel, as Clausewitz insists.[33] The appropriate test of the quality of defence planning should not be its ability to guess correctly which dangers will erupt and exactly which forms they will assume. The right test is rather the assessment of the ability of one's defence preparation to cope with deep uncertainty, adjust to adapt survivably to unpredicted moves by adversaries, and carry the friendly cause on to politically meaningful success. In other words, we can and should learn from strategic history that although error is normal, the likelihood of error being nationally fatal is far from certain. For Britain in 1940, error in the conduct of continental warfare in Europe proved only operationally decisive in a single campaign. By way of contrast, strategic excellence in homeland air defence enabled operational success briefly in the Middle East that had strategic value in helping sustain Britain as an active belligerent pending a necessary benign change in the overall political and strategic context.[34]

Defence planning in its actual and potential contexts of statecraft and war cannot afford to rely upon good fortune, particularly in the invaluable coinage of enemy political, strategic, and operational error. However, strategic history does suggest strongly that strategy's temporal context can play an important role in belligerents' performances when allowed to do so. Specifically, because one knows that in the duel that is war mistakes at all levels certainly will be made by both sides, it is only prudent to conduct defence planning with both a 'Plan A' for the short term and a set of 'Plan B' options for the longer term, in mind. Every conflict, let alone every war, is very much a learning experience for all sides.[35] Also, one should be willing to learn that while there are possible tasks in some wars to which the maxim that 'the impossible really is impos- sible' applies, there are many conflicts where strategic effectiveness achieved through a process of honest competitive learning from near-real-time experi- ence can be advanced decisively. The practice of warfare teaches both sides how to be more effective, and one side may well learn more quickly than the other. The education that some immersion in strategic history can provide will not usually be of specific analogical value. Indeed, to examine the past in a quest for details of similarity to today, let alone a hypothetical tomorrow, would be foolish. Strategic historical data should yield evidence of the experience of confrontation with the under-expected and outright unanticipated, and some understanding of how and why belligerents on balance succeeded or failed to cope with surprise.[36] We should not seek to learn from the past how politicians and generals coped with the challenges of their day. Rather should we learn from their successes and failures, including the reasons for them, about the political and strategic difficulties of a categorical kind with which they were obliged to strive to cope. Contemporary policymakers and soldiers need pre-eminently to be educated as to the questions to ask of potential challenges in the future. The answers will need to be as specific to time, place, adversary, and circumstance, as they will be near eternal in their relevance to strategic historical experience. Marcus Licinius Crassus should not have been defeated catastrophically at Carrhae in 53 bc, had he benefited from strategic education. We can learn nothing today from his tactical or operational level errors, but we should be able to learn a great deal from an education in strategy that would have foreclosed on Crassus' fatal expedition to the Euphrates.[37]

Turning closer to contemporary concerns, the conflict in Afghanistan offers classic features to illustrate the argument here. Because Afghanistan is unique in vital respects, it would be unwise to venture without extreme care into the realm of possible 'lessons' for the future that its course might provide. Nonetheless, at the levels of politics and strategy we should be able to learn much that is well attested and has plausible relevance for the future. The strategic history of the 2000s-plus in and about Afghanistan cannot and will not be repeated, but as a kind or category of strategic challenge Afghanistan in that decade is entirely plausible as a type likely to feature in the future. What we can learn from Afghanistan in the 2000s is that foreign intervention on behalf of unpopular politicians whose regime is systemically corrupt will be resented and eventually opposed. The American and NATO intervention(s) in the country were always so likely to fail to achieve positive results at all commensurate with their costs that they ought to have been rejected as policy. The US and Allied (re)learning of enduring truths about the tactical countering of insurgency was futile, because success with COIN requires a permissive political context in order to empower sensible strategy enabled by high tactical expertise and competence. Defence planners will not be better educated for their duty by means of mastery of the techniques of COIN in Helmand Province in the late 2000s, but they should be able to learn from the evidence of that experience why, and therefore when, COIN would be likely to work well enough in the future.

Wherever one looks at strategic history, temporally distant or close, the relevance of experience as evidence with utility for future planning depends critically upon the categorical level. This author's understanding and misunderstanding of the record of arms control and disarmament in the statecraft of the past century illustrates the argument advanced here. For some years I was prepared foolishly to believe that the detail mattered in the on-off-on process of negotiation about the possible control of competitive armament. Furthermore, I was willing to believe that the subject of arms control was important. Plainly, this could and probably should be a topic with profound significance for future defence planning. Happily or otherwise, belatedly I came to understand that the entire edifice of arms control—official bureaucracies, negotiating processes, diplomatic activity, and even creative intellectual effort—was at worst a charade, or at best relatively unimportant political theatre. Arms control (and disarmament) is not really about war and peace, rather is it a largely decorative supportive appendix to the serious business of statecraft and strategy. It is important that defence planners should know this. It is even more important that they should understand why they can have high confidence in the argument presented here.

Winston Churchill understood the problem of disarmament with exemplary clarity in 1934 when he said that '[i]t is the greatest possible mistake to mix up disarmament with peace. When you have peace you will have disarmament'.[38] Churchill's austerely reductionist maxim conveys an inexorable logic that is amply evidenced historically and has noteworthy value for defence planning: it summarizes the argument for the political nature of war and peace. This is not quite to claim that the political theatre of arms control negotiations can have no politically worthwhile value, and nor is it to argue that every possible measure of arms control must be insignificant. But were one to insist that arms control and disarmament are only adornments to statecraft and strategy, there would be small risk of serious error being committed. The case of arms control is but a minor variant of argument close to the reasoning of Michael Howard when he observed that it is so challenging a task to maintain an army in peacetime in good-looking military order, that it is all too easy to forget about the purpose of that army.[39] By analogy, so enthralling can be the often contestable highly technical details of potential arms control agreements, that it is easy to forget in practice the extreme dependency of technical agreement upon political will. Arms control has no autonomous merit for peace; it is an instrument of diplomacy that expresses the motives in the political theatre of the moment. When political relations are permissive of strategic agreement, unsurprisingly arms control then emerges from the shadows and may even appear important.[40] Our reading of the meaning of strategic history provides unambiguous evidence of Churchill's wisdom. There is no need to burrow into the archives in search of the minutiae of offer and counteroffer in an historical arms control negotiating process. While some value may be gleaned from past experience of chicanery over battleship tonnage or ICBM throwweight, the lesson that matters pertains to the persisting dominance of matters political over issues military-technical. Weapons neither make war nor keep the peace, rather is it human beings with their politics that do both, inter alia with their military instruments.

It should not be concluded that technical detail is unimportant. The detail of competitive armament does matter, in the same way and for the same reasons that the triadic strategy architecture of ends, ways, and means does not imply disdain for means. When using strategic history as an educational tool for defence planners, it is essential to emphasize the nature of the challenges read about in times past, rather than to focus upon their precise character. The challenges and responses repeat generically over time, while much of their character does not. We can be confident in our ability to identify categories of challenge for which we may need to be prepared, even though particular detail cannot be anticipated with confidence as likely to be most appropriate as an effective response. There is no reliable substitute for expertise on and even somewhat over the anticipated edge of the militarily feasible, but history is more likely to mislead than to educate wisely about such detail.

By way of the concluding note on this consideration of statecraft and war, yet again I wish to indicate strongly the inclusivity of this discussion of strategic phenomena. In particular I believe it is important for future defence planning that we appreciate the weight of strategic historical support that is there privileging the following proposition: events anticipated to be only small have a substantial record of escalation into episodes that can blight decades and more. Small events quite commonly trigger large events by means of second (and beyond) order consequences that were neither foreseen nor anticipated. The human agents of strategic history are not always reasonable, nor necessarily are they even rational. A distinctly modest scale of violence in the Balkans somewhere, say, bounded by clear particular political ends, or action to dethrone a monstrous regime on the Tigris, for example, may be 'briefable' tidily to political authority. But, time after time the sheer complexity of the agents and agencies that insist on playing a role in the course of history leads effectively to chaos. This was a consequence of liberal intervention in Iraq in 2003, notwithstanding what ought to have served well as the good enough intentions of would-be movers and shakers in the great stream of time. Friction happens, chance strikes unexpected blows to the confidently laid plans of purposeful action—and protracted chaos may ensue. This is to flag an essential lesson that can and should be learned from strategic historical experience: it repeats categorically, not in particulars.

STRATEGY AND MILITARY POWER

The general theory of strategy derives empirically from understanding of the whole course of strategic history and is authoritative for all times and places.[41] The theory is not normative, rather only explanatory. The entire record of strategic experience in the great stream of time is the database about which general dicta can be drawn. What can be learnt, if often contestably, from historical experience is what was attempted, what succeeded or failed, and why that was so. The contemporary detail of how strategic history was done, including the strategic and operational choices made and the tactical skills exercised, is of only modest interest and importance. Because of the timeless nature of the strategy function, the strategic history of any place or period can safely be assumed to be framed conceptually in terms of the ends, ways, and means particular to the then-contemporary situation. The wide range of cultural and other variety in historical experience did not, indeed could not, preclude or cancel the relevance of a strategic frame of reference, no matter the linguistic usage of the time. Unless historians are familiar with the general theory of strategy, their typically contextually well-situated, and perhaps culturally alert and even empathetic, scholarship will be hard for our contemporary defence planners to use with educational value. It is unlikely that our planners of today for tomorrow will be in need of knowing how to manoeuvre a Roman consular army for battle, for example. However, the contemporary defence planner should be interested in learning what a Roman expeditionary force or garrison attempted to do in order to quell an insurgency. We can and should 'talk strategy' across the centuries and millennia, because the Romans, inter alia, were obliged to attempt to satisfy the requirements of the strategy function, as are we today. They too had political ends, some choice of strategic ways, and a variety of available or obtainable means. Cultural assumptions certainly have differed enormously, but we can be alert to that fact, though it will be a challenge to make due allowance for it.

I have risked invoking the ire of many professional historians who may believe that I am unduly disrespectful of the authority of specific historical context. In some measure I may merit rebuke, because there can be little doubt that the assumptions, motives, and reasoning behind behaviour in times past that today we can identify fairly plainly as strategic, is apt to be chronically anachronistic, or so it appears in our terms today. It is necessary that I lay emphasis on the importance of recognition of the strategy function that obliged people in all periods to advance their political interests in ways that made effective use of their available means. History in all periods and places provides evidence of the often grim reality of this function. Considered grand and military strategically, the experience of the Duke of Marlborough is a gold mine of education for today's defence planners. But, details about the fitting of the tactically innovative and vital ring bayonet on the muskets of his infantry now is only of antiquarian interest as a tactical improvement, though this major advance had long-lasting operational level significance with implications for decisiveness of battle and hence for the prudent scope of strategic and political ambition.[42]

Military power always needs geographical, for geopolitical and geostrategic, specification. It is highly significant for this enquiry that a general theory of strategy suffices to explain the strategic meaning of military power tailored to the opportunities and limitations of each and every particular geographical environment. Conceptually regarded, strategy per se is an imperial authority. Beyond the austere homeland of general theory, however, lies a growing realm of conceptually satellite, or franchised holdings. We need not, and certainly should not, resort expediently to 'riding rough-shod' over profound as well as minor but telling historical differences across time and place, in the interest of imposing a foolishly asserted comparability upon disparate phenomena.[43] Happily for the mission of defence planners today, the reason why we can be somewhat relaxed about historical detail is because for them that knowledge is not an end of high interest in and of itself. What they require far more, not quite instead, is knowledge and understanding of how military power, in its available forms and with the local character of time and culture, performed with meaning for the strategic effect then sought.

The strategic implications of physical geography have changed over time, largely as a compounded consequence of technological, social-cultural, and political agency. But the fact remains impressively steady that specific general theory explains very well the abiding qualities with strategic meaning of armies and navies, indeed more inclusively expressed as being of land power and sea power. Contemporary cartography for strategic historical examination identifies only two geographies that featured prior to the first decade of the twentieth century, land and sea, but no fewer than three subsequently additional: air, orbital space, and the electromagnetic spectrum (EMS) for cyberspace. It is possible, as well as strongly desirable, for us to regard the strategic historical contribution of each geographically specialized form of military power essentially as a unity across time, place, and particular circumstance. With no wish or need to ignore the diversity of detail as between, say, Roman and Carthaginian sea power in the Punic Wars of the third and second centuries BC, and the Anglo–American sea power of the two World Wars in the twentieth century, it is true to claim that sea power remained easily recognizable as such, the same kind of military power, in both cases.

It is unsurprising to discover that each of the five contemporary geographies for military power today lend themselves to comprehension by explanation in theory with persisting authority.[44] Not all the military power in strategic history is as well explained theoretically as it could be for contemporary value for future defence planners, but that is only our fault. For reason most significantly of distinctive physical geography(ies), general strategic theory explaining the nature of military power specific to the five distinctive geophysical contexts is possible. Defence planners are able to examine strategic history and appreciate the military thought and behaviour of the then-present moment, not only in the context of its time, as professional historians rightly insist, but also as phenomena illustrative of enduring reality. There is no need to sacrifice respect for then contemporary historical necessity, in the interest of allegedly grand analogy. Rather would one be arguing that armies are armies that are land power, and they place many boots on the ground, usually up close and personally, regardless of their armament, logistic arrangements, and social composition. Strategically regarded, armies are land power across time, place, and culture. It is self-evident that armies have differed hugely. Moreover, it is no less apparent that the strategic effectiveness of armies depends critically upon the coherence of the whole local historical actuality of the architecture of strategy. Military means have to do strategy tactically, and it is legitimized and enabled, and possibly ennobled, only by the political purpose in the ends that provide what sense there is in it.

The unity of strategic history that binds it together across time and space, and is explained in the general theory of strategy, allows us to seek in the past and present for guidance that could be valuable for the future. From strategic history we ought to be able to learn why some armies fight harder than do others, why military training tends to be rewarded by advantage in combat, why some armies are able to adjust their culture in order to adapt to novel challenges, and why others cannot. Appreciated globally, strategic history is replete with examples of conflicts that were asymmetrical in several major, even defining, respects. Steppe-founded horse-heavy armies have confronted (largely) foot armies, maritime dominance has met and contested with continental hegemony, irregular guerrilla fighters have fought conventional armies. The diversity of detail across time, place, and culture, is scarcely more impressive than are the broad commonalities that enable strategic history to be exploited carefully for educational assistance in helping us understand what needs understanding for the unavoidable task of planning for security. What defence planners require is such comprehension of future context as reasonably can be gleaned from empirical theory, not from studies that are short of necessary detail and are not driven by, or decorated with, history-light for absent analytical metrics.

The argument of this chapter and the preceding one is summarized by the claim that there is but one stream of time, and that the past, the present, and the future in their nature are categorically both ever distinctive characteristically, yet effectively are the same. The necessity for deep historical knowledge for contextual understanding is unquestionable. Happily, there is a small army of professional historians who generally can be trusted to police their turf against raiders with 'presentist', let alone 'futurist', agendas.

Naturally, concerns for the future must translate into present anxieties, given our inability to function in the future. The future eternally is 'now'.

Education from Experience (preferably of others)

The accessibility of so much of strategic history to study for current use looking to the future is fortunate. However, we are less fortunate in that the quality of our understanding of the past as candidate evidence is amply hindered by the qualities that render us human and in need of potential education from our all too strategic history. That history cannot be viewed, appreciated, and rendered useful for education for our contemporary need to plan for the future, unless it is somewhat liberated from unduly close guardianship by professional historians. This is a serious problem. Inappropriate understanding of loyalty to a particular scholarly tribe can have the consequence that historical understanding needing translation into categories for education today, is not licensed with full authority. It is plausible to argue that the twenty-first century will not record strategic phenomena unknown to Thucydides, Sun-Tzu, and Clausewitz. This argument reflects consideration of strategic historical experience over millennia. The challenge is to find ways to access the strategic experience purchased so expensively for so long.

Mastery of historical contextual detail is essential, but it is a hopeless task as an educational aid for prudent defence planning. No matter how much more is known about more strategic historical contexts, there will always be more to know. How much is enough? To rephrase Michael Howard, 'how wide, how deep, and how much context' should we seek?[45] One of the more important tasks of this examination of strategy in relation to defence planning is to reaffirm the merit in the claim that the impossible is impossible, and therefore should be avoided when feasible. To know more and more strategic history, particularly in the form of military history, is not necessarily to know much sensibly usable for defence planning. There is a need for translation. As usual, the most pressing question that the future focused strategist must ask of the historian is 'so what?' Historians understandably are apt to be nervous of generalizing from what they believe they know, to hypothetical circumstances about which they can know with confidence nothing of importance. Professional modesty all round usually is appropriate. But defence planning cannot be unduly permissive of scholarly modesty. The reason is because planning requires that contending professionals in the arts (for example, history) and social sciences address scholarly terrain that is either forbidden or at the least is known to be acutely hazardous.

A defence planner wondering how best to think and act with prudence for the future, finds himself, *faute de mieux*, engaging in pattern anticipation which must rest upon the quality and quantity of strategic historical knowledge and understanding. Past events cannot repeat, but past circumstances by type can and do. The whole contemporary landscape of security and therefore of interest to defence planning, is connected in patterns of thought and behaviour that have endured as contextual features in history. Today's planners do not confront future uncertainty with a mental *tabula rasa*; rather do they bring their understanding of the strategic meaning of the past (and present) to projection of the future(s) they anticipate. This is not and cannot be either science or social science, it is intuitive guesswork that should rest firmly on education by exposure to long human experience. The experience available includes all that is accessible through historical enquiry. Today's planner must provide guesses about the future that rest upon both his grasp of plausible meaning from historical experience and some detail that is speculative extrapolation from recent and contemporary trends. Defence planners cannot see the future; they know that historical events will not recur in detail. But they can be confident in their grasp of the most relevant concepts and categories that can provide order for prudent preparation for the uncertain future. Educated planners usually will not be deeply knowledgeable about a temporally extensive range of strategic history, but such expertise is not necessary except for professional historians. Rather is the process of defence planning well enough served by historical understanding if planners are educated in understanding the nature and changing character of inter alia such concepts as politics, strategy, alliance, war and peace. The need is to have learnt from past experience the identity of the more vital questions they must ask for the future. Thinking with the aid of grand categorical analogy, planners for possible COIN challenges in the future will want to know when and why such ventures succeed or fail, and the practical meaning of those frequently unduly casual terms, as well as what historical experience suggests the cost and duration of COIN campaigns tend to be.

The maxim that the impossible really is impossible has appeared already in this text, but it bears repeating. Contemporary social science seeks heroically to refute natural laws, but alas to no good effect. What defence planners cannot enjoy is certain understanding of future events rich in discretionary possibilities. Thoroughly reliable—'bet the nation on it'—knowledge about future security is unobtainable by any method. There is no kind of analytical technique, no form of organization that can achieve reliable predictive quality understanding of the strategic future. A candidate example of mission impossible is the advocacy in a recent article that apparently is outstanding in its historical narrative, but unfortunately refuses, or neglects, to recognize that certain knowledge about the future is not gleanable by any available method. Specifically, Dimitry Adamsky tells the frightening story of the November 1983 crisis that could have transmuted into World War III, a task which he performs quite well.[46] But, unfortunately he proceeds beyond historical understanding, and even beyond the pattern recognition across time favoured in this book. Instead, Adamsky urges that we seek for method and implementing organization that could enable us to 'pinpoint' a 'culminating point of deterrence', beyond which the would-be deterrer is more likely to provoke an anticipatory pre-emptive or perhaps preventive war than to deter.[47] The idea that desperation is apt to be dangerous is not exactly a novel one to strategic history. What would be new would be the ability to 'pinpoint this tipping point' with reliable prediction quality knowledge for understanding. Of course the idea is dangerous nonsense. It is nonsense for the reasons explained in this and the preceding chapter why the future cannot be known with certainty. It is dangerous because the pretensions of social science in this case are apt to appeal strongly to officials and a public who want to believe that their future is knowable, and therefore possibly reliably controllable in some of its less agreeable possible features.

Education in strategic history cannot enable impossible futurology, but it would equip defence planners to cope with the kinds or categories of contextual challenges that across millennia certainly have existed before, albeit not always dressed in a toga or fighting with a gladius.

NOTES

1. Jakub Grygiel, 'Educating for National Security', *Orbis*, 57 (Spring 2013), 211.
2. See Colin S. Gray, *Perspectives on Strategy* (Oxford: Oxford University Press, 2013), chs. 3–5.
3. Williamson Murray, 'History, War, and the Future,' *Orbis*, 52 (Fall 2008), 545.
4. Michael Howard has offered this pertinent thought: 'The trouble is that there is no such thing as "history". History is what historians write, and historians are part of the process they are writing about'. *The Lessons of History* (New Haven, CT: Yale University Press, 1991), 11.
5. I recognize that some readers will not want to believe in all the elements in my theory here. In particular, I suspect that there could be considerable resistance to the proposition that politics always is about relative power, understood as influence. I believe that this argument enjoys unarguable empirical merit: I do not advance it in a normative spirit or with normative intent. Also, the final logical piece in the whole theoretical assembly here might appear unduly obscure unless one understands the inclusivity of the concepts of strategy and strategic process. One bank anchoring the bridge of strategy is charged primarily with developing and promoting political ends. Logically, it has to follow that the process of making and executing strategy always should accommodate the political process that alone, though not unaided, generates the obligatory ends, whatever they are chosen to be.
6. Grygiel, 'Educating for National Security', is a particularly clear and uncompromising statement of the thesis that national defence is an art and cannot be a science. Robust and generally convincing support for this view is advanced in John Lewis Gaddis: 'International Relations Theory and the End of the Cold War', *International Security*, 17 (Winter 1992–1993), 5–58; and *The Landscape of History: How Historians Map the Past* (Oxford: Oxford University Press, 2004).

7. See Victor Davis Hanson, ed., *Makers of Ancient Strategy: From the Persian Wars to the Fall of Rome* (Princeton, NJ: Princeton University Press, 2010).

8. See Alvin Bernstein, 'The strategy of a warrior-state: Rome and the wars against Carthage, 264–201 BC', in Williamson Murray, MacGregor Knox, and Bernstein, eds., *The Making of Strategy: Rulers, States, and War* (Cambridge: Cambridge University Press, 1994), 56–84; and Edward N. Luttwak, *The Grand Strategy of the Byzantine Empire* (Cambridge, MA: Harvard University Press, 2009). Long historical perspective on strategy is provided in Beatrice Heuser, *The Evolution of Strategy: Thinking War from Antiquity to the Present* (Cambridge: Cambridge University Press, 2010), ch. 1; and Colin S. Gray, in 'Conclusion', in John Andreas Olsen and Gray, eds., *The Practice of Strategy: From Alexander the Great to the Present* (Oxford: Oxford University Press, 2011), 287–300.

9. Again, I express my thanks to Richard Danzig, *Driving in the Dark: Ten Propositions About Prediction and National Security* (Washington, DC: Center for a New American Security, October 2011).

10. See the argument developed in Colin S. Gray, *The Strategy Bridge: Theory for Practice* (Oxford: Oxford University Press, 2010), 267–77, 'Appendix C, 'Conceptual "Hueys" at Thermopylae? The Challenge of Strategic Anachronism'.

11. Since the Second World War cumulatively immense analytical effort has been expended upon the challenge of deterrence to statecraft and strategy. The challenge was not new, but the atomic bomb elevated its relative importance to an unprecedented height. Nearly seventy years on, it has been recognized by a few scholars and officials that although we can plan to attempt to deter in the future, we cannot be certain of success. The factors that either will or may be active in a context of attempted deterrence are simply too many, too uncertain, and too inherently problematic, to enable deterrent effect to be predicted with assurance. This does not mean that deterrence does not occur and cannot be attempted. But, it does mean that there will always be a fragility about expectations of deterrence that cannot be removed by prudent defence planning. The fundamental reason is because the one intended to be deterred needs to agree to being deterred. The success of our policy and strategy of deterrence is discretionary for the adversary. He should be deterred, but he may decline, at whatever cost. Not all social scientists have been willing to accept this fact concerning the impossibility of predicting the future. Scientific certainty cannot be secured by any methodology for analysing unique events beyond the present. We may be confident of success with deterrence, but that reveals more about us and our credulity, than it possibly can about foreign choices. The depths of the challenge posed by plans to deter in the future can be gauged usefully from the insight provided in Keith B. Payne, *The Fallacies of Cold War Deterrence and a New Direction* (Lexington, KY: University Press of Kentucky, 2001); and 'Special Issue: Understanding Deterrence', *Comparative Strategy*, 30 (November–December 2011).

12. Emile Simpson, *War from the Ground Up: Twenty–First–Century Combat as Politics* (London: Hurst, 2012), 25. This important insight on the effective autonomy of war, regardless of the truth in the Clausewitzian definition of war as an act of policy, also is to be found in Patrick Porter, *Military Orientalism: Eastern War Through Western Eyes* (London: Hurst, 2009), 65.

13. See Howard, *The Lessons of History*, 6–20.

14. Jeremy Black writes helpfully about 'cultural assumptions' that are highly relevant to attitudes towards the conduct and outcome of war. *Rethinking Military History* (Abingdon: Routledge, 2004), esp. 13–22. Writing eight years later, Black reflected helpfully and somewhat retrospectively on *War and the Cultural Turn* (Cambridge: Polity Press, 2012).

15. Rationality is a theme central to Patrick M. Morgan, *Deterrence Now* (Cambridge: Cambridge University Press, 2003); and Keith B. Payne, *The Great American Gamble: Deterrence Theory and Practice from the Cold War to the Twenty–First Century* (Fairfax, VA: National Institute Press, 2008).

16. Strategic theorists need to take more than passing note of the facts that assumptions are as inalienable from the basic architecture of strategy with its fundamental and unchanging trinity of elements, as they are mandatory in considering the future. This is a rather unsettling reality of defence planning for the future.

17. Clausewitz, *On War*, 605.

18. Clausewitz, *On War*, 87, 'It is clear, consequently, that war is not a mere act of policy but a policy instrument, a continuation of political activity by other means'. This sentence loses some of its necessary potency simply by virtue of its familiarity.

19. Clausewitz addresses the question of political influence on the character of warfare in the following way: 'War in general, and the commander in any specific instance, is entitled to require that the trend and designs of policy shall not be inconsistent with these [military] means. That, of course, is no small demand; but however much it may affect political aims in a given case, it will never do more than modify them'. *On War*, 87.

20. The employment of Unmanned Aerial Vehicles (UAVs), navigated and piloted remotely is the most recent exemplar of this trend. Such 'drone' use, however, is a source of some moral unease, pertaining both to the absence of human decision-making for action at the scene, and to the certainty of occasional error in targeting for armed UAVs. The use of armed drones to strike from altitude without warning is still growing, but it will meet tactical, political, legal, and moral opposition. UAVs are here to stay and they will acquire autonomous capability that is bound to be controversial—charges of robotic warfare will proliferate, with some reason. The debate about drones is still in its early stages, with the technology currently running ahead of strategic comprehension. See P. W Singer, *Wired for War: The Robotics Revolution and Conflict in the 21st Century* (New York: The Penguin Press, 2009); and Jeffry S. Thurner, 'Legal Implications of Fully Autonomous Targeting', *Joint Force Quarterly*, 67 (4th quarter 2012), 77–84.

21. It should not be forgotten that the scale of violence in warfare may bear little relation to the dominant military technology of the time. For example, the still contemporary nuclear age of the post-Cold War early 1990s recorded a death toll in excess of one million in Rwanda and Burundi, executed in significant measure by the precise and deeply personal use of the sharply effective machete. In addition to precision use of violence delivered by robotic drones and deadly machetes, it is well to remember that British and American Special Forces tried hard to kill their way to victory in Iraq and Afghanistan in the 2000s. Precisely targeted

assassination of important insurgents was a major adjunct to the politically more palatable efforts at hearts and minds. For an account of the campaign of precisely targeted killings by Special Forces in Iraq, see Mark Urban, *Task Force Black: The Explosive True Story of the SAS and the Secret War in Iraq* (London: Little, Brown, 2010). Optimistic social science that claims to know that human behaviour is becoming less violent, is not to be trusted. An example of such social science, is Stephen Pinker, *The Better Angels of Our Nature: The Decline of Violence in History and Its Causes* (London: Allen Lane, 2011).

22. As usual, Clausewitz did his best to warn us. He wrote as follows: 'If you want to overcome your enemy you must match your effort against his power of resistance, which can be expressed as the product of two inseparable factors, viz. *the total means at his disposal and the strength of his will.* The extent of the means at his disposal is a matter—though not exclusively—of figures, and should be measurable. But the strength of his will is much less easy to determine and can only be gauged approximately by the strength of the motive animating it'. *On War*, 77 (emphasis in the original).

23. See Colin S. Gray, *Weapons Don't Make War: Policy, Strategy, and Military Technology* (Lawrence, KS: University of Kansas, 1993), 95–9.

24. Strategic ethics are addressed in detail in Gray, *Perspectives on Strategy*, ch. 2.

25. See R. J. Overy, *Why the Allies Won* (London: Jonathan Cape, 1995), ch. 9; and Michael Burleigh, *Moral Combat: A History of World War II* (London: Harper Perennial, 2007).

26. See Michael O'Hanlon, *The Science of War: Defense Budgeting, Military Technology, Logistics, and Combat Outcomes* (Princeton, NJ: Princeton University Press, 2009).

27. See Ken Booth and Nicholas J. Wheeler, *The Security Dilemma: Fear, Cooperation and Trust in World Politics* (Basingstoke: Palgrave Macmillan, 2008).

28. The somewhat unusual, but very appropriate, idea of causing peace is explored productively in Michael Howard, *The Invention of Peace and the Reinvention of War* (London: Profile Books, 2001).

29. See Seyom Brown, 'Scenarios in Systems Analysis', in E. S. Quade and W. I. Boucher, eds., *Systems Analysis and Policy Planning: Applications in Defense* (New York: American Elsevier, 1968), ch. 16; Herman Kahn, *On Escalation: Metaphors and Scenarios* (New York: Frederick A. Praeger, 1965); and Andrew F. Krepinevich, *Deadly Scenarios: A Military Futurist Explores War in the 21st Century* (New York: Bantam Books, 2009).

30. In the context of counterinsurgency, it can be important to endorse the idea of warfare as theatre with a constructed narrative as script, as opposed to approaching the violence as a military struggle with a strategic outcome to be in military terms secured by military action. Simpson, *War from the Ground Up*, ch. 1, risks overstatement of this argument, but the theory is not implausible.

31. Clausewitz, *On War*, 87.

32. The literature dedicated to strategic folly and incompetence is not as extensive as probably it should be. Study of these topics tends to be overly inclusive and to be unduly permissive of prejudice by the author. Admittedly, it is not always easy to be just to a principal in strategic history who may have been more blighted by the

folly and incompetence of subordinates, or of his soldiers, and by ill *fortuna*, than by his own failings. And it would not do to be dismissive of the competitive quality of strategy in execution as an adversarial project. An exceptionally capable or fortunate enemy leader may condemn his foe to the design of plans and execution of action that are all but condemned in advance to fail. This perilously broad subject is addressed in different ways in the following works: Norman F. Dixon, *On the Psychology of Military Incompetence* (London: Jonathon Cape, 1976); Barbara W. Tuchman, *The March of Folly: From Troy to Vietnam* (New York: Ballantine Books, 1984); Eliot A. Cohen and John Gooch, *Military Misfortunes: The Anatomy of Failure in War* (New York: Free Press, 1990); and Robert Pois and Philip Langer, *Command Failure in War: Psychology and Leadership* (Blooming-ton, IN: Indiana University Press, 2004).

33. Clausewitz, *On War*, 75.
34. Williamson Murray, *Military Adaptation in War: With Fear of Change* (Cam-bridge: Cambridge University Press, 2011), is the leading study of its subject.
35. See Porter, *Military Orientalism*, 195.
36. John A. Nagl, *Learning to Eat Soup with a Knife: Counterinsurgency Lessons from Malaya and Vietnam* (Chicago: The University of Chicago Press, 2002), esp. ch. 1, 9.
37. See John France, *Perilous Glory: The Rise of Western Military Power* (New Haven, CT: Yale University Press, 2011), 89.
38. Winston S. Churchill, *The Gathering Storm* (1948; London: Penguin, 1985), 92.
39. Michael Howard, *The Causes of Wars and Other Essays* (London: Counterpoint, 1983), 214.
40. See Colin S. Gray, *House of Cards: Why Arms Control Must Fail* (Ithaca, NY: Cornell University Press, 1992), ch. 6.
41. See Table 2.2. Explanation at length is provided in Gray, *The Strategy Bridge*, ch. 1–2.
42. See Jeremy Black: *War in the Eighteenth Century* (Basingstoke: Palgrave Macmil-lan, 2013), 43; and 'A Military Revolution? A 1660–1792 Perspective', in Clifford J. Rogers, ed., *The Military Revolution Debate: Readings on the Military Trans-formation of Early Modern Europe* (Boulder, CO: Westview Press, 1995), 95–114, for the whole military context of the tactical innovation of the ring-socket bayonet.
43. As alleged in Hew Strachan, 'Strategy in the Twenty–First Century', in Strachan and Sibylle Scheppers, eds., *The Changing Character of War* (Oxford: Oxford University Press, 2011), 505–6. Plainly, we cannot both be correct.
44. I explain the nature of geographically specific general theory in my *Perspectives on Strategy*, 18.
45. With apologies to Michael Howard concerning *The Causes of Wars*, 215–17.
46. Dimitry (Dima) Adamsky, 'The 1983 Nuclear Crisis—Lessons for Deterrence Theory and Practice', *The Journal of Strategic Studies*, 36 (February 2013), 4–41.
47. Adamsky, 2013, 33.

5

Political Process and Defence Planning

THE MISSION

The 'stovepipe' thinking inimical to joined-up endeavour in the conduct of war is fully matched in the analogous condition of thought about defence planning. By this I do not refer to the obvious privileging of particular kinds of military power alleged to be the keys to strategic and political success. Strategic worldviews and culture both shape and are shaped by the preference for particular kinds of military power. Strategic cultural preference reflecting nationally distinctive physical geography appear to be both universal and universally readily explicable. Much less well recognized or understood is the 'stovepiping' of approaches to defence planning by scholars and others who seem all but blind to the 'tribal' character of their often narrowly professionally competent thought and behaviour.

The playing field of human actors eager to be influential on the broad subject of national defence contains a host of would-be human and institutional players. I choose to collapse the contending categories (or teams) of players to just four: politicians, soldiers, historians, and defence analysts. The most important category of player in defence planning should be that of the strategist, but typically that is the least well peopled among the combative tribes. My austere short-list of principal contenders is accompanied by, rather than contains, the category of strategist, essentially in practice almost as a rogue outlying contender. It is ironic that the outlier category of strategist should be judged the most important for the mission here. Strategy as an intellectual and a practical matter suffers because of the very inclusivity of domain that should mandate its sovereign relative importance. It is the master concept and provides the model that should enable one to conduct defence planning purposefully with a reasonable prospect of success.[1] This is not to deny that an irrationally and unreasonably stochastic world can thwart prudent thought and behaviour. Random happenings attest convincingly to the wisdom of Clausewitz on the subject of change and indeed also of Nassim Taleb with his *Black Swan* theory. Highly improbable events do occur, sometimes with appalling consequences.[2]

Because neglect of careful definition of mission endangers the prospects for success, it is advisable to restate the definition of defence planning provided early in the Introduction '*By defence planning I mean purposeful preparation for the defence of a polity in the future*' (near-, medium-, and far-term). Different countries, at different times, have employed different words, but my preference should be clear enough, as is its intentional inclusivity. Defence rather than security is specified in order to indicate that military concerns are my primary focus. However, the full wording of the sentence is designed to suggest some willingness to venture beyond military topics.

Strategic theory has unique utility in its provision of the only model that enables understanding as fuel for practical behaviour in defence planning adequate to meet the challenge of uncertainty. Whereas four of my player categories primarily are identifiable as job descriptions—politician, soldier, historian, defence analyst—strategist is a functional label, not a category of employment. Strategy is so inclusive a concept that strategist is endangered as a distinctive species. If we all attempt to think and behave strategically, which is at least a partial truth, the consequence is that strategy fails to be recognized as necessary thought and behaviour. Since the ubiquity of functionally strategic behaviour is matched fully by its difficulty of competent achievement, it is not very surprising that the honour roll of great strategists is so sparsely peopled.

Lest readers believe this study to be largely an exercise in abstract theory, it may be important that I flag the empirical bases for this exploration and examination of defence planning. Research for this investigation has comprised: experience from 45 years of professional life in three countries (Britain, Canada, and the United States), and in a variety of institutions (universities, government, and think-tanks; and contributions to the literatures more or less distinctive to and among the categories of employment here identified. Scholarship on defence planning, broadly defined as here, is evident principally in two clusters of studies, with outlying contributions from three others. The core of the subject, indeed its centre of gravity one might claim, resides in the efforts of professional defence analysts and of those with disciplinary identity in the humanities, largely in history and the study of politics by methods only lightly, if at all, dependent on 'metric' methodology from the social sciences.

This study is not sociological, neither is it autobiographical. However, the analysis here is flavoured by some first-hand knowledge and experience gained over a long period in hugely different political and strategic contexts. To explain, I have worked on defence subjects in a (strategically evaluated) small power (Canada), a medium-sized (lapsed great) power (Britain), and a superpower (the United States). In addition, I have worked in the political and strategic contexts of Cold War and post-Cold War. What follows is calibrated to be as non-specific to time, place, and political and strategic circumstance as feasible, but omniscient objective observance of defence planning is unlikely to be achieved or indeed achievable. This chapter proceeds on the working proposition that there is an essential unity to the subject of defence planning that is not well reflected in the thought and behaviour of those who undertake its study and advise about it. Given that this study is an examination of the nature of the subject of defence planning for the purpose of identifying a superior way in which its challenges might be met successfully, historical narrative is used solely to illustrate argument.

Politics and Policy Ends

Defence planning is not a technical enterprise conducted by expert defence analysts with some inputs from the military agents who actually have to do it—whatever, wherever, and however the 'it' happens to be. Such inputs from expert analysis and military experience can be vitally important, but policy, meaning politics, is or should be sovereign. Defence planning for the protection of the polity does not confine political authority to a consultative prerogative, with a duty to warn or encourage.[3] One could hardly exaggerate the relative importance of policy for defence planning, or the contribution of politics to policy. Because defence debate lends itself so readily to discussion of military topics amenable to analytical, usually metric, treatment, it might be supposed that most of the field under examination can safely be left to technical experts. The elementary strategy model of ends, ways, and means, does not always enjoy the understanding that it merits, overwhelmed as it can be by a deluge of statistics.

Clausewitz wrote that '[w]ar, therefore, is an act of policy', and a little later 'that war is not a mere act of policy but a true political instrument, a continuation of political activity by other means'.[4] Defence planning in hope of peace, though necessarily in readiness for war, must be governed by the same logic and political authority as war itself. However, the policy ends in the severely reductionist strategy model should not be regarded largely as decoration on the real business of defence planning. Far from being a kind of imperial guard, colourful and perhaps essential to the dignity of the state, policy ends are the most important element in the interdependent trinity that comprises the model of strategy. As noted here already, historical experience provides evidence persuasive of the proposition that errors in policy and strategy are vastly more difficult to survive than are weaknesses in operational skill and tactical capability. But the nature of the challenge that unsound policy poses for those who must attempt to do strategy tactically in combat or in the prevention of war in time of crisis, is not as obvious as it needs to be. A fundamental problem, possibly even the fundamental problem, is that although the concept and real-world function of strategy is a logical unity in its trinitarian neatness, in practice it need not be so.

Even if a government is admirably strategic in its thinking, deciding, and planning, it is extraordinarily difficult to achieve a mutually supporting united endeavour of strategy, with strongly compatible ends, ways, and means. In addition to the proclivity of enemies to be uncooperative, the normal villainies of ill-chance in the form of random friction will hamper what might have been smooth strategic performance. But, even when one acknowledges Clausewitzian friction and the importance of chance, the conceptual and practical terrain is still strategic. By way of a major caveat upon such strategic appreciation, it is necessary to consider seriously the contradictory argument that the policy ends in the strategy model are often in essence thoroughly astrategic. By this I do not mean that policy necessarily is unwise, and certainly not that it would have no strategic meaning; the claim is rather only that policy is made in a political process that is uninterested in strategic reasoning with genuine concern for national defence.

When there is a domestic political consensus favouring the view that the polity does not and probably will not face a dominant danger in the near future, it can be hard to impose strategic discipline on defence planning. If an expediently useful organizing dominant threat is absent, how does one prepare national defence? Against whom, what, where, when, and with what, should one prepare? In historical practice polities are never entirely free of menace, but acute national security alarm most typically is episodic at worst. This means there are frequent periods wherein polities believe their strategic contexts are sufficiently benign as to permit discretion on a large scale over defence planning. Britain, in the 1920s, adopted as a rolling assumption for defence planning that it would not be involved in war against a great power for the next ten years. This assumption, not unreasonable in 1919 and for many years thereafter, was dropped in 1932.[5] For a more recent example of a national discretionary case, the United States in the 1990s needed to adjust to a strategic context assumed no longer to contain a peer or near-peer superpower adversary. The American defence planning process adapted to the shock of Soviet absence by adopting—over a decade and more—what is known as a capabilities-based approach to a future strategic context noticeably short of certainty concerning major menace.[6]

What needs to be appreciated more fully is the quality of the relationship between defence planning and policy, with particular reference to the salience of domestic political context. It is necessary to think inclusively about strategy, a theme important to this text. Government and its society, or vice versa according to ideological preference, have no choice other than to function grand strategically. Policy ends in strategy's trinity, oriented towards goals attainable by planned military effort, are apt to be modest in relative political significance when perceived in peaceful times. When non-state Jihadist terror is perceived to be a danger, in comparison with the dangers understood to repose in Nazi Germany or the Soviet Union, the apparent scope for discretion in defence planning is challengingly wide. Given that defence planning is about politics, foreign and domestic, it is scarcely surprising, in a democracy at least, that government licenses and conducts such planning in ways responsive, at the least attentive, to the public mood regarding danger.

It is an understandable error, but error nonetheless, in effect to approach matters of defence planning in a narrowly self-referential manner. This is akin to the examination of armed combat in isolation from its political purpose. We know that in practice policy frequently follows the military verdict of the fighting, but it is sensible to recognize the astrategic phenomenon of policy-making effectively uninterested in military-strategic consequences.[7] In a period apparently permissive of discretion over military employment, politicians are likely to be unmoved by arguments for defence plans that are heavy on prudential reasoning, but light on evidence of specific danger. Although the security of the nation is essentially unchallenged, indeed is unchallengeable, in polities around the world as the most senior of official concerns and duties, public discourse on the subject typically consists largely of assertions and platitudes. Defence planning for the national security needs careful performance, but on what kind of evidence can it be anchored and calibrated?

Because the subject here is defence planning for national security, the boundary for our attention is inconveniently inclusive. Thinking back to 1907 and also 1939, the question of whether or not there should be a British Expeditionary Force (BEF) for continental war was one that required clear political answer, possibly before issues of quality of desirable military commitment could properly be posed and answered.[8] Although the details of military planning were vitally important, the military planners could not ply their expertise optimally to useful effect prior to the political decision to commit a BEF to the European continent. What the historical record shows is that in both 1907–14 and 1939, the supremely important British decision to send an expeditionary force to the continent betrayed a noteworthy disconnect between British statecraft and British military planning. In both historical cases, notwithstanding contextual differences, the political decision did not rest upon careful strategic or military planning. Before the First World War Britain prepared to dispatch the size of force that it could most readily assemble and transport; while in 1939–40 the BEF comprised the scale of force which was available and could be spared from imperial duties, under-trained, hastily ill-armed, and recently conscripted. The military instrument was obliged to make the best job that it could of the consequences of politicians' momentous decisions. Military planning in Britain immediately prior to both world wars followed political orders to the sense of which it had not contributed significantly. My intention is not to add to arguments about British preparedness or otherwise for the wars that broke out in 1914 and 1939, but rather to highlight the incoherence of the political guidance for the military planning defence contribution to the planning for national security.

In both years the British Army was committed to a war for which it was not remotely ready.[9] However, to be fair, none of the participants in either world war can be said to have been prepared adequately for the war(s) in which they participated with variable freedom of discretion.

Selection of the BEF of 1914 and 1939 as exemplary negative examples of relative poverty in prudent pre-war anticipation and preparation, should not be considered extraordinary episodes of official incoherence. A poor fit between military preparation and the actuality of future political need and demand, is commonplace. Indeed, irreducible uncertainty about the future virtually ensures some measure of unreadiness for future challenges. The answer has to lie in a combination of prudent 'portfolio' style investment in a range of military capabilities that hopefully will prove sufficiently adaptable to meet the particular circumstances of the unknowable future.[10]

Every historical case must have unique details, but that political decision or oscillating tendency (for example, policy) moves at its own speed, usually largely unrelated to national readiness in defence preparedness. The temporal dimensions to political and to military affairs can be substantially unharmonious. Adolf Hitler expected Germany, if need be, to be ready enough for general war by 1943: it came in full spate or more in 1941. The Wehrmacht went to war on the largest of scales with what it had and what it could steal, when it was ordered to do so. Its infantry by and large was unmotorized, its artillery was heavily reliant upon literally horse power, and it was always too small for the grandiose strategic mission demanded and commanded by political authority. Elsewhere I have argued for recognition of the problem of 'currency conversion' of military effect into strategic and especially political effect, the latter after all being the purpose of, and justification for the violence.[11] The conversion problem requires recognition as inherent in the differences between political behaviour and defence planning. This gap is more than somewhat obscured by Clausewitz. For all his clear declarations that '[w]ar therefore is an act of policy' and a 'true political instrument',[12] it would be all too easy to read and assume that policy (politics) and war (the military instrument) should have little difficulty goose-stepping more or less together.

When actual war indicates beyond much room for dispute who is fighting whom, where, with what, and about what, the mission of defence planning of course is much simplified. But, when the defence planning challenge is hampered by great uncertainty, because it is geared to be able to meet variables with values not exactly known, then the possibility can be acute of severe cracks appearing between extant policy and military capability. This is situation normal for most polities most of the time. In peacetime it is usual for countries not to know whether or not their defence planning is good enough. However, just because some large issues in defence planning are beyond objective scientific analysis, it follows neither that analysis should not be conducted, nor that it must be unhelpful. But what cannot be achieved is certain understanding of future needs for national defence: that would be mission impossible, and would be offered only by fools or charlatans. Surprisingly, perhaps, sensible defence planning should be possible, even though it can never be assumed to be correct, just as it cannot be tested reliably ahead of real-time action in crisis or war.

Defence planning always is the dynamic product of a no less dynamic domestic policy process that is quintessentially political. All political processes have relative winners and relative losers, while the scale of victory and defeat will vary from polity to polity and from one issue to another. The issues of the day may be high and momentous in their consequential reach, but the political process by which they are settled, regardless of the character of political system under discussion, will be substantially common across frontiers and cultures. Because decisions about the future defence of countries are taken in a process that is in its nature everywhere political, approximately the same factors compose a fairly generic policy process, distinctive though each country's policy (political) process will be. The point of importance here is the need to recognize the universality of political process, notwithstanding the rich diversity of actual political systems. The Russian, the Chinese, and the American policy making and policy executing systems are plainly distinctive in organizational and bureaucratic process terms. However, those three powers all must make decisions about defence planning in a process that is in its nature political. This may appear a banal claim, so much rich diversity in granular and other detail does it ignore. That appearance should not be so judged, because by unavoidable implication a substantial claim is contained within it.

Specifically, a political process has political outcomes for political reasons. No criticism of politics is intended or implied by this argument. Such would often be appropriate, but that is not my point here. The structure of the subject under examination needs recognition. This structure is explained as follows:

1. Right, often even just right enough, answers to important questions about defence planning for future national security, are neither attainable nor scientifically demonstrable (were they subsequently to be revealed by events to have been right).

2. Political systems contain people and institutions who, by their nature (and in the character locally permissible), contend for relative power (understood as influence).

3. There is ineradicable uncertainty about how much defence preparation, and of what kind(s), to purchase. Given that the contending human and organizational players have distinctive interests to advance for their particular advantage, a necessarily political struggle about defence planning ensues, wherein issues of defence substance are less important in practice than is relative political gain and loss.

4. The political process that governs national defence planning may be dominated by people and institutions less than deeply concerned about the military dimension to national security.

Budgetary allocation to defence planning for the security function can be decided somewhat arbitrarily by the 'remainder' method. This translates as meaning that the financing of the military aspects of national security is determined arbitrarily by the remainder of public money after other, higher, priorities are deemed satisfied. Defence is allowed what is left in the public purse. It may be needless to say that the remainder method (to risk unduly dignifying such inelegance) can be applied in directly the opposite way, to license non-defence spending only after the believed needs of national security are fully funded. Short of plausible demonstration by the unmistakeable evidence provided by negative events, it can be exceedingly difficult to provide convincing evidence of error in defence planning. As Nassim Taleb argues in his Black Swan theory, the non-occurrence of severe adversity appears to confirm the rightness of contemporary practice.[13] It is simply a fact that the probability of occurrence of awful events is utterly non-computable. In the face of the incalculability of grave risks, notwithstanding the prevalence of official language that implies some science, rather than mere guesswork, one should not be surprised to discover that defence planning in peacetime provides a happy hunting ground for political contenders.

Ironically, policy ends are rarely anything of the sort. Goals, the 'ends' in the strategy model, typically have sell-by dates, whether or not that feature of their nature is made publically explicit. Politicians and civil servants understand that there is no end-state to their labours. Policy emerges episodically and usually lumpily from a political process that can have no end. Similarly, defence planning is always a work in progress; even when regarded historically it has no beginning, middle, and end. Politicians as policymakers satisfice when they settle, for now, on some number for a military capability that is judged good enough to meet the need of the moment and the near term. Quite commonly, a particular 'metric', say the forward garrison-deployment of four British divisions in a BAOR (British Army of the Rhine), agreed in 1954 and sustained through the decades of Cold War, enjoys an iconic value upon which defence preparation can anchor.[14] This is not to claim that such numbers are thoroughly arbitrary, but rather that judgement about the rightness of particular numbers is rarely the product of careful defence analysis undirected by political and financial guidance. When this text makes a sweeping claim for the prevalence of politics in all matters pertaining to preparation for national defence, the link to Thucydides may not be as clear as it should be.[15] His model of motivation for statecraft has a unique utility in enabling plausible exploration of what otherwise might appear chaotic or even random. The explanatory reach and grasp of Thucydides' austere trinitarian summation on motivation is extraordinarily satisfactory for inclusive explanation: 'fear, honour, and interest,' accommodates all we need to know about the motives that fuel the political process that generates defence planning behaviour. This fact is easily revealed.

1. *Fear* in its several forms (concern, anxiety, alarm) is a variable condition ever liable to haunt defence planning: sometimes it is expressed metrically, as in the American DEF CON rating system, 5–1, which in descending rank order expresses and demands the readiness states of US armed forces judged appropriate to the contextual dangers of the present. Whether perceived reasons for fear are acute or much less so, the entire enterprise of defence planning finds political and moral licence in the belief that there is always some danger to the polity, even if it is deemed at present only to be distantly possible, rather than actual or near-term probable. No matter what analytical system is adopted as a technical aid for defence planning, some possible danger from foreign threat generally will be assumed; this is fundamental for the function of defence preparation if not literally necessary, because of the possible peril of internal conflict. The 'threat' concept word may be avoided, along with the specification of state-villain names in scenario design, but there has to be a trail connecting defence planning today with sources of possible anxiety for the future.[16] Thucydidean 'fear' is generously inclusive in its coverage.

2. *Honour* as a concept covers well enough the broad range of behaviours addressed in defence planning that bear most particularly upon the high-calorific idea of reputation. Much of the military activity, even simply the local or rapidly deployable military presence that it is hoped yields evidence of a sufficiency of moral commitment, can be understood in good part as being political. There is politics in Thucydides' concept of honour. In Thomas C. Schelling's theory of the art of commitment in regard to an inter-state process of bargaining pertaining to deterrence, reputation is critically important.[17] When political commitment can be inbred with moral value it is deemed far more credible. Schelling and Kahn in particular, were eloquent in their theorizing about the importance of honour-as-reputation, in statecraft.[18] Although expediency, as well as necessity, is a frequent feature of politics, we humans are apt to guess about tomorrow on some of the basis of behaviour yesterday. Politicians know that the past is raided constantly as evidence allegedly bearing on contemporary decisions about preparation for the future. For example, in 1914 and 1939 Britain's potential European continental co-belligerents needed to decide whether or not the British really would be fully with them, locally, in the event of German aggression. Pragmatically regarded, honour means reputation, which translates into the relative power that is the realm of polities.

3. *Interest* The third of Thucydides' categories of motivation for combative behaviour in statecraft virtually defines itself tautologically. The values of people and organizations determine their interests, all of which are advanced or defended in relationships that either are actually adversarial, or at least are potentially so. That which we care about either is, or becomes a political interest of variable weight. Most things that humans value therefore either actively or latently have a political quality. Most interests, both those that are personal and those more appropriately understood to be collective, are not in danger of a kind interesting to defence planners, at least not actively so. But, the particular virtue in this third category of motive specified by Thucydides is that it serves in a warning role against undue optimism in inter-state and intercommunal relations. What this category achieves is convincing coverage of currently unknowable sources of hostility and perhaps needed military action. There is not much over which human beings cannot find apparently good enough reasons to quarrel and perhaps fight. It is an elementary error to peer into the future, and discover—contrary to the unpredictability that nature imposes on us—that little of self-evidently sufficient importance for war lurks menacingly out there in decades to come. Aside from the folly that cannot help but attend most efforts at futurology, regardless of methodology, seers, social science or whatever, it is a mistake to attempt to identify possible issues between polities that could be a cause of acute conflict and even war in the future. The reason is because issues of any and all kinds over which communities disagree are inherently and actively political in nature. No matter how remote from military violence the subject of a particular disagreement may be at one time, it may have the potential to fuel antagonism that finds military expression. The military dimension to this logic is strictly a dependent variable. Interests are the source of military conflict when their political nature is believed to demand active measures. Historians try to tell us that there is very little over which people and their polities will not find reason enough to fight. Military force cannot settle directly deep disagreements about truth and virtue, but it can and does resolve political disputes over who has the political authority to decide whose version of truth and virtue is to command the most respect for a while. War cannot resolve philosophical or theological matters directly, but it does decide whose philosophy and theology will prosper in a post-war world. In this brutal sense therefore, morality and its ethics is both political and strategic.[19]

It may not much matter whether a perceived national interest is moral-cultural-ideological, geographical, economic or whatever, if it is identified as an issue in a subject of national importance it becomes political in nature and might be deemed worthy of advancement by military means. In his view of the potential for conflict in the human political condition, Thucydides left no easy escape routes for those sufficiently imprudent as to envisage an irenic future.

The politics of and about the policy 'ends' in the structure of the universal and eternal strategy model can have no stable frontiers as a category; but nonetheless it does refer to themes of national concern that fit plausibly into the Thucydidean trinity. When or if one probes for higher meaning to the issues that command the attention of defence planners, one finds that the very large and intimidatingly inclusive concepts of fear, honour, and interest, have plainly recognizable icons perhaps contentiously in need of protection with defence planning. For leading categorical examples, defence planning most usually will be about geography, culture, and indeed relative power its ever dynamic self. Defence planning by definition is conducted with a view to helping shape a polity's security context in the future. Whatever the locally authoritative view may be of the good enough life, the direct purpose of defence planning must be to promote the relative power position of the polity. Defence planning for any polity therefore is about the achievement of a satisfactory power relationship with those who may be motivated to attempt to change the terms of competition in their favour to its disadvantage. Defence planning cannot help but be about politics.

Civilian Authority and Military Experience

Military power and war should not be conceived as self-referential. They do not compound to constitute a masterful independent variable, with politics demoted logically to a dependent status that expresses the consequences of the course of military strategic events. But, planning in preparation for defence in the future is not a subject and agenda that can prudently be left to those who are strategically illiterate. The primacy of politics and the political cannot sensibly be challenged as a principle. What can be difficult to understand is the nature of what needs to be an unequal yet cooperative relationship between the two banks which the strategy bridge connects, the political and the military. The cases in history when political and military authority were fused in people and institutions that combined command of political and military power, commonly have not had benign outcomes for the polities in question. A dominant reason for the consequences of failure of strategic bridging lies in a systemic difficulty that probably is inalienable from a military approach to strategic challenges. Specifically, political purpose tends not to combine well, that is to say to fuse, with military power and authority without, as a consequence, becoming confused and all but mislaid.

A heavy and proper focus on the development of military expertise can be difficult to constrain to its essential role as the enabler of political purpose. The theory of the strategy bridge outlined elsewhere by this author may be appealing in principle, but always and everywhere it is applied by people and institutions who do not commonly share all goals with an equal priority.[20] The two banks that anchor the strategy bridge do not share a truly common prioritization of concerns. Without claiming or even implying that politics and its military instrument pursue divergent paths in quest of distinctive goals, the fact remains that the worlds of politics and of military preparation do not easily combine in a united effort in the interest of national security. It tends to be difficult to explain this point without inadvertently giving offence to a military audience, but fundamentally there are no strictly military challenges. In preparation for national defence there are few issues wholly innocent of military implications. It is not possible to evade the need for political decision by means of seeking to find comfort in experts, military or other. One is unable to delegate to military experts the larger, and potentially therefore the more consequential, choices about contentious issues of national security in the future. Expert defence analysis of some kinds indeed is possible, if far from usually found to be entirely practicable as well-informed technical advice, but it cannot shoulder the most important of the tasks inalienable from the responsibility for defence planning.

Because war is a political act, civilian authority should always be superior to military experience. This is not quite the case with respect to warfare, concerning which there ought not to be controversy over who is the expert professional and who is the amateur.[21] Furthermore, given that I understand defence planning to mean purposeful preparation for the defence of a polity, that endeavour must include considerations that may far transcend the usual professional bounds of military expertise. Defence planning in this wider sense has to engage with the whole field encompassed by the perilously inclusive concept of grand strategy. Many of the assets of a country may need to be exploited if it is to see off present and future dangers, and exploit opportunities that appear unanticipated as windows that open at random, rather than as rewards merited by cunning plots. The core of this discussion has to be military concerns about preparation for future security, but it would be a challenge to seek plausibly to exclude consideration of the political context for defence planning. If the subject could be bounded intelligently by the criterion of direct military content, there would be no argument over the necessity for dominance of defence planning by those with professional military expertise. However, defence planning is not primarily a military subject, rather is it political. There is critical need for defence planning to be anchored upon military experience and strategic education, but there are exceptionally good reasons for Eliot Cohen's characterization of civil-military relations as an 'unequal dialogue' weighted in favour of the civilian.[22] In the heat of domestic defence argument it is not uncommon for contending champions to forget how different, indeed legitimately different, are the two banks that should be connected by the bridge of strategy. It is useful to organize the argument about civil-military relations into four rather porous categories of issues, pertaining to: responsibility; military-political currency conversion; prudent statecraft; money and other domestic opportunity costs.

Responsibility

In principle, at least, there can be no helpful comparison between the scope and scale of responsibility of civilian political and military authority. The former licenses, sponsors, and pays for the latter. Although the soldier is obliged to protect the polity if necessary in conditions of extremity, the intensity and criticality of the military effort does not alter a chain of command that at its most elevated has a national community delegate decisions bearing upon its protection to a government authorized to behave with strategic prudence on its behalf. Regardless of the importance of the expert knowledge about military affairs presumed to reside in the brain of the military instrument, nothing changes the legal and political norm that military forces should only be an instrument; they are not to be wielded for reasons strictly endogenous to their own nature. It is commonplace for soldiers periodically to be angry, at least dissatisfied, over the apparent disregard by politicians of expert military advice on military matters of defence planning. Although such anger is not infrequently merited, scarcely less frequently is it appropriate to notice that the military critics and their political allies appear not to understand the full context for civilian policy making. In most polities, most of the time, in other words when they are neither at war nor in a condition of acute crisis, it proves difficult for military defence interests to accept that central government must decide among competing demands for priority in budgetary allocation.[23] Soldiers tend to see themselves as deserving of preferential priority because of their unique importance to the first charge on political authority, physical protection of the polity. But, soldiers, among others, are likely to be light in understanding, really understanding, the differences there are between their particular responsibilities to the country, and the general responsibilities of the central government.

Currency conversion

Elsewhere I have explained the problems of currency conversion between military power and ultimately political effect.[24] While these problems can be severe in the conduct of warfare, they appear also in peacetime, especially in a condition believed to be one of 'deep peace', a concept popular in much of EU Europe at present.[25] The problem is fundamental to all strategy for the military genus of national power. The threat and the use of military power does not and cannot have calculable political effect. In time of war the relationship between particular military outcomes of action and political consequences usually is more readily anticipated than is the case of military menace in peacetime. In wartime, belligerents are likely to secure some useful physical limitation on an enemy's freedom of realistic political decision. But given that a condition of more or less limited war is historically typical, as contrasted with variants of the idea of 'total war', the scope for adversary political discretion is by no means readily reduced and agreeably channelled by warfare: this is so even when it is applied cunningly with advice from sophisticated defence analysis.[26] Just as historical experience demonstrates that military victory cannot be relied upon to deliver, as in lock-step, a consequential political success, so also, if less dramatically, military defence planning cannot assure delivery of a desired and intended political result. The point is not that the military power envisaged in defence planning cannot have the effect that was the political purpose of its political parents, but rather that the scope for political discretion on the part of the Other cannot be disciplined with thorough reliability by foreign military power. As the latent menace lurking in peacetime defence preparation, that power may be potent as a political persuader in contrast to its presence inflicting harm with its sharp end in warfare. Although the immediate costs of political non-compliance will be much smaller in time of peace than in time of war, the political consequence of violent coercion could promote a quality of resistance unanticipated by military planners. This argument emphasizes the enduring fact that the currencies of political and of military achievement are categorically distinctive. Scholars have learnt to recognize that the winning of a war militarily does not have to convert easily into the political winning of the peace that should follow. This challenge appears generically as a close relative in the relationship between competitive adversarial efforts at defence preparation in peacetime and desired political consequences. Defence plans ahead of action in war cannot be opposed and thwarted in the field by worthy enemies. The desirable quality to that necessary fact is lightly offset by another fact: anticipated military success cannot be shown by events to be improbable because of folly in our planning that we failed to identify. Given that adequate performance in national defence planning in peacetime inherently is preferable to success in war, it is important that both civilian policymakers and soldiers understand the challenge of currency conversion identified above. I will hazard the speculative thought that neither bank connected by the bridge of strategy—civilian politicians on the one side, military experts on the other—may comprehend well enough the difficulty of converting military threat or action into desired political consequences. The character of this convertibility challenge differs between time of war and time of peace, but its nature is the same species of difficulty.

Prudence

The different natures of the responsibilities of civilian policymakers and professional soldiers is apt to fuel sincere and intense differences of opinion between them. Arguably, the most important value for both of these tribal identities is that which is known rather loosely as prudence. Prudence should be the cardinal virtue in the ranks of both the political and the military class. Following Raymond Aron, as is my wont, I deem prudence to be the most appropriate quality needed in statecraft and its defence planning.[27] Unfortunately, prudence is not analytically accessible with metric tools that enable doubts to be replaced scientifically by reliably determined calculated answers to uncertainty from which mathematics can rescue us. Correct equations should enable us to find correct solutions. Would that it were so, perhaps. For better or worse, the nature of the uncertainty that besets and sometimes confounds us over security issues for the future, is such as to preclude virtually any certainty of knowledge about future events and, therefore inevitably, their consequences. This is the wondrously opaque world that will contain some unknown unknowns that will merit labelling as Black Swans, and which of course must have unknowable consequences.

It is one thing for the politician and the soldier to agree on the high relative value of prudence, but it is quite another for them to agree on how prudence applies to their distinctive domains of responsibility. Because the politician is responsible for future security in its entirety, prudent behaviour pertains to due diligence over matters that extend far beyond the domain of the military. Defence planning must have future military security as a principal concern, but national security cannot prudently be reduced to an issue-area all but entirely military-strategic in content and reference. Exceptions would be those relatively brief rare 'strategic moments' of national peril when it may indeed be prudent to behave strategically by discounting concern for tomorrow, in the immediate interest of physical and political survival today. But, even in moments of appalling national peril, when military strategic issues unarguably are of overriding significance, statecraft is not usually able to be reduced with thoroughgoing rigour to the single issue of military strategic effect. Government can hardly help itself from needing to think and act grand strategically very occasionally, whether or not it manages to do so competently.

It is not quite inevitable that prudence should be applied with distinctively different results by the two banks of the strategy bridge, but it is almost so. The differences in responsibility render unavoidable a clash of prioritization over military security that can contribute noticeably to the frustration of scientific method in earnest and numerate defence analysis. It would not be entirely unreasonable to discern in the attitudes towards prudence of most concern to this discussion some elements of thought and behaviour functionally characteristic of Asperger's syndrome. Specifically, there can be an inability to view and understand the world from the perspective of people and institutions different from one's own. Given that politicians are responsible for the whole country going into the future down every path of national activity, while soldiers have responsibility only for the country's future military security, it is scarcely surprising that the strategy bridge sees much military authored traffic destined for politically negotiated or commanded decision. Of course, strategy-making typically is a more or less dynamic process in the context of unequal dialogue privileging civilian policymakers with superior authority. It would seem to be difficult for some to understand that where people sit in governance drives their judgement on the ranking of priorities. Once one has grasped that there are never objectively correct (mathematically testable and demonstrable beyond reasonable argument) precise answers to the strategic problems in future defence planning, one begins to be ready to address the subject productively.

Money

The lingua franca of defence planning has to be money, not strategy. The reason for this is fairly describable as banal. Theoretically the leading alternative to money as the currency of choice for debate has to be strategy, but in practice that is a much inferior subject for debate for several compelling reasons. To debate national defence in terms of the budget is to prefer not to argue about unknown, often even literally unknowable, matters of the kind inescapable in strategic discussion. Instead, the strategic world of interest is translated both in and by a currency conversion into money. This conversion achieves a certainty of material reference, a concretization, which can prove seriously misleading, but when that is the case at least it will be comprehensible in its own monetary terms. Strategy-making is easier to achieve when all major participants, civilian and military, can reduce the process of negotiation to the common denominator of budget share. As a practical matter of doing the country's governance business, it is important for contending interests to employ a common currency in argument, and that has to be money, the budget. With argument about defence planning reduced, or should I say converted, into budgetary terms expressed both as absolute and relative (percentage share) amounts, negotiation becomes much easier than would be debate with alternative terms of reference.[28] Strategic ideas are inherently rather opaque as to their budgetary meaning.[29] In addition, when people and organizations strive hard to sell their expensive ideas, the concepts *du jour* and the hardware they are claimed to justify are apt to acquire iconic status in the minds of their advocates. Beyond the icons of the present day lurk institutionally tribal and functionally all but sacred strategic tenets and hopes that do not lend themselves expediently to compromise in negotiations over subjects important to defence planning. Strategy and its expression in preparation for security in the future through defence planning quintessentially is both about politics and is inherently political in nature and dynamic character. However, it is unusual for that political process actually to be dominated by strategic argument, inclusively understood. More often than not, defence planning, even when conducted with the serious aid of a civil-military strategy bridge, is argued and debated in budgetary terms as money. Except for the context of political consensus over the gravest of believed perils to national security, there will always be some civilians who are relatively indifferent to possible military strategic dangers. There will also be soldiers who remain relaxed about budgetary menace to military capabilities other than their particular own.

Although it is an eternal verity that money always is essential as the vital enabler of defence for security, it is true also that money tends to be the expedient default choice as the focus for debate. Budgetary discussion enables intra-governmental negotiation to evade some of the more emotive terms that attend perilously explicit yet financially uncertain contention over strategy.

The 'stovepiping' consequences of particularly encultured perspectives are in the nature of a defence planning process that combines the distinctive responsibilities of different functional and legal responsibilities in a single process of decision for strategy-making. Participants will defend what they understand to be their bureaucratic turf and personal career prospects; as senior people they are certain to be deeply encultured in the values and consequent assumptions, as well as the understood but unarticulated interests of the organizations they must represent. Those military persons who must cross the strategy bridge to argue about defence preparation, have to be understood not only as leaders of strongly vested interests, but in addition as leaders with dependent followers whose quality of followership cannot be taken for granted as a matter of discipline and essential common interest. However, it would be a serious error to be dismissive of institutionally influenced bias in perception, of the future as indeed of much else. It is no less necessary that a military strategic prudence should characterize the attitudes of military representatives, than it is for civilian contributors to the making of strategy to ensure that possible military dangers are appropriately contextualized. Central government is required to take seriously most of the actual or potential perils to national security. Indeed, adjectival enrichment of the notably subjective quality of what may lie in the large conceptual tent of security, is apt to expand exponentially. Security lends itself as a convenient all-purpose abstract idea that provides useful cover to all kinds of concern. Seemingly, there is an endless expensive list of variably important asserted concerns that can be added limpet-like to the concept of security. Security truly is so subjective, while being abstract and vague, that it is a perfect conceptual conscript for allegedly good causes.[30] Security is a value with meaning not commonly understood to be subjective. Surely my finances, physical and mental health, property, employment and so forth, either is or is not secure? In reality, security is rarely considered as an objectively determinable quality; rather is it a judgement, even a feeling. A sense of security captures well the element of inherent uncertainty about it.

Civilian politicians and soldiers inhabit different cultural spaces with respect to consideration of security in the future. The soldier knows, perhaps uniquely, his profession in violent action is the realm of chance and uncertainty. He ought to know also that warfare either is, or always could be, at risk of becoming chaotic. The near universal and eternal military demands for clarity of political and strategic purpose, and for discipline in military behaviour, are very much an often despairing effort to promote, indeed endeavour to enforce, a desirable certainty upon the future. This feature of military culture is readily understandable, even though it guarantees friction with civilian political authority, and is doomed to yield much disappointment. Its effect is to oblige the professional soldier to row upstream against the often desperately uncertain features of military duty. The military planning within the much broader functional category of defence planning is perpetually and unavoidably ill-fitted for its future context of high concern. Given the awesome heights of personal and particular organizational stakes in military planning, it is easy to understand why soldiers seek certainty and consistency of purpose and decision, and favour steady identification of well-enough comprehended adversaries. Ideally, those adversaries should be closely associated with definite territory of exactly known location, and would be so encultured to well-enough known consequence in ways of warfare as to be usefully helpfully permissive of a friendly style by us sufficient to impose defeat.[31] Civilian policymakers and soldiers typically are sufficiently distinctive in their enculturation, as a result both of self-selection of preferred career path, as well as of formal responsibilities, that tension and controversy commonly attend performance of the defence planning function.

The concluding section below explores the possibility of locating helpful reliable certainties of high utility for orderly defence planning. The relevance of strategic thought and method as potentially the key enabler for success in such a hazard-prone mission is emphasized.

ARCHITECTURE OF ARGUMENT

The challenge posed by the necessity to conduct defence planning under conditions of great uncertainty can best be met by people and organizations educated in general strategic theory, in history, and in methods of defence analysis. When properly understood, the basic architecture of strategy provides the master key that unlocks explanation for understanding of what otherwise can be an ungovernable mess. Appreciation of strategy's essential bridging role is the only credible foundation upon which purposeful defence planning can be conducted. There are alternatives, but they are not advisable. For example, one may believe that strategically the country is secure enough against military menace, and that as a consequence of this pleasing conviction it does not much matter what the country does by way of its defence planning. Since abrupt changes in military posture might provoke unwanted, unexpected, and undesirable reaction abroad, and possibly in some quarters at home, the policy course of 'steady as she goes' will be attractive. The political rationale being that current estimation of national security concludes that it is probably good enough and there are no pressing and convincing arguments for a change in course. Politically the least troublesome grand design would be simply to allow the momentum of inertia to guide us as if in effect we were on autopilot. Variants of this approach are possible and may have much to recommend them. 'Steady as she goes' has the virtues of its apparent vices. While a steady course may be evidence of inappropriate resistance to changing circumstances, it does provide a stability important for orderly process in equipment acquisition and personnel training, as well as make for important predictability by foreign partners and potential adversaries.

It is correct and can be significant to distinguish clearly between policy and strategy, but for the purpose here it is necessary to signal a highly desirable connectivity between them. The whole house of strategy in its general theory provides normative guidance in what is truly a gestalt.[32] The trinity of ends, ways, and means probably should be displayed prominently on the wall of every office whose occupants believe that they are striving to do defence planning. It is essential to the sense in argument of this text that each category in the trinity should be recognized on its own terms. This point is crucial for understanding, because if it eludes one's conceptual grasp much of the episodic debate about strategic, operational, and tactical choices will be deprived of appropriate frames of reference and methodological aids to assessment. What follows are summative comments in the interest of a weapons' check before battle is fully joined in this text. The succeeding conceptual and methodological explanation clears the way for understanding of the argument that develops in the closing chapters. What comes next are the principal threads in this narrative.

Grand Strategy (or national security)

This is the master concept that accommodates all else in its different, but connecting rooms. Although strategy usually is understood to stand in a position necessarily subordinate to policy, it is important to appreciate the structure of strategy as encompassing political policy ends, as well as strategic ways, and military means. The purpose and indeed the nature of strategy are not violated by understanding the true authority of the strategy trinity of ends, ways, and means. Indeed, the relationship between strategy and policy is so interdependent that it is not possible to have the former without the latter. Strategy cannot comprise simply a marriage between ways and means: policy purpose is literally essential.

Ends: Political process and policy

This book has emphasized the role of politics in policy choices concerning planning for national defence. I argue that policy choice is the dynamic product of political process. This process is only variably influenced by professional expertise in defence matters. In part the explanation for this lies in the fact that politicians are obliged by the nature of their roles to attempt to design and conduct grand strategy rather than military strategy. It so happens that the more important questions for defence planning are not amenable to scientific investigation in the pursuit of reliably correct answers. Two reasons serve utterly to disable foolish aspirations to make a science of strategy (understood here as including politically forged policy ends). First, because by definitional certainty the future has yet to happen, it is unable to be mined or manipulated methodologically in fruitful pursuit of reliably correct knowledge. Second, even if we ignore the non-trivial problems of philosophy and physics that should discourage us, future strategic contexts are far too liable to unpredictable, including random, happenstance to lend themselves to creative futurological examination. Advanced metric methodology cannot help us secure a trustworthy grip on the strategic future. Human beings, their politics, and friction, assuredly will work to thwart our would-be expert futurists. Strangely perhaps, this does not mean that we have to be ignorant of all understanding of the future useful for defence planning but, what it does mean is that we have to be exceedingly careful, and modest in ambition, about what we can and should place reliance upon as candidate evidence about the strategic future. There is need for historical knowledge, but not in the form of possibly analogous events. The policy ends selected politically today essentially comprise judgements, (meaning guesses) that are a mixture of value-flavoured creative endeavour, imagination, and historical education—duly encased, one hopes, in a requirement for prudence. Prudent policymakers know they must be careful to attempt to control and limit the possible negative consequences of defence planning effort.

Ways: strategies and operations

Historical experience reveals readily that while selection of strategy(ies) is of high importance, it is not possible to have a strategy without, *ipso facto*, having a policy end also, even if only as an unpremeditated consequence. Because military behaviour always and unavoidably must have strategic meaning, even when specifically unintended, it follows also that it must carry political meaning, even should policy appear to be missing from the scene. The many 'ways' that are strategies must have political consequences that should fuel political issues of policy. However, it is possible to eschew or just neglect strategic purpose, and simply leap into the mode of 'doing something' forceful, with whatever elements of military power are available for use at the time. When military force, generally on a considerable scale, is directed hopefully to gain an attainable objective, one is in the realm of operations and operational artistry.[33] Whether or not operational effort is prudently conducted is, of course, a matter for critical assessment. Operations, understood as tactical effort directed to achieve substantial principally military ends, must depend for their strategic valuation strictly upon the strategic effect of their operational level effort. If strategy, the higher and literally essential guide and purpose is lacking, operations will at best be a waste of effort expended (lives and other scarce valuable assets).

Means

At its core, defence planning has to be about the suitability, adaptability, and readiness of a polity's military instrument to protect its nation. Means usually is the third item in the standard model of strategy, if only because it is the category of behaviour and activity at the lowest level of authority. If 'ends' captures in policy the political purpose of strategic behaviour, while 'ways' identifies how that purpose should be secured, 'means' may appear to the casual theorist as a dependent variable that expresses the implications of decisions made higher up. Strategic experience accessible through historical study, as well as defence analytical examination—not to mention commonsense—reveals that relative weakness in military means is entirely capable of rendering even prudent policy and cunning strategy futile. There is good reason why policy and strategy must stand higher in conceptual rank-order than tactics. But, all political and strategic effort is achieved only by behaviour that is by necessary definition tactical in the doing.[34] As a practical matter, defence planning always may be about the fitness or otherwise of friendly military forces to defend the polity. The inclusive subjects treated here have a brutal core of meaning that liberal societies usually decline to emphasize or even, for understandable reasons, recognize very explicitly. Public discourse about defence planning and preparation commonly does not highlight the fact that the defining feature of the activity under discussion is violence, or more politely, force. Public debate about warfare tends to focus on issues of legality, ethics, and occasionally politics. But the activity itself is all about the threat or application of violence. Similarly, the core meaning of political behaviour rarely is much more or less than relative power. The entirety of the strategy model's architecture of ends, ways, and means fits effortlessly into and for a context of individual and collective human (political) competition. The political ends and the strategic ways critical for the prudence in purposeful defence planning, are likely to prove hubristic at best, or lethally vain at worst, if military means are not competent to enable them.

This chapter has focused primarily on the inalienably political nature of the policy process that guides and then conducts defence planning. I have argued, certainly I have implied, that defence planning is not and cannot be an objective rational enterprise. It is not an endeavour in which rational and reasonable people, a crucial if underappreciated distinction, expertly seek competently and honestly for the correct answers to their polity's security needs in the future. As the text thus far should have made clear enough, every significant idea in the previous sentence is deeply problematic. Both rationality and reason can be strangers to defence planning; a polity's security needs are inherently subjective, incapable of being answered correctly with reliability; and the future is not at all permissive of penetration in aid of convenient foreseeability, no matter how glittering, elegant, or metric the methodology applied.

Despite the somewhat discouraging argument advanced immediately above, all is not lost as there are grounds for hope for a wise prudence. There are ways to educate ourselves for the conduct of sensible defence planning. History and somewhat scientific defence analysis can be conscripted in hope of assistance, provided one recognizes their limitations as sources of potential evidence. The hindrances to prudent planning caused by insuperable ignorance are easily identifiable. They are not all evadable, but nonetheless we are forearmed with the immense asset of access to millennia of strategic history. If that history is utilized intelligently for plausible understanding of the future, we will be far from naked in the face of dangers that literally are unknowable in specific detail. Whether or not we can be well enough educated strategically to be sufficiently adaptable to meet challenges to security in the future, is an open question.

NOTES

1. It would be difficult to exaggerate the contemporary popularity and therefore ubiquity of the concept of strategy, at least its apparently universal appeal as a

term. One wonders if the idea of strategy now has talismanic value. The literature on strategy in relation to business and politics is so prolific that the contrast between apparent clarity of theory and mixed results at best in official and commercial practice, is particularly stark. The main reason for the contrast between theory and practice, of course, is the sharpness of the distinction between the relative ease with which the logic of strategy can be explained, and the often awesome difficulty of actually behaving strategically with competence. The popularity of the idea of strategy is readily appreciated via any brief review of the business literature. For example, see: Peter Schwartz, *The Art of the Long View: Planning for the Future in an Uncertain World* (Chichester: John Wiley, 1998); Henry Mintzberg, *The Rise and Fall of Strategic Planning* (Harlow: Pearson Education, 2000); and Henry Mintzberg, Bruce Ahlstrand, and Joseph Laupel, *Strategic Safari: The complete guide through the wilds of strategic management*, 2nd edn. (Harlow: Pearson Education, 2009). Both in defence and business, the words 'strategy' and 'strategic' have become so familiar in popular (mis)use that this strategic thinker is inclined to believe that they have lost much of their proper meaning. If we all think and do strategy, in practice it is likely that few of us are worthy of the claim.

2. Nassim Nicholas Taleb, *The Black Swan: The Impact of the Highly Improbable* (New York: Random House, 2010). Taleb writes approvingly and appropriately about Andrew Marshall and Andrew Mays at the US Department of Defense, Office of the Secretary of Defense, Office of Net Assessment: 'The impulse on the part of the military is to devote resources to predicting the next problems. These thinkers [Marshall and Mays] advocate the opposite: invest in preparedness, not in prediction. Remember that infinite vigilance is not possible'. 208.

3. Thinking of the semi-engaged role allowed the British monarch by Sir Walter Bagehot. See his book, *The English Constitution* 1867; London: Oxford University Press, 1961), 67.

4. Carl von Clausewitz, *On War*, trans. Michael Howard and Peter Paret (1833–4; Princeton, NJ: Princeton University Press, 1976), 87.

5. See N. H. Gibbs, *History of the Second World War: Grand Strategy, Vol 1: Rearmament Policy* (London: Her Majesty's Stationery Office, 1976), chs. 1–3.

6. Such is the challenge of uncertainty about the future that even superior examples of methodologically expert defence analysis inexorably acquire an unmistakeable period-piece quality. See, for example: Paul K. Davis, 'Planning Under Uncertainty Then and Now: Paradigms Lost and Paradigms Emerging', in Davis, ed., *New Challenges for Defense Planning: Rethinking How Much is Enough* MR–400–RC (Santa Monica, CA: RAND, 1994), 15–57; and 'Strategy and Defense Planning for the Coming Century', in Zalmay M. Khalilzad and David A. Ochmanek, eds., *Strategic Appraisal 1997: Strategy and Defense Planning for the 21st Century*, MR–826–AF (Santa Monica, CA: RAND, 1997), 7–34. Capabilities-based planning is defined and described comprehensively in Paul K. Davis, *Analytic Architecture for Capabilities-Based Planning, Mission-Systems Analysis, and Transformation*, MR–1513–OSD (Santa Monica, CA: RAND, 2002); and also, tersely but effectively, in Paul K. Davis, 'Uncertainty-Sensitive Planning', in Stuart E. Johnson, Martin C. Librecki, and Gregory F. Treverton, eds., *New Challenges, New Tools for Defense*

Decisionmaking, MR–1576 (Santa Monica, CA: RAND, 2003), 141–43. There is important truth in the maxim that 'nothing dates so rapidly as yesterday's tomorrow'.

7. Simpson, *War from the Ground Up*, explains this rather unClausewitzian context. His argument rests heavily, though not exclusively on his personal experience of 'war'—or was it?—in Afghanistan.

8. See Michael Howard, *The Continental Commitment: The Dilemma of British Defence Policy in the Era of the Two World Wars* (London: Temple Smith, 1972); and Keith Neilson, 'Great Britain' in Richard F. Hamilton and Holger H. Herwig, eds., *War Planning 1914* (Cambridge: Cambridge University Press, 2010), 175–97.

9. See John Gooch, *The Plans of War: The General Staff and British Military Strategy c.1900–1916* (London: Routledge and Kegan Paul, 1974); and Williamson Murray, 'British grand strategy, 1933–1942', in Murray, Richard Hart Sinnreich, and James Lacey, eds., *The Shaping of Grand Strategy: Policy, diplomacy, and war* (Cambridge: Cambridge University Press, 2011), 147–81.

10. A 'portfolio' approach to military planning is explained helpfully in Davis, Analytic Architecture for Capabilities-Based Planning, Mission-Systems Analysis, and Transformation, 11–14.

11. Colin S. Gray, *The Strategy Bridge: Theory for Practice* (Oxford: Oxford University Press, 2010), ch. 5.

12. Clausewitz, *On War*, 87.

13. Taleb, *The Black Swan*, 50: 'This is the distortion of silent evidence'.

14. Paul Cornish, *British Military Planning for the Defence of Germany, 1945–50* (Basingstoke: Macmillan, 1996), provides essential historical context to what became eventually an open-ended British continental commitment.

15. Thucydides, *The Landmark Thucydides: A Comprehensive Guide to the Peloponnesian War*, ed. Robert B. Strasler, rev. trans. Richard Crawley (*c*.400 BC: New York, Free Press, 1996), 43.

16. Scenarios are best understood as 'stories about how future events might come to pass'. Andrew F. Krepinevich, *7 Deadly Scenarios: A Military Futurist Explores War in the 21st Century* (New York: Bantam Books, 2009). This is the clearest and most economical explanation of the function of scenario design. It is admirably simple, but not simplistic. For human, political, and defence analytic reasons, all arguments about national defence in the future are conducted more or less explicitly in the light of some narrative that provides intelligible, if not necessarily plausible, strategic context.

17. Thomas C. Schelling: *The Strategy of Conflict* (New York: Oxford University Press, 1960); and *Arms and Influence* (New Haven, CT: Yale University Press, 1966).

18. In Herman Kahn's immortal words: 'Usually the most convincing way to look willing is to be willing'. *On Thermonuclear War* (1960; New York: Free Press, 1969), 287.

19. I have explored the connection between 'might' and 'right' in the following publications: *Defining and Achieving Decisive Victory* (Carlisle, PA: Strategic Studies Institute, US Army War College, April 2002); 'Moral Advantage, Strategic

Advantage?' *The Journal of Strategic Studies*, 33 (June 2010), 33–65; and *Perspectives on Strategy*, ch. 2.

20. Gray, *The Strategy Bridge*.

21. The past is replete with examples of civilian political leaders who had difficulty confining their leadership role to the political. The trouble is that sound strategic judgement is not sourced reliably from among those most experienced in the conduct of warfare. The reason is because soldiers cannot be educated reliably to be wise in understanding how the threat and use of military force should advance the likelihood of desired political consequences. It need hardly be said that deep and long experience of political process is also incapable of providing reliable education in strategy. Civil-military relations in practice nearly always amount to a 'shotgun marriage' of necessity between distinctive tribes with different cultures. History is short neither of politicians who fancied themselves as generals, nor of generals who were convinced that they should have been in political charge of national effort. There is little natural harmony between the civilian political and the military banks of the strategy bridge. Personality and circumstance always matter, but often the two are more co-belligerents than a united team. See Eliot A. Cohen, *Supreme Command: Soldiers, Statesmen, and Leadership in Wartime* (New York: Free Press, 2002); and the excellent collection of essays in Stephen J. Cimbala, ed., *Civil-Military Relations in Perspective: Strategy, Structure and Policy* (Farnham: Ashgate, 2012). The literature on civil-military relations is forbiddingly large, not least because its subject necessarily is central to the conduct and meaning of all war and warfare. The Churchill case is admittedly rather extreme, almost an 'outlier', but nonetheless it has great utility in highlighting the major threads in this particular issue-area. See Geoffrey Best, *Churchill and War* (London: Hambledon and London 2005); Carlo D'Este, *Warlord: A Life of Churchill at War, 1874–1945* (London: Allen Lane, 2009); and Max Hastings, *Finest Years: Churchill as Warlord, 1940–45* (London: Harper Press, 2009).

22. Cohen, *Supreme Command*.

23. Defence debate may be joined by senior military figures who are still serving; by recently retired soldiers (but with positive name and reputation recognition; by spokespeople for particular branches of military activity; by the spokespeople on behalf of the variably dependent industries for the military; by politicians whose electoral fortunes may be influenced by defence-related job gains or losses; by a few expert scholarly commentators; and by sundry inexpert journalists as well as explicit lobbyists for particular causes believed to be impacted by national defence decisions. Rationality in defence planning may be hampered by human emotional facts that can intrude inconveniently to make rational policymaking appear unreasonable. For example, the British electorate, although typically uncaring about much of contemporary military detail, can be stirred for political trouble-making quite readily on such an iconic issue as fair play for Ghurkha retirees who wish to live in Britain. Similarly, Iraqi and Afghan translators who served with the British armed forces and fear a lethal retribution should they remain in their homeland, provide fuel for anger in British politics. To disregard the vital personal interest of such loyal servants of the Crown can be retailed credibly for political

effect as disloyalty that dishonours us and harms our reputation. Thucydides would have understood this.

24. Gray, *The Strategy Bridge*, 135–36.

25. The concept of a deep peace does not quite mean that war has been abolished, but it does signify the belief that war is all but unthinkable. Most of Western and Central Europe was at peace in 1913, and again in 1933, and yet again in 1953, and 1983. However, a like condition of 'peace' does not unite those dates in their strategic meaning very usefully with 2013. Just as a condition of war can be said to have varying states of intensity, so also might peace be qualified similarly. There is, of course, an abiding evidential difficulty attending designations of depth of peace. Events of a 'Black-Swan' nature can upset overconfident faith in peace. There is no way in which peace (for the future) can be verified. See Taleb, *The Black Swan*, for a reminder that the future may be negatively surprising with deep consequences.

26. Clausewitz could hardly be clearer on the reality of limitation in war. He writes: 'It is not possible in every war for the victor to overthrow his enemy completely'. *On War*, 566. This is a factual claim about the reality of strategic history, it is not a normative statement.

27. Raymond Aron, *Peace and War: A Theory of International Relations* (New York: Doubleday, 1966), 285.

28. Compare two important views of methods in strategic studies written 24 years apart by the same scholar: Bernard Brodie: 'Strategy as a science', 1st pub. 1949, in Thomas G. Mahnken, *Strategic Studies: A Reader* (Abingdon: Routledge, 2008), 8–21; and *War and Politics* (New York: Macmillan, 1973), ch. 10. The erroneous belief that strategy could be approached as a science, was based substantially on the more basic convictions that economics was or should be a science, and that strategy could be addressed economically and therefore scientifically. The syllogism is sound enough as logic: if economics is a science, and if strategy is really economics, then strategy also must be a science. The difficulty here lies not in the logic, but rather is empirical. There is far more to strategy than economics; that which is embraced by economics comprises only a part of the whole. Iconic period-piece publications for the rise of RAND include: Charles J. Hitch, *Decision-Making for Defense* (Berkeley, CA: University of California Press, 1965); and Hitch and Roland N. McKean, *The Economics of Defense in the Nuclear Age* (New York: Atheneum, 1966). Useful perspective is provided in Alex Arbella, *Soldiers of Reason: The RAND Corporation and the Rise of the American Empire* (Orlando, FL: Harcourt, 2008), which is better than its occasional populist overstatement might mislead one to expect; and Bruce Kuklick, *Blind Oracles: Intellectuals and War from Kennan to Kissinger* (Princeton, NJ: Princeton University Press, 2006). The peril to strategy posed by an unwisely metric approach to war and warfare is illustrated in truly granular detail in Gregory A. Daddis, *No Sure Victory: Measuring U.S. Army Effectiveness and Progress in the Vietnam War* (New York: Oxford University Press, 2011).

29. It should be needless to say that one can always reduce or even remove opacity at will, by making discrete metric assumptions. Elegant mathematics, honestly and competently applied, can obscure the fact that the analysis makes little strategic sense. With this sceptical view in mind, see Edward S. Quade, ed., *Analysis for*

Military Decisions: the RAND Lectures on Systems Analysis (Chicago: RAND McNally, 1964); E. S. Quade and W. I. Boucher, eds., *Systems Analysis and Policy Planning: Applications in Defense* (New York: American Elsevier, 1969); and Alain C. Enthoven and K. Wayne Smith, *How Much is Enough? Shaping the Defense Program, 1961–1969* (1971; Santa Monica, CA: RAND, 2005).

30. Security is a meaningless idea without value for defence planning for two fundamental reasons: it is inherently subjective and is without boundaries. This is not to mean or imply that the concept is without meaning, only that it lacks meaning which can be extracted by analysis. It is normative, discretionary, can be highly emotional, and it consumes its own contexts. To be blunt, it is not a useful concept, notwithstanding its global popularity. Indeed the width and depth of its popularity provides more than a hint concerning its impracticability. The fact that the most senior sometimes executive body of the United Nations Organization was called and remains the Security Council, should alert us to the utility long understood to inhere in the opacity of the concept. For illustration of my argument, see the table of contents of Paul D. Williams, ed., *Security Studies: An Introduction*, 2nd edn. (Abingdon: Routledge, 2013).

31. The challenge of seeking to succeed strategically in armed combat that is not de facto agreed among belligerents and other relevant audiences to be a war as we know and prefer it in the West, is developed impressively in Simpson, *War from the Ground Up*, in which he argues that what has occurred since 2001 in Afghanistan is 'armed politics outside war'. 66. Obviously, his argument stands or falls on the basis of understanding when what appears to be a war actually needs understanding as something else. I have yet to be entirely convinced that Simpson is sufficiently correct in his theorizing, but I admit willingly to being intrigued by the questions that he raises.

32. See Gray, *Perspectives on Strategy*, ch. 6.

33. For an outstanding review and critical analysis of the theory and practice of the operational level of war in modern strategic history, see John Andreas Olsen and Martin van Creveld, eds., *The Evolution of Operational Art: From Napoleon to the Present* (Oxford: Oxford University Press, 2011). The concept of an operational level of war remains somewhat controversial, as I indicated in *The Strategy Bridge*, 20–1. Melvin, *Manstein*, has much to offer that is empirically enlightening to those of us who tend unduly to the theoretical.

34. The vital argument is explained well in Antulio J. Echevarria II, 'Dynamic Inter-Dimensionality: A Revolution in Military Theory', *Joint Force Quarterly*, 15 (spring 1997), 29–36. It is remarkable how resistant many defence professionals are to accepting the admirably clear meaning, with high utility, of Clausewitz's distinction between strategy and tactics. '[Tactics teaches *the use of armed forces in the engagement*; strategy, *the use of engagements for the object of the war*'. *On War*, 128 (emphasis in the original). It is something of a mystery why the terms continue to be grossly abused.

6

Guidance for Defence Planning

LEVELS OF ANALYSIS

Despite the prominence accorded to politics in Clausewitz's *On War*, much missionary work remains to be done in explaining its ownership role over strategy.[1] Although politics and strategy are by no means synonymous, the relationship is more intimate than is commonly recognized. Because this book has adopted an inclusive understanding of the meaning of defence planning, it is exceptionally important here to be clear about the relevant domain of interest. My subject is purposeful preparation for the defence of a polity in the future. This understanding of defence planning may be characterized as a definition with attitude. Although little is excluded, the choice of wording is far from casual. The intention is to emphasize the need to take a contextually rich view of the subject, rather than to burrow deeply into the particulars, which though important, necessarily are subordinate to a purpose that must be political and requires strategic expression. This text endorses the thesis of Williamson Murray, inter alia, that choice of policy and strategy typically is far more consequential than are operations and tactics.[2] Murray's argument should be regarded as incontrovertible, but it does lend itself to misrepresentation, at least by possible implication. The misrepresentation can take the form of straw targets liable to mislead. A noteworthy example of exaggeration in argument mars the first page of Michael O'Hanlon's useful study of *The Science of War*. Having first granted generously and accurately the imprecision of the defence analyst's quantitative methodological tools, he moves on rapidly to argue as follows:

> We have little choice, however, but to try to refine the science of war as much as possible. What would the alternative be? To base defense budget levels on pure guesswork or politics? To develop any weapon that seems technically within reach without regard to its likely cost, effectiveness, or other strategic effects? As imprecise as the science of war may be, we must attempt to understand it.[3]

The words just quoted are critically important, both in what they get right and in what they do not. On the positive side, O'Hanlon surely is correct in insisting upon the expenditure of analytical effort 'to try to refine the science of war as much as possible', and in his admonition that 'imprecise as the science of war may be, we must attempt to understand it'. So much, so unexceptional. Unfortunately the remainder of the quoted words are far less admirable. Inadvertently, he is both confused and confusing in ways that illustrate the case for the main argument in my book. Specifically, although there is a great deal of science about war, and O'Hanlon performs valiantly in its explanation, neither physical (and mathematical) science nor social science contributes very helpfully to its understanding. Being an all too human endeavour, driven or at least shaped by contingency, war and its strategy cannot be studied scientifically: certain and thoroughly reliable knowledge of war is not obtainable by any methodology. This is not to claim that military challenges, including the warfare in war, are by their nature immune to useful metric analysis, but it is to argue that strategic choice does not lend itself to scientific examination in a quest for correct answers.

First-order consideration of strategy has to be political and is always certain to rest upon guesswork. O'Hanlon's pejorative deployment of guesswork, politics, and intuition in the words quoted, reflects an apparent misunderstanding of the subject of war and of future planning for national defence. Politics is not sensibly to be contrasted with science and defence analysis, because they have distinctive functional responsibilities. Similarly, intuition, provided it is educated by experience and perhaps study (of the experience of others), is not to be despised in political leaders, military planners and commanders. Long and deep experience can equip policy makers and strategists with the intuitive, though educated, wisdom described by Clausewitz in his concept of the *coup d'oeil*.[4] No refinement of the science of war is able to reveal that which is not open to scientific examination. Earlier chapters in this work strove to explain that no science of war or defence planning in anticipation of future war can know the unknowable. No matter how elegant or complex the mathematics of defence analysis, such would-be scientific effort must depend for its relevance on the guesswork and the intuition of politics and strategy. Would that it were not—perhaps so! Arguably, it would be convenient were governments able to out-source their strategic problems to defence experts who could fire up their computers and generate reliably correct answers. It should be needless to say that this cannot be done. Political responsibility cannot be delegated to technically proficient cognoscenti. Regardless of the character of political system, the issues of strategy most significant for future national security are decided by the political will, even the mood, of the domestic stakeholders. There is large scope for quantitative analysis of defence issues, but that analysis can only be relevant once politics and its policy and strategy have decided on the course of the community's effort.

When history and scientific defence analysis are contrasted and compared, as here, it is necessary to realize that as a general rule they should not be considered competitively with respect to their possible contributory advice. Science cannot offer prudent advice for the future, not even when it seeks to manipulate historical data. In its turn, history also is hugely limited in its utility as a source of reliable evidence for defence planning, but at least it has the relatively advantageous qualities of being a human, political, and strategic domain. The future may fascinate, even compel and oblige intended anticipatory behaviour, but—yet, by definitional dependence on the laws of physics, really it is no domain at all.

Defence Analysis and its Limitations

The calculation of reliably correct answers by metrically demonstrable methodology is feasible with respect to challenges with values that are certain. For example, ICBM survivability is readily calculable, provided one knows the accuracy of the enemy's missiles, their number, their reliability, the scale of their MIRV-ing for warhead numbers and their explosive yields, and the blast resistance of the silos that house one's own ICBMs.[5] Fortunately or not, however, such a scientific example of the elementary mathematics of a nuclear 'exchange' is not quite as strategically revealing as it may appear, and the possibility of consequential mis-education with dire implications for the human race is troubling. The relevance to my argument of the example just given of alleged certainty of calculable knowledge, is that it points up the importance of adopting a broad rather than a narrowly technical view of defence planning. The quotations from Michael O'Hanlon supplied earlier, typified an approach to defence planning that overreaches in its quest after 'the science of war'. It is instructive to offer a thought by Ken Booth that similarly somewhat overreaches, though in his case rather more plausibly. Booth offers the memorable aphorism that '[u]ltimately strategy is a continuation of philosophy with an admixture of firepower'.[6] He explains that:

> Strategy is certainly brutal, but it is also concerned with profound moral questions. These questions are more important than simply life and death: they are also concerned with individual and group values, including definitions of freedom and aspirations for justice.[7]

Strategy may appear to be a highly technical subject, as indeed it is in important respects. But, it is essential never to forget that it is also a strongly human subject that can be driven by ideational, psychological, and circumstantial influences.

Two kinds of peril hover over scientific defence analysis, neither of which is reliably controllable by the analysts. The first is the technical uncertainty that must limit the faith that policymakers should place in quantifiable analysis. Mathematical method per se is not so much the problem; rather is it the accuracy of the values assigned in the equations. By analogy, an advanced culinary technique is of little utility if the necessary ingredients are missing and cannot be supplied. The second hazard inherent in defence analysis is the fact that political, strategic, operational, and tactical behaviour is human. Human beings acting under strict discipline, even combat discipline in all the conditions exposed by Clausewitz in his 'climate of war', cannot entirely be trusted to think and behave as Universal Soldiers should.[8] Plainly this is an inconvenient historical reality apt to derail careful calculations of military balance and imbalance. This is not to argue that combat metrics are meaningless, but it is to insist that human will, as well as the contingency of circumstance and simply accident, can render analysis of little value. In fact such analysis may be dangerous, because it will suggest as highly probable combat outcomes that do not occur, largely because combatant behaviour was eccentric to the analytical model. Needless to say, perhaps, the hazards of combat modelling are enhanced when they seek to accommodate not Belligerents 'A' and 'B', but rather security communities with divergent and asymmetric political and military cultures. While warfare and its lethal dangers is common to all periods of strategic history and to all peoples, still just about every war has differed from every other one. Although the features of war and warfare that have been shared across time and culture are important for general understanding of the phenomena, the differences can be vitally important. This is why the challenge to try and understand the relationship between continuity and change is critical. The problem is that wars do not come in standard sizes, let alone a single standard size, and nor do the military means thereto most appropriate, or their consequences. Thoughts of this kind that flow from the study of military history are valuable as caveats that need to be placed on anticipatory calculations of combat and combat support, but for the multi-cultural legion of defence analysts around the world it can appear as a show-stopper. Let me hasten to add that the show of metric defence analysis should not be stopped. Notwithstanding my earlier criticism of Michael O'Hanlon's overstatement of the prospective benefit attainable by scientific analysis, there is no good enough reason to be definitively sceptical of the value of using mathematical models in the anticipation of combat—always provided one remembers that Military Man as the Universal Warrior is no easier to find than is Strategic Man.

It is usual for experts inadvertently to shrink the domain they allow to intrude on their professional world. That domain of experts is ruled intelligently and often emotionally also by the conviction that their expertise should govern, polish, and may decorate and then be employed to promote. Genuine communication across disciplinary boundaries and cultures sadly is rare, even in cases where institutions boast of an interdisciplinary ethos and assets. The occupants of lunch tables tend to cluster for cultural, if not gastronomic, comfort with like-minded colleagues. A core challenge to the understanding of prudent defence planning is how to allow guidance for policy to accommodate the different kinds of expertise that contend for priority. On the one hand, the political bank of the strategy bridge is both legally and morally in the driving seat for a security community's policy toward its defence preparation for the future. This unequal dialogue permits defence experts to play at politics and its choices, but in principle at least only when those people are functioning as citizens, not as experts. On the other hand, defence professionals are essential if policy choices are to be compared competitively and competently. Difficulty arises in distinguishing between critically important subject expertise, which must be subordinate as a contributor to political choice, and the content of policy. When effectively there is fusion of choices made and the quality of advice offered and accepted, explicitly or implicitly, there is some danger that 'means' and their usual 'ways' will achieve undue influence over 'ends' of policy that properly are the product of politics.

Defence planning must have a substantial basis in defence analysis, but that analysis cannot have stand-alone integrity—in effect in splendid isolation from its domestic political context, climate, and therefore mood. Because defence planning is treated here as a national issue area, it is plausible and appropriate to claim that the international political context for this planning activity is reflected for good or ill in domestic political action and reaction. In other words, for example, foreign phenomena that are candidates for influence on American defence planning, only become significant if Americans and their domestic political process decide that that should be so. This point highlights both the importance of national discretion and the sovereignty of policy choice through the local political process.[9] The critical issue is the highly subjective matter of the practical limits to political discretion. The relevance to the subject here pertains to the relative influence of defence subject experts, as well as to the objective frontier of knowledge and understanding.

A non-trivial challenge to prudence in defence planning is the need to grasp the reality of the political and moral legitimacy of sharply different points of view. It is relatively easy, even if the mathematics are complex and forbidding, to model situations with known, perhaps very confidently assumed, quantities and values. But, little reflection is required to alert one to the conundrum that that which is most readily quantifiable, even with replicable scientific certainty, tends not to embrace much of the strategic domain vital to national security. Notionally to illustrate my argument, each of the following questions are or would be hypothetical triggers for American defence planning interest and activity:

- Should we seek to negotiate a minimum nuclear deterrent? (for what purposes?)
- Should we assist in the defence of Taiwan were China to attempt invasion?
- Should we intervene in a war that has Israel under nuclear threat or attack?
- Should we encourage Georgia to apply for NATO membership?
- Should we punish North Korea for its aggressive military harassment of South Korea?
- Should we strive to establish, or at least support, political moves towards the creation of an intended NATO-equivalent in Asia?

The above items are intended simply to illustrate the critically important point that it would be challenging to try to identify an issue of interest to defence planning that would lend itself to unarguably correct answers. In our strategic world that is thoroughly, if not quite reliably, Clausewitzian, the hypothetical conflictual context essentially is always one of limited war and warfare.[10] Given that in war the enemy always has a vote, his discretionary authority over competitive military effort should reduce aspirations to conduct combat modelling in expectation of confidently deriving future knowledge that could be certain. Different personalities, divergent military and strategic doctrines, significantly asymmetrical cultures, friction, chance, and accident, are any and all capable of reducing hopes for achieving useful predictability of the course of strategic history to an expression of vanity. The point is not that defence planning is unable to model combat, which is not true, but rather that the quantity and quality of combat that will characterize any war depends critically upon decisions and behaviour that are beyond confident prior analysis by either side.[11] There are ways in which belligerents may seek to enhance the predictability of victory at tolerable cost, but as a general rule it is no exaggeration to say that war is a gamble. There is simply too much that will prove consequentially unpredictable that is important in the competitive dynamics of warfare, for a decision to fight to be other than a roll of the dice.[12]

How defence analysis can and should feature as a vital aid to defence planning is in its helping policymakers understand the possible net military effectiveness of alternative force postures. Analysis may be pressed to suggest how much the attainable alternative postures should cost, and with what lead-times. Indeed, almost anything is rationally analysable, provided key parameters are specified. However, the principal challenges of uncertainty of dominant significance for this enquiry are beyond confident parametric specification.

In a simple explanation illustrating the military dimension of uncertainty, Clausewitz explained that while one can count and compare numbers of fighting men, it is far more of a challenge to estimate how hard those men should be willing to fight.[13] The defence planner today will derive much no doubt useful information about potential enemy capabilities, including doctrines and even cultural tendencies, as well as his technical preferences and probable competencies. Nonetheless, the fact will remain that the lion's share of the needed understanding will be missing or at best highly dubious. It is important to know about the military forces an enemy could bring to the fight, but will he bring them? How strongly motivated, and by what considerations, will he be to escalate or constrain combat?

Defence analysis at all levels of military organization can and certainly will inform its chain of command of everything which it is capable about an enemy's ability to fight, indeed as it will educate friendly commanders and their staffs about all aspects of friendly combat engagement and its logistical sustainment. But the larger and far deeper questions must always be beyond totally reliable expert analysis, because they require judgement of people, politics, and strategy. It is far simpler to estimate the anticipatable loss rate likely to be imposed by air in an interdiction campaign, for example, than it is to do other than guess whether or not the Other will choose to continue to resist, let alone escalate possibly to the level of a nuclear exchange, should he have that option.[14] Unique decisions made by flawed or inspired individuals operating under great pressure of time amidst the chaos and stress of crisis, are close to impossible to anticipate with confidence. But defence planning by and large is dominated by the possibility of contingencies that have to be approached largely as challenges to our ability to anticipate political behaviour by individuals and even groups who may or may not be open to rational, let alone responsible, strategic argument.[15] Given that defence planning has to look to an unknown and literally unknowable time and issue-set in the future, this book, although respectful of technical defence analysis, must maintain that the higher slopes of the defence planning challenge are out of first-order reach of defence analysis. The strategic mind insists upon receiving a plausible answer to the most general purpose of default questions, so what? The numbers crunched in analysis require strategic explanation. This is not to demean the importance of second-order issues concerning the feasibility and affordability of alternative military solutions that policy and strategy decide need to be attempted, or interrogated, rigorously. Questions of strategy may be reducible to numerate expression, and indeed they should be so informed, when such is practicable. But strategic decision requires consideration that is pre-eminently political and moral, rather than mathematical.

Quantitative skills of defence analysis are essential for the understanding and selection of the operational ways and military means of strategy, but they can only contribute in a supportive, including critical, role to the choice of strategy's political ends. Defence analysis cannot usually be a source of timely and prudent advice on the 'what' of strategy. Of course, the strategic choice of what to attempt should benefit from such analytical support as quantitative analysts can provide but strategy cannot be a prudent pursuit of the doable as an end in itself. Defence analysts are not competent professionally to choose the political purposes that should be translatable into the goals of strategy that may enable them.[16] Since defence planning is understood to refer most significantly to preparation for the defence of a country in the future, in its highest reaches one must grant in practice discretionary authority to the collective political, moral and, in a somewhat subordinate role, strategic, will of a polity. Political preference in strategy is not exercised by expert professional defence analysts, at least not when performing as such. Even an outstanding level of understanding of military matters does not qualify a person to make political decisions on behalf of his community. The expert's knowledge and understanding must be valuable, if it is sound—though how can one be sure, short of a live-fire test in the field. However, war is not about what can be done, no matter how competently, but rather about the consequences of violent action. In other words, regardless of the technical skills of the professional defence analyst, only the general public through its elected representatives can decide for and against strategic action. That public owns both its armed forces and their deeds in combat, and the political consequences of that violence for net good or ill.

A Defence Planning Guide

The remainder of this chapter is devoted to identification and critical discussion of the matters most fundamental for understanding of the challenges inescapable from the function of defence planning. Most of the topics specified here have been discussed earlier, though sometimes in ways that did not privilege strategic comprehension of the whole enterprise. What follows is not presented as a theory of defence planning, but rather as a critical review of what needs to be understood about the challenges of the mission. Insofar as possible, this discussion is developed without bias or prejudice, favour against or towards particular polities. All security communities are obliged to satisfy the function of defence planning. Unavoidably I cannot prevent traces of my Anglo–American DNA from being occasionally detectable. Nonetheless, the intention here is to analyse and discuss strategy and defence planning as global and even an eternal field of necessary human political thought and behaviour. This is my understanding of what would-be defence planners need to know. The engine of this serial topical discussion is driven by five elemental questions: why, what, when, where, and how? Some of the topics most obviously address just one of the master quintet, but many require answer to three or more. Analytically it is convenient to focus seriatim upon particular aspects of the subject, hence the topical identities. But, distinctions must not be

---

Understanding Defence Planning: Summary of Topics

• Motivation	• Science and certainty
• Priorities	• Politics and economics
• Tolerance of error	• History and strategy

---

permitted to conceal the true essential unity of the entire subject of defence planning. Box 6.1 gives a topical summary by category of what follows.

MOTIVATION: THE DRIVERS OF POLITICAL AND STRATEGIC BEHAVIOUR

The strategic and political history of the human race reveals plainly what amounts to evidence of a boundary-free realm for the exercise of discretion. Just about every conceivable belief about, or hope concerning, the conduct of relations between communities has been field-tested many times, in many places, and across cultural and civilizational as well as political divides. The frontier, if there really is one, between biological nature and cultural nurture, is not of noteworthy relevance here, because of the high consistency of typical political and strategic behaviour over a very long period. Whether or not Man (with apologies for the gender expediency) might one day evolve, or learn, to prefer a default condition of political life that would be thoroughly and deeply astrategic, there are currently no grounds convincingly extant for such speculation. If this judgement is sound it has necessary implications for the future of fundamental importance to the context for defence planning. There is likely to be essential continuity in strategic history, from the past, through the present, into the future.[17]

One is not over-simply re-stating the old half-truth that history repeats itself. There is no doubt that our history has shown great discontinuity in nearly all matters of detail, and indeed ones of higher moment regarding beliefs and values. Nonetheless the motives behind conflict and war, and therefore the reasons for defence planning in whatever form in a particular time and place, have not altered significantly over millennia. Athenian general Thucydides managed to achieve one of literary history's greatest feats of inspired reductionism when he claimed that fear, honour, and interest, could provide the dominant explanation for political behaviour. Regarded suitably as broad inclusive concepts, this famous triptych from the end of the fifth century BC, offers entirely persuasive explanation of why defence planners in the twenty–first century, which is still largely to come, would be well-advised to consider prudence to be their highest professional value.

If one respects empirical evidence of strategic historical continuity, while not excluding Black-Swan theory, it is beyond plausible doubt that our future strategic context should be anticipated to be war-prone. That can only be the beginning of the acquisition of necessary understanding for defence planning, but it is nonetheless truly essential for all that.

PRIORITIES: GETTING WHAT IS MOST IMPORTANT RIGHT ENOUGH

Unfortunately for defence planners, it is not always the case that the relative importance of an issue is so clear as to be self-evidently so. It has to be prudent to seek to get the biggest issues right enough, but how does one identify the relative strategic importance of a question, and how can one determine the character of answer that should be right enough? When posed thus, it is no great achievement to understand why at least one of the two questions does not lend itself to scientifically analytical assault. The biggest of issues for national defence planning must concern perceived menaces to national security. But, when awesome menaces are not convincingly current, the scope for policy discretion is almost inconveniently large. Serial German menace in the twentieth century, succeeded functionally by Soviet danger, concentrated the minds of understandably troubled foreign observers. Germany and then the Soviet Union, attracted threat estimates abroad which, as an essential minimum, usefully simplified the defence mission of Others. If only one character of strategic context is permitted to serve as master narrative, which is to say as the 'plot', policy authority has a relatively easy time. If, however, that authority is at best only weak, then the defence analyst essentially is adrift with no home port providing safe harbour that is a confident source of understanding as to the requirements of contemporary, let alone future, security.

If the threat horizon lacks a plausibly dominant cloud, defence planners cannot advise prudently and persuasively on how their political community should prioritize defence issues. Super dominant threats for the 'West' at least: Persians, Huns, Ottoman jihadists, Nazi and Soviet imperialists, have been the exception in strategic history, though perceptions of danger and even anticipation of war have been common indeed. Existential peril that would place political and possibly even physical survival at risk, has however been only distinctly episodic. This plausible historical reality understandably has had high importance for performance of the defence planning function.[18] When contemporary existential menace is not perceived, even though its distant possibility may be acknowledged, how does one prioritize both as between defence and other kinds of important community benefit, and among alternative investments in defence posture?

The more closely the issue of prioritization is examined, the more it becomes clear to see that expert defence analysis is out of its depth. National security always is subjective; it is evident that scientifically verifiable answers to questions about defence prioritization cannot be generated. Choice of priorities cannot be delegated to technical experts, because the rank-ordering is a matter of political choice. Defence planning is an exercise in strategy, and strategy is about politics, not science. That said, it is both necessary as well as fortunately possible to identify and apply some discipline in political debate about national defence. The historical record shows that sometimes choices in defence planning were easy to make. Whether or not an extreme contemporary menace was discerned as existential, particular kinds of extreme military threat have been identified and generally agreed, if not always in very good time, to be such. A golden rule for defence planning has been, and continues to be, the absolute necessity of defeating or at least evading an existential and plausibly super threat.

Many polities have been in little strategic doubt that their most important military asset either was an army capable of thwarting continental invaders, or a navy able to prevent either amphibious assault or economic (and financial) strangulation at sea. Since 1945, political and cultural frontiers have not much impeded understanding that nuclear weapons are in a class of their own as all but guarantors of a nation's security. No one knows, or can know, exactly what quantity and quality of nuclear threat and counter threat will achieve deterrent effect in the future. But, it is widely understood that it would be imprudent to take avoidable risks of potential inadequacy.[19] One can soon reach the further shores of improbability in speculating about the political leverage of nuclear threat, but there is no sound basis for doubting the prudence in the assumption that nuclear forces, able to survive surprise attack and intended to deter, have critically unique political and strategic value. Even if one disagrees with that argument, it would be only prudent to go along anyway, given the possibility that one might be wrong. Nuclear possession is not without its risks, but neither is nuclear disarmament.

Another example of a crown jewel for defence planning was British homeland air defence in the era of the two world wars. The Battle of Britain was neither predicted nor predictable, but it was anticipated as a possibility. RAF Fighter Command proved good enough in 1940, and that strategic fact was the product of nearly a quarter century of British official acceptance of the strategic and political logic of this vital argument about protection of the highest priorities.[20] Fighter Command was smaller than strategically desirable, and it acquired both the Spitfire and radar assistance later than it might, but still it proved good enough when the test came. That granted, it cannot be denied that much defence planning activity, much of the time, concerns matters that truly are discretionary. Regarding the political connection, as a general rule defence planning is conducted in support of foreign policy that is to an important degree chosen for it. This is not always so, but it is well to remember that when politicians debate the attraction of this or that behaviour abroad, it follows logically and should follow practically, that there ought to be consequences for defence planning. Many risks to national interests are the result of gambles in intervention that were strictly discretionary. As a general rule, much of the content of defence planning is the consequence of political choice, not strict necessity.

TOLERANCE OF ERROR AND ADAPTABILITY TO CIRCUMSTANCE: STRIVE TO BE RESILIENT DESPITE SOME LEGACY OF PAST MISTAKES

Error is professionally inescapable for the defence planner. The fundamental reason why this has to be so is because war and its warfare is not a science. Future war, the focus of defence planning, cannot be studied and analysed sensibly for the purpose of eliciting reliably correct answers from the data. The problem is that there is not and never can be data to be analysed about the future from the future. This is simply a truth of physics. Of course, futures can be, and are, invented not discovered by social science, but they are never reliable; they are guesswork. Educated guesswork, perhaps, but they cannot find reference for the future except by extrapolation from the past and the present.

As a source of potential error in anticipation, the total absence of data from the future has argument arresting quality. One must also, though, cite the nature of the research challenge posed by war. Even if some near miracle of forecasting science, social science, and art could reveal basic facts about future strategic history, the nature of war and the character of its warfare must frustrate a search for understanding with reliably predictive quality. War is a creative venture that has the nature of a duel. Two or more belligerents, singly or in more or less binding combinations of co-belligerency with formal or informal allies, contend in an adversarial relationship. The course of war is always unpredictable, even if outcomes quite often either were, or, with the benefit of hindsight should have been, predictable. This fact is readily supportable from the strategic historical experience of all times, places, and participants. The relevance of this appreciation of the unique character of every conflict and war to the subject of defence planning could hardly be more obvious. If each war is a unique creation of contending wills and capabilities among belligerents, with a course of struggle literally unknowable in advance, and probably rather mysterious even in retrospect, how can defence planning possibly be conducted rationally? Is war a stochastic and chaotic realm?

It is necessary to accept the fact that there is a vital sense in which wars make themselves in their content, once the sponsoring policymakers and societies have pressed the button for a green light ordering 'go' on strategic action.[21] Peacetime military establishments and the politicians who control them, tend to have difficulty grasping ahead of the day of battle in the future just how alien to nearly all other experience is the context of war. This context is a zone of political experience characterized exceptionally by contingency, friction, and chaos. And yet, indeed especially because of the extremity of challenge, planning is essential. There is an important sense in which the course of war tends to unfold as 'one damn thing after another', but both sides in a violent strategic contest will strive purposefully, by necessity in competition, to exploit the circumstances apparently opened by contingency, even if unanticipated in advance. Defence planning has to provide prudently for a future strategic history that in important respects cannot be anticipated with confidence in plans.

The need for military adaptability to enable resilience in the face of unexpected demands from politicians, comes close to serving adequately as a description of a challenge perennially characteristic of civil-military relations on and across the strategy bridge, surprised by the strength of their unanticipated need for military muscle of particular kinds. Given that perfect knowledge of future policy demands upon defence planning is always unobtainable, plainly an approach to the subject is required which somehow can offset unhelpful laws of nature, while succeeding well enough in performance in aid of the vital mission. The challenge should be understood to require an approach to national security for national survival on tolerable terms, despite the certainty of past error and its legacy in ill consequences in defence planning. This argument may appear closer to philosophy and psychology than to defence analysis and management. Also, it involves recognition of persisting cultural realities that are apt to encourage friction in the civil-military relations key to the functioning of the strategy bridge as a working construct, despite its reification of an abstraction. Politicians and soldiers inhabit and are the product of very different milieus. The politician as policymaker wants freedom to choose, preferably from many options, useful ambiguities, and the ability, intentionally if not necessarily purposefully, to order swift action or to delay such. He is likely to favour some deliberate opacity in policy language lest he overreaches in commitment before circumstances make preferred choice easier to identify and to explain and justify to a possibly sceptical domestic public.

The soldier responsible for doing the policy-supporting military event also is vitally interested inter alia in the political, legal, and moral justification for the political decision, but those cannot be his prime concerns. Instead, his overriding duty is to do as well as he is able with the military instrument available, on behalf of his political and societal masters and sponsors, while speaking military truth to political power. But, inevitably in every conflict, there will be some mismatch between political 'ends' and available 'means'. Wizardry with cunning alternative strategic 'ways' may reduce the asymmetry usefully, but still it is a constant feature of strategic history that polities' military means are obliged to do the best they can in the conditions in which they find themselves placed. Even if *der Tag* has been chosen by home-team policymakers, the creative adversarial nature of war all but ensures that the military force posture planned will not prove ideal for the real test that is provided only by actual combat. This is not to deny that military 'ways' and 'means' have important, indeed sometimes critically important, roles to play in international political relations short of war. Relationships of mutual nuclear deterrence are just one recent example of possible strategic leverage secured in peacetime because of anticipation that the consequences of action would be unacceptable.[22]

It is a crucial challenge to defence planning and its political masters to recognize frankly, if not usually too openly, that no scale and quality of defence preparation ever approaches a perfect fit with the strategic needs of future policy. It has to follow that the fair yet realistic test of adequacy is whether or not it has been, or is likely to prove, good enough to cope with the always somewhat unpredictable demands that will be made upon it. A prime virtue for competent defence planning has to be adaptability to unexpected events and anxieties. However, as with all virtues, adaptability is subject to some necessary, indeed unavoidable, discipline. There are always limits to practicable military preparation for national defence. Even in time of war, when many constraints on the generation of military effort are suspended, choices are not unconstrained. Recognition of the high virtue in the value of the principle of adaptability in defence planning is entirely appropriate.[23] That said, its recognition does not foreclose on the need for debate and decision about priorities. Adaptability is a key concept, but it is naked of specific measuring and it carries the risk of misleading the unwary: indeed, uncritical acceptance of the idea carries risks. One such is the danger that undue confidence in adaptability to the defence needs of unpredicted future challenges may encourage a perilous slimness of assets suitable, adaptably, for employment. Adaptability can be genuine and economical of scarce resources but, as a claim, it can also provide a semi-plausible excuse for imprudent official parsimony.

Because future strategic history is not predictable, and can only be anticipated with uncertainty, it is essential that defence planning be geared to provide policymakers with the means for ways likely to support policy well enough. Adaptability is fundamentally important. Since strategic need in the future is unknowable in detail today, defence planning must be adaptable. That said, defence planning cannot be adaptable as a boundary-free value, because it comes at a cost and resources always are bounded. Given that error-free defence planning is never an option, anywhere at any time, the practical challenge is to provide advice on the tracing of the frontier for necessary adaptability. In common with many other austere sounding trinities, the tripartite architecture of strategy is as fundamental for understanding as it can deceive for reason of its apparent simplicity. Forbiddingly complex though defence planning certainly can be, the three categories basic to the theory and practice of strategy provide a key that should enable many of the dilemmas in the subject to be met tolerably well. Central to this claim is the recognition that no single category among the trio of ends, ways, and means, is permissive of the ignoring of constraints that apply in a particular place, at a particular time, and in particular circumstances. But the complex relations among ends, ways, and means, in principle provide rich opportunities for substantial inter- and intra-categorical adjustment through compensation.[24] For example, over-ambitious political goals need not foreclose on strategic advantage, because they should be capable of prudent reduction for lesser, but still worthwhile ends, given what experience in the field can teach about the feasibility of particular means employed in selected ways. If one accepts the prudence of a strategic approach to defence planning, it should be practicable to realign ends, ways, and means when the whole enterprise is under intolerable stress. For some greater nuance that can matter, it is significant that, in principle at least, a polity proceeding strategically should enjoy the luxury of 'mixing and matching' among the three foundational categories. If policy is revealed by events to be unsound, it may well be the case that some ratcheting down or up of the strategic ways and the quantity of military means committed will be able to restore a sufficiency of holistic fit, if not a Chinese ideal of harmony.[25]

Of course, all of this is usually far more difficult to achieve in practice than in theory. The American conduct of conflict in Vietnam after 1963, or, forty years later, the American dilemma in Iraq in 2006–7 were classic examples of strategic dysfunctionality.[26] Understanding of the logic and working of strategy can point to an approach to defence planning that is fundamentally sound. Of course human error, personal and institutional, is capable of resisting the logic for coherent strategy. I can only suggest ways to approach the challenge posed by the uncertainties of the defence planning mission and function. If political decision makers and their military advisor-executives insist upon making unsound choices and persisting with them, no strategic theory will assist national security. What follows is a short list of desiderata relating directly to the need to minimize either the likelihood of the commission of unsurvivable error in defence planning, or some of the ill consequences of errors that were not avoided, and may not even reasonably be judged in retrospect to have been avoidable.

1. Avoid literally irretrievable potential mistakes.

2. Identify national strategic missions that must be satisfied or at least seriously attempted.

3. Identify high risk defence investments for vital missions, and strive to locate and invest in Plans 'B' and 'C' as tolerably adequate, albeit inferior, substitutes if Plan 'A' fails.

4. Identify and favour capabilities that have genuine multi-functional promise, without undue sacrifice of particular effectiveness.

5. Identify and preferentially protect distinctive national military strengths, especially the ones that enjoy international recognition for excellence.

6. Encourage and even reward genuinely open unclassified debate on priorities and resources, with the discipline provided by the framework of the theory of strategy.

The purpose here is to help equip readers with an approach to the challenge of uncertainty in defence planning. Education in strategy can prepare people and should enable them to cope with what is unknowable about future problems in national defence (meaning any nation's defence).[27] The items of advice are so drafted as to be applicable to any polity, whether it is a country modest in ambition and not unduly worried about predatory Others, or whether it has reasons to be fearful for its national security. The advisory list does not assume or possibly even require high competence in national security decision-making and executive performance. Rather is it advice that rests empirically upon longstanding study of strategic history, and personal exposure to experience in and of argument about many issues of defence planning.

SCIENCE AND CERTAINTY: SEEK GOOD ENOUGH ANSWERS TO THE RIGHT QUESTIONS

Precision is an attractive quality but is attainable only in the category of military actions and some of their tactical effects. In contrast, politics and strategy are not zones of human endeavour that lend themselves to scientific examination, unless one so relaxes the definition of science as to render it readily achievable, but critically at the cost of being meaningless. This is inconvenient and it can be embarrassing, because many participants, including special-interest stakeholders, in national defence fail to appreciate a dilemma central to all debate about defence in the future. Although there are plausibly 'right enough' answers to defence questions, there are none that can be demonstrated analytically ahead of the time of test through trial under fire in the field, to be reliably correct. It follows necessarily that the project of defence planning needs to be understanding of the right questions in need of answer. It is important to approach defence planning comprehending that it cannot sensibly be regarded as a quest for correct answers, because there is no reliable way in which good enough questions about the future can be found. Instead, defence planning must seek good enough answers to questions or challenges, the details of which are always uncertain because they will emerge out of a dynamic adversarial process in years to come. The Holy Grail of defence planning has to be the key that opens the door to understanding what is likely to prove to be good enough.

If we could identify the questions that need to be answered, defence planning choices could be treated scientifically. We could seek demonstrably correct answers with such mathematical exactitude as this subject permits. However, because the need to dissuade, prevent, determine, or actually defend uncertain values at unknown dates in the future cannot be settled in the present, the role of defence analysis in planning has to be regarded as modest. Such analysis is useful, even essentially so, but nonetheless definitively subordinate to broader considerations that are obliged, *faut de mieux*, to rest most heavily on factors that are not permissive of scientific examination. Each of these factors will be more or less active as a source of some contextual influence upon the process that delivers a nation's defence planning.

Inevitably, analytical argument is produced in support or opposition to political and strategic preferences. With preferred assumptions providing a mock certainty that enables calculation, anything developed as a result of argument in the 'A' list of Box 6.2, can be analysed quantitatively. However, aside from the numeracy itself, such an exercise owes nothing to scientific method. Much debate about defence planning treats allegedly pertinent numbers simply as more or less useful ammunition for political supporters, not in any scientific sense as data that deserves translation as evidence.

Major Factors with Influence on Defence Planning

A. On choice of 'policy ends' and (some implementing operational and strategic) 'ways'
   Politics
   • Domestic
   • International
   Strategy (and geography)
   History
   Particular people and institutions
   Culture
   Circumstance, contingency
B. On (national) selection of military 'means'
   Defence analysis

The mathematics of honest defence analysis can yield important insight into the possible, if not probable, implications of the political and strategic preferences that a polity debates when influenced by the 'A' list of potent factors. Defence analysts can 'read the runes' on possible armed conflict by examining rigorously, indeed scientifically (if one can tolerate dependence upon discretionary, though not altogether arbitrary, assumptions) how friendly forces of particular kinds currently are believed likely to fare. Calculation of anticipated loss and kill rates, logistic sustainability, and the rest, is all fuel for the edification of those who need to try and support their educated political and strategic instincts with some approximation to reliable and replicable analysis.

'Hitchcraft', referred to the relatively new techniques of economic analysis introduced into the Pentagon by RAND economist Charles J. Hitch, when he was appointed Controller of the Department of Defense by President Kennedy in January 1961. His eponymous contribution to the McNamara revolution in Pentagon management techniques and style can hardly be exaggerated. For both good and ill, defence analysis came to stay in the Pentagon in the 1960s, and continues to this day. It is necessary to say that numerate analysis was copied and adopted abroad, if in some places in a manner that was mainly 'faint but pursuing'. It has to be said, though, that the new civilian American metric rigor in analysis behind defence decisions was found intimidating by those who could not compete methodologically. It was not recognized sufficiently at the time in the 1960s, that although defence planning requires numerate analysis, its most important issues are those of politics and strategy, in which regard mathematics is only of distinctly limited utility. The awesome reputation of McNamara's 'whizz kid' econometric defence analysts suffered substantial decline late in the 1960s and early in the 1970s, as the Vietnam war cast a deep shadow of presumed guilt over those apparently closely associated with its misdirection and mismanagement. Whatever the new style of defence analysis may or may not have contributed that was positive to the management of the strategic arms competition with the Soviet Union, plainly and unarguably it had contributed to the immense American failure in the war of the decade. Considered overall, problems with defence analysis arise only when it is mis-employed to provide evidence in support of political and strategic decisions that lie beyond its proper domain of methodologically rigorous competence.[28] Given that every special interest in a defence bureaucracy will be highly motivated to produce analytical outputs that privilege the assets of its own domain of responsibility, healthy competition may be the result. However, given the political nature of major defence planning decisions, one must offer as a caveat the thought that a system of competitive analysis itself provides no guarantee of honest concluding political and strategic decision. Politicians will be tempted to select the analyses that best support their existing preference. Of course, this can be politically dangerous. Decisions that future events appear to show to have been ill advised will be certain to motivate domestic opponents of the failed policy to seek out earlier analyses that later are found to have been prescient.

What defence analysis can and should do is calculate that which is calculable and worth knowing. And what sensibly are calculable are most aspects of military force posture, including its prospective performance in combat, always granting obvious weaknesses that cannot be diminished significantly. To be specific, models have to be simplifications of extreme complexity in the context of adversarial behaviour.[29] The critical list of necessary assumptions required if there is to be numerate analytical method, is awesome indeed. Defence planning is closer to a leap into the unknown and unknowable than it is to an orderly realm permissive of rational decision making reliant upon scientific method to generate correct answers in which one can repose high confidence. The production of genuinely methodologically impressive analyses of defence planning issues, such as those almost routinely generated at the RAND Corporation, could mislead one into the error of believing that correct answers can be found, provided only that good enough methodology is employed expertly and honestly. But, for good or ill, defence planning in its most important respects does not lend itself to ministration by the methods of science. The subject is deeply political, though the measure of political parentage of defence planning choices is not always as obvious as it needs to be.

POLITICS AND ECONOMICS: DEFENCE PLANNING IS MORE POLITICAL THAN ANYTHING ELSE

When I claim repeatedly that choices in defence planning are political, I am no more being disdainful than was Clausewitz when he observed that '[p]olitics is the womb in which war develops'.[30] He argues that 'war is not a mere act of policy but a true political instrument, a continuation of political activity by other means'.[31] Defence planning is governed by politics. Far from being a source of weakness, politics are necessary, desirable, and inevitable. What they are not is an alternative to expertise, scientific or other. There is no science of war capable of substituting for political debate and decision. As argued earlier in this chapter, it is a fundamental error to suggest, or at least imply for ironic effect as does O'Hanlon, that 'pure guesswork or politics' and the 'intuition of generals (or secretaries of defense)', might be the practical alternative to a 'science of war'.[32] In fact there is no science of war (or strategy), though there is a great deal of science in warfare.[33] Scientific defence analysis can answer many questions that lend themselves to mathematical treatment. Forage for horses, fuel for vehicles, food and drink for soldiers, duration of burst by eight Browning 0.303 inch (7.7 mm) machine guns needed to be dwelled by a

Spitfire to render a German medium bomber unflyable (2 secs), and the like.[34] But all the tactical behaviour that lends itself to mathematical modelling is chosen for analysis because it is anticipated to play some part in decisions about operations, strategy, and ultimately the high politics of the policy that licenses the violence. No science of warfare can decide issues of strategy and policy.

Experts ply their specialized analytical trades but defence planning and decisions for war or peace are always settled by some political process. This is not an aberration and weakness; instead it is a strength of human social organization. Our species governs itself by politics. Even the more techno-cratic seeming of polities find that political process is mandatory for govern-ance. Politics reflect the reality that nearly always there is some room for policy choice, which means there will be room for argument. The choice may well be one entailing selection of which risks to brave and which to attempt to moderate through appeasement, but there will be some scope for choice nonetheless. Whenever one looks in the basket of defence planning concerns, one finds prior decision and usually argument about national political, and therefore strategic, purpose. Every topic for expert defence analytical examin-ation is a zone for expression of judgement that requires political reasoning.

Of course, much political discourse is misinformed by poor technical understanding of defence planning issues, just as international strife follows a course that owes little to calculably allegedly correct ways to threaten or employ armed force. Having more rather than fewer nuclear-tipped missiles believed to be survivable to a first strike should be a plan helpful for deter-rence, but it cannot serve as a guarantee. War, decisions for it and in it, cannot be regarded as reliably rational happenings, because they will show lethal quantities of apparently unreasonable thought and behaviour. The content of rational thought and behaviour is not universal: it is the work of reason which is influenced by biology, culture, and the accidents of contingency.[35]

It is necessary to consider politics both as the governing process for all our thought and behaviour, and also as somewhat distinctive domestic processes. Politics is about power, meaning legitimate or other authority, and it is 'ends', 'ways', and 'means'. Just as there is no final act (in the near future, we hope!) to human strategic history, so there is and can be no fully satisfactory lasting condition of national security. Regardless of how deep a contemporary con-dition of peace is believed to be, the continuum of the great stream of time is known to be capable of producing reasons for anxiety that had previously been thoroughly unanticipated. When foreign developments do not appear to be likely to manifest themselves in ways that would menace the national security alarmingly and guesswork is often perceived reassuringly as trends, the scope for domestic defence planning debate widens markedly. Whereas national defence rightfully can be considered as meriting first-priority draw on the national wealth when the polity is believed to be in peril, such a condition of alarm does not persist. Domestic politics governing resource allocation for defence planning rapidly desanctifies debate over preparation to meet threats that few now believe existential or near-term probable. Public debate about the alleged affordability of defence preparation is apt to be exceptionally misleading. The concept of affordability sounds as if it is a commonsensical economic idea that speaks to a discipline that plainly should be mandatory on public officials. However, the reality is different. Instead of being largely an economic concept, expressive of an easily understandable idea, it is in actuality largely a political concept. Economic and financial logic lurk close-by, but in the main, affordability is a matter of society-wide political choice.

There are usually excellent reasons why economic affordability is a serious constraint or, less pejoratively, an important discipline on the funding of defence planning concerns. The core of this matter is the real or anticipated relationship between political tolerance of economic pain and the perception of danger expressed in anxiety and fear. When people are frightened, let alone alarmed, they will accept, or at least temporarily tolerate, fresh economic hardship. The process described here is psychological and political, it is not at heart economic. There will be real economic limitations on the ability of any and every national security community to spend wealth—however acquired, by savings, borrowing, capture from enemies, or as 'gifts' from abroad—on the defence function. But, a condition of 'total war', or even total societal defence preparation short of war, mercifully is rare in strategic history. It is universally true that societies recognize the importance of national security, indeed how could they not? But, a mandatory bow to the demands of national security almost invariably is followed swiftly by practices in budgetary allocation that plainly do not reflect public alarm. All polities at all times have many calls made upon public finance that have little, or at most only tangential, relevance to issues typical of focus in defence planning. In other words, notwithstanding probable formal political acceptance of the authority of defence demands on the public purse, when peril is believed to be slight and distant defence will be regarded in effect as just another expensive draw on limited national re-sources. Much of the presumption of important discipline encouraged by reference to alleged affordability is, in fact, largely a matter of political choice. Defence officials have little leeway for orderly economies in defence if high spending departments of government with social welfare and educational responsibilities enjoy competitive protection for their budgetary plans.

It can be difficult to convey with sufficient clarity the degree of freedom that truly lurks in government budget-making. If most of a state's tax revenue is regarded as untouchable because of the possible or even probable domestic (political) harm that might ensue, then defence planning must be impacted as a direct consequence. In a period believed to be one of deep and enduring peace, it is easily understandable why defence expenditures come more and more, de facto, to be regarded as just another competitor for scarce resources.

When societies and their politicians decide in effect increasingly to de-singu-larize defence, they are making a political choice that is rational, but not necessarily reasonable. Public political attitudes and mood, in democracies at least, determine the general level of defence effort that is tolerable and therefore is tolerated politically. Expert calculation feeds defence debate, but alternative purposes and relative weights of effort are matters settled by political process with help and harassment from cultural sources, not by conclusions reached by defence analysis.

STRATEGY AND HISTORY: CHANGE IN CONTINUITY

Understandably, it is tempting to be over impressed by physics and worried unduly by the danger of anachronism, when considering the value of the vicarious experience that may be derived from the educational exposure to strategic history. It is an inconvenient and academically uncomfortable fact that history is the only variably accessible source of relevant data available to defence planners, typically contentious though competing historians tend to be. The process of defence planning is inalienably political, while its strong dependence upon detailed analysis encourages a search for calculable demon-strability of correctness, given the more or less mandatory political and strategic parameters of the time, place, and circumstance. But neither political process nor scientific (and social scientific) method themselves are replete with knowledge and understanding of strategic behaviour. That behaviour is the adversarial product of particular people in unique places, with arguable differences in thought and deed that lend themselves to some helpful measure of cultural identification. There is much to be said in praise of historical education, notwithstanding the often unrecognized risks of ethnocentrism in theory and understanding.[36] The historical narratives preferred in most soci-eties are those that privilege the home team at some cost in empathy lost for Others in the asserted national story. It is not hard to find reasons for scepticism about the merit in the average quality of historical education. That granted, the awkward fact remains that defence planning quite literally has nowhere to go except to the past, for understanding of contemporary and prospective future national challenges.

The fact that strategic history is not and can never be a source of evidence to be mined in search of reliable guidance for the future, is simply beside the parametric point that history is all we have. By way of a somewhat strained analogy, readers are invited to think of the strategic historical experience of their nation much as they would of a highly unreliable relative or close if troublesome foreign ally. Neither is entirely to be trusted, but they share a unique value in quality of potential support. First-hand experience and understanding is necessarily a very limited, if undoubtedly potent, source of evidence. People retire, die, and their personal comprehension of what should be done and why, dies with them. Institutional memory endures a little longer, but even that tends soon to move into a half-life condition, as it ages rather than matures. It has to follow from the argument just outlined that more respect than one is fully satisfied in according needs to be conceded to strategic historical narratives. I do not assume that history, unlike historians, repeats itself: at least it is not reliably anticipatable that it will do so. But, history, the narratives told by historians, and also the stories regaled, by and large to but not only to, the young, have substantial value for the stamping and reinforcement of national (or tribal) cultural identity. For good and ill, ethnocentrism is encouraged, if not implicitly mandated, in classrooms world-wide.

There is no magic key that assuredly unlocks useful understanding of historical experience for defence planning. There is no formula, let alone equation enabling calculability, capable of revealing reliably what experience demonstrates to be virtuously prudent and what is not. This bad news concerning the impracticability of approaching defence planning as a science, must however be accepted regretfully and not permitted unduly to discourage. Above all else, it should not provide the fuel of enthusiasm born of desperation, let alone feed enthusiasm for methodological patent medicines that offer what amounts to snake oil as an alleged cure for uncertainty; allegedly the answer to uncertainty and the risks that may live there. Aside from the unalterable absence of alternatives, it is important not to forget the major reasons why strategic history contains stories of defence planning prowess and folly that resonate through millennia. The defence planning function:

- Has been a permanent feature in history, regardless of time, politics, place and culture.
- Always could be analysed within the conceptual framework of the general theory of strategy: whether or not contemporaries articulated explicitly any version of that theory. The logically interdependent ideas of ends, ways, and means, can be employed to make strategic sense of historical practice, without anachronism that would be harmful to understanding.[37]
- All human communities have thought and behaved politically; politics are not cultural, they are socially human; indeed they may simply be ubiquitous in animal behaviour.
- Human thought and behaviour has changed greatly in historical times, but not (yet) in ways that imperil the importance of the strategic narrative in our general history.

Given that the future is unknown in detail, and that the present is a source of experience as yet undigested for understanding, history is the sole repository of precious metal for use in defence planning. Because strategic history is the only resource available to defence planning as a repository of relevant experience, the abuse of analogy is all too common an anachronistic blight in public defence debate. Much earlier, I explained the unsoundness of historical analogy as an alleged source of relevant understanding about the future. Since the future has yet to happen and therefore has to be unknown, there is no way in which past events can be deployed as analogical evidence. Because we cannot know potentially vital detail about possible future happenings, it has to follow that we cannot identify reliably particular strategic historical experience, no matter how well we believe we comprehend it.

There is, however, an approach that can be taken to strategic history that should yield a quality of understanding critically useful for prudent defence planning. Specifically, strategic historical education needs to be delivered and received not in a 'presentist' spirit of 'lessons for today and tomorrow', but rather in the 'depth, breadth, and context', identified as appropriate desiderata by Michael Howard.[38] The strategic challenges faced by Pericles, Marlborough, Abraham Lincoln, Winston S. Churchill, and David Petraeus differed radically in most detail, but when regarded as challenges to strategic thought and behaviour, many of the historical distinctions fade in relative significance as constraints on utility for education. Purposefully strategic behaviour effectively has been a constant theme in the history of the human race. The defence planner of today cannot look to the past for reliable guidance as to how to think and act in regard to the challenges of tomorrow. But, education in strategic history yields familiarity with generically similar problems, and evidence on the fate of the answers provided by those who then confronted the challenge of uncertainty.

Necessity and Discretion

Defence planning conducted with little or no reference to politics must lack both purpose and legitimacy, while when conducted with no substantial regard for strategy it can make no sense. Politics are necessary for defence planning but they cannot be sufficient. By definition, politics are devoid of substantial content about issue areas. When one insists, as here, that defence planning is thoroughly political, it needs to be understood that politics per se is an empty vessel: it is the method by means of which societies organize and operate their governance. But, regarded strictly as a method, politics itself makes no contribution to the understanding of how one should plan national defence preparation. Of course, politics at one level is always 'about' issues of, or at least alleged to be of, substance. The currency of debate and negotiated exchange may well genuinely be contending propositions concerning defence preparation. However, because of biology, sociology, and circumstance, the mechanism and process of debate has its flavour of specific subject content added. Should America's professional politicians choose to argue about such currently fashionable big strategic concepts as 'AirSea Battle' or a 'Pivot to Asia', these ideas certainly have content in strategic implications, but debate about their prudence is only political with respect to method. This is not intended to demean politics. Politics, like strategy, is what it is. Political experts are those deemed knowledgeable about the process of governance. By analogy, to be respected for one's understanding of strategy need carry no necessary imputation of political wisdom about the policy 'ends' that one prefers.

One can offer education in strategy, without intending to forward any particular agenda of strategic desiderata. This book is written on the basis of the belief that strategy and defence planning can be studied, taught, and understood as a challenge to prudent governance for any polity. Most people do not consider defence planning as a challenge generic to human political communities. Instead, naturally and appropriately, they apply general theory to the specific concerns of their day, place, and culture. The matters discussed here were chosen for their inherent relative high importance, and also because they all lend themselves to local application for any polity. None of the subjects here are relevant only to British and American defence planning. This work seeks to aid the understanding of defence planning that strictly is necessary, regardless of the discretion effected and pursued locally by the favoured methods of politics.

NOTES

1. In his possibly important supplement to Clausewitz, Emile Simpson advises: 'Once actions in war (both violent and non-violent) are seen as a form of language used to communicate meaning in the context of an argument, there is a possibility of being misunderstood. In order to use war successfully as an instrument of policy, one's actions in war ultimately need to be interpreted in accordance with the intent of one's policy. Thus strategy in relation to war seeks to link the meaning of tactical actions with the intent of policy to deliver the desired policy end-state. To do this, strategy seeks to invest actions in war with their desired meaning. Hence strategy has to harmonise both of the "instruments" that are contained in the idea of war as an extension of policy by other means. Strategy does not merely need to orchestrate tactical actions (the use of force), but also construct the interpretive structure which gives them meaning and links them to the end of policy'. *War from the Ground Up: Twenty-First-Century Combat as Politics* (London: C. Hurst, 2012), 28. Simpson argues that 'Afghanistan is one example of the consequence of confusing Clause-witzian war with armed politics outside war', 66. Others may disagree, but I find Clausewitz's understanding of politics and of war to be sufficiently inclusive for the accommodation of 'armed politics' as war. Obviously, choice of authoritative

assumptions is key to decision as to what is and what is not, 'war'. As a mildly subversive thought, one might with profit ask the strategist's question, as usual, 'so what?'

2. Williamson Murray, *War, Strategy, and Military Effectiveness* (Cambridge: Cambridge University Press, 2011), 33.

3. Michael O'Hanlon, *The Science of War: Defense Budgeting, Military Technology, Logistics, and Combat Outcomes* (Princeton, NJ: Princeton University Press, 2009), 1.

4. Carl von Clausewitz, *On War*, trans. Michael Howard and Peter Paret (1832–4; Princeton, NJ: Princeton University Press, 1976), 102.

5. For many years I had some personal familiarity with calculations of ICBM survivability. I discuss this subject in *Modern Strategy* (Oxford: Oxford University Press, 1999), chs. 11–12. Also see Lawrence Freedman, *The Evolution of Nuclear Strategy*, 3rd edn. (Basingstoke: Palgrave Macmillan, 2003), 369–75; and Glenn A. Kent, *Thinking About America's Defense: An Analytical Memoir* (Santa Monica, CA: RAND, 2008), chs. 2, 4, 6.

6. Ken Booth, *Strategy and Ethnocentrism* (London: Croom Helm, 1979), 9.

7. Booth, 1979.

8. Clausewitz, *On War*, 104.

9. 'Rationality has its place, but Strategic Man does not, except in the context of a particular nation, and then only with the utmost caution'. Booth, *Strategy and Ethnocentrism*, 140.

10. Clausewitz, *On War*, ch. 1. Today in the 2010s it is easy to forget how substantial has been the change in dominant strategic ideas. For example, Bernard Brodie, who was in a position to know, wrote as follows about the concept and practice of limited war in regard to Korea 1950: 'The United States *backed* into a limited war in Korea, because the kind of doctrine about limited war that is so completely familiar today not only did not then exist but would have been utterly incomprehensible. Public discussion of and ruminations upon limited war did not begin until about 1954'. *War and Politics* (New York: Macmillan, 1973), 63 (emphasis in the original). William W. Kaufman, 'Limited Warfare', in Kaufman, ed., *Military Policy and National Security* (Princeton, NJ: Princeton University Press, 1956), 102–36; and Robert Endicott Osgood, *Limited War: The Challenge to American Strategy* (Chicago: The University of Chicago Press, 1957), were landmark publications for modern strategic studies. However, the idea of the limitation of war is anything but modern. The practice of waging limited war for limited political objectives appears to be lost in the ancient mists of strategic history. To the best of this theorist's knowledge, there are not, and possibly cannot now be, any new strategic ideas. This rather depressing point has some relevance to arguments about the utility or inutility in seeking evidence of experience from times past, for their possible relevance to today and tomorrow. Obviously, the perils of anachronism and seriously unsafe analogy must loom large. See my examination of this contentious topic in *The Strategy Bridge: Theory for Practice* (Oxford: Oxford University Press, 2010), 267–77, Appendix C: 'Conceptual '"Hueys" at Thermopylae? The Challenge of Strategic Anachronism'.

11. Readers unimpressed by my scepticism may find solace in: E. S. Quade and W. I. Boucher, eds., *Systems Analysis and Policy Planning* (New York: American Elsevier, 1968); Stephen Biddle, *Military Power: Explaining Victory and Defeat in Modern Battle* (Princeton, NJ: Princeton University Press, 2004); and O'Hanlon, *The Science of War*, ch. 2.

12. Clausewitz, *On War*, 85, 101.

13. Clausewitz, *On War*, 77.

14. The key uncertainty, as Clausewitz and indeed all strategic historical experience tells us, is the human factor. We can calculate well enough when soldiers will expend all of their ammunition, but how they may choose to fight in a condition of kinetic austerity, is going to be guesswork. For a similar thread of thought, we may seek to educate ourselves about the prudent requirements of our nuclear forces, on the basis of apparently projecting rational cost-benefit analyses onto an adversary, but we ought never to believe that deterrent needs are calculable. Highly numerate defence analysts are prone to capture by their own mathematical prowess, believing it to be capable of answering questions that should never be posed to it.

15. For more than somewhat contrasting examinations of the arguable scope of detectable cultural variation in strategic behaviour, see the following excellent studies: on the one hand, Booth, *Strategy and Ethnocentrism*, esp. 64; and on the other, Patrick Porter, *Military Orientalism: Eastern War Through Western Eyes* (London: C. Hurst, 2009), and John France, *Perilous Glory: The Rise of Western Military Power* (New Haven, CT: Yale University Press, 2011).

16. See Clausewitz, *On War*, 81, 585.

17. For an intelligently somewhat ambivalent analysis written at one of modern history's more 'pivotal' of strategic moments, see Robert Jervis, 'The Future of World Politics: Will It Resemble the Past? *International Security*, 16 (winter 1991–2), 39–73.

18. See Colin S. Gray, *Weapons Don't Make War: Policy, Strategy, and Military Technology* (Lawrence, KS: University Press of Kansas, 1993), esp. 95–9, on 'Super Threats'.

19. For a good contemporary example in supportive illustration of my argument, see Keith B. Payne (Study Director), *Minimum Deterrence: Examining the Evidence* (Fairfax, VA: National Institute Press, 2013). I cite this study not because I was associated with it, but rather because it offers argument against the policy and strategy option of minimum deterrence that includes my concern not to be imprudent. The study does not purport to know just how much residual strategic nuclear force will be sufficient in order to deter in the future. But, it makes unmistakeably plain the fact that the advocates of large-scale nuclear reduction have no plausible idea just how little might prove sufficient to provide the strategic effect required for deterrence in the future. If risk management is a high priority desideratum for defence planning, unverifiable claims for the strategic benefit of a substantial scale of nuclear disarmament merit sceptical examination.

20. See Colin S. Gray, 'Dowding and the British Strategy of Air Defence, 1936–40', in Williamson Murray and Richard Hart Sinnreich, eds., *Successful Strategies: Triumphing in War and Peace from Antiquity to the Present* (Cambridge: Cambridge University Press, forthcoming).

21. *War from the Ground Up*, Emile Simpson takes necessary account of the ability of war, even his alternative characterization of 'armed politics outside war' (66), to make and serve itself, rather than 'policy' (126–9). As a caveat, one should consider the possibility that foci on dialogues, audiences, and violence as a language in competing narratives might privilege unduly the importance of local narratives of political meaning, at the potentially serious cost of discounting the somewhat autonomous dynamics of particular armed conflicts. Arguments against reification (i.e. 'the war...'), though valid, may encourage imprudent underappreciation of the danger of war, or war-like politics, itself becoming a significant actor in strategic history. The abstraction, war, created by and as competitive acts of violence, may construct and reconstruct itself on the opportunistic logic of dynamic contingent military events. For all his intellectually rather belated vital appreciation of the political nature of war's meaning, Clausewitz remained in no doubt that when human beings choose to fight, or, I suspect, conduct armed politics, they are riding a tiger that can escape political control. Simpson rightly draws attention to the political theatre of politics with guns for distinctive audiences who hold to distinctive narratives of strategic meaning. However, one ought not to lose sight of the Prussian's instance that war is the realm of chance.

22. See Keith B. Payne, ed., *Understanding Deterrence* (Abingdon: Routledge, 2013), on a subject that ages, but does not fade into insignificance over time.

23. The outstanding study is Williamson Murray, *Military Adaptation in War: With Fear of Change* (Cambridge: Cambridge University Press, 2011).

24. Gray, *Strategy Bridge*, 155.

25. Simpson, *War from the Ground Up*, offers useful analysis of this critically important issue. Mechanistic adjustments among ends, ways, and means, ones not usually feasible in practice, substantially because the entire political project of a war may not be expediently reducible so as to match much better what proves to be military achievable through forceful action.

26. See Andrew F. Krepinevich, Jr, *The Army and Vietnam* (Baltimore: Johns Hopkins University Press, 1986); C. Dale Walton, *The Myth of Inevitable U.S. Defeat in Vietnam* (London: Frank Cass, 2002).

27. See my *Schools for Strategy: Teaching Strategy for 21st Century* (Carlisle, PA: Strategic Studies Institute, US Army War College, 2009).

28. Amidst a large literature, see the following for some grasp of the American defence analytical effort made over the past half century: Charles J. Hitch, *Decision-Making for Defense* (Berkeley, CA: University of California Press, 1965); Charles J. Hitch and Roland N. McKean, *The Economics of Defense in the Nuclear Age* (New York: Atheneum, 1966); E. S. Quade, ed., *Analysis for Military Decisions* (Chicago: RAND McNally, 1964); Roland N. McKean, ed., *Issues in Defense Economics* (New York: National Bureau of Economic Research, 1967); Quade and Boucher, eds., *Systems Analysis and Policy Planning*; Alain C. Enthoven and F. Wayne Smith, *How Much is Enough? Shaping the Defense Program, 1961–1969* (1971; Santa Monica, CA: RAND, 2005); Paul K. Davis, ed., *New Challenges for Defense Planning: Rethinking How Much Is Enough* (Santa Monica, CA: RAND, 1994); Paul K. Davis, *Analytic Architecture of Capabilities-Based Planning,*

Mission-Systems Analysis, and Transformations (Santa Monica, CA: RAND, 2002); and *Lessons from RAND's Work on Planning Under Uncertainty for National Security*, technical report (Santa Monica, CA: RAND, 2012).

29. See O'Hanlon, ch. 2.
30. Clausewitz, *On War*, 149.
31. Clausewitz, *On War*, 87.
32. O'Hanlon, *The Science of War*, 1.
33. Notwithstanding its title and argument in praise of economics as a science, there is little in Bernard Brodie's brilliant 1949 argument in 'Strategy as a science', in Thomas G. Mahnken and Joseph A Maiolo, eds., *Strategic Studies: A Reader* (Abingdon: Routledge, 2008), 8–21, with which I disagree. Brodie's argument, as it were from the 'Stone Age' of defence analysis in the late 1940s, needs to be read in the light of the argument in his last major work, *War and Politics*, esp. ch. 10. Barry Scott Zellen, *State of Doom: Beyond Brodie, the Bomb, and the Birth of the Bipolar World* (New York: Continuum, 2012), is essential. The finest appreciation of Bernard Brodie I have read is Ken Booth, 'Bernard Brodie,' in John Baylis and John Garnett, eds., *Makers of Nuclear Strategy* (New York: St. Martin's Press, 1991), 19–56. Booth is empathetic, yet insightfully critical where necessary. I should acknowledge the fact that I discussed issues pertaining to methodology in Strategic Studies with Bernard Brodie in 1974.
34. Stephen Bungay explains well how the Spitfire needed to be designed as a flying gun platform, *The Most Dangerous Enemy: A History of the Battle of Britain* (London: Aurum Press, 2001), ch. 5.
35. Booth, *Strategy and Ethnocentrism*, is a potent source of insight on the fallacies that can attend and follow misguided ethnocentric notions of what is or should be rational.
36. Booth, *Strategy and Ethnocentrism*. Booth is a generally successful pioneering effort to look beyond argument about culture in order to direct attention to the self-inflicted harm in the widespread cultural malady of ethnocentrism. Also, there is much merit in Robert B. Bathurst, *Intelligence and the Mirror: On Creating an Enemy* (London: SAGE Publications, 1993).
37. Such, at least, is my belief, as I argued in some detail in *The Strategy Bridge*, 267–77.
38. Michael Howard, *The Causes of Wars* (London: Counterpoint, 1983), 215–17.

7

Between Prudence and Paranoia

THE PUBLIC MOOD

Raymond Aron was right to argue that prudence is the quality that deserves to be most admired in statecraft.[1] But a problem appears when one seeks to implement the wise Frenchman's undoubtedly good advice. What does it mean to be prudent in defence planning? Prudence is the standard that requires us to be careful of the consequences of our actions or inaction. The practical challenge does not lie in selecting the superior value by which to judge official defence planning endeavours, it is rather in understanding the relative prudential merit in the schemes proposed. As Ken Booth claims wryly: 'One man's prudence is another man's overkill',[2] and no quantity or quality of expert study can establish in advance and beyond doubt which of the two is the more correct. Because of the many continuities in history, the true quality of the challenge that needs to be overcome in meeting well enough the uncertainty of the future, typically either is ignored or at least is understated and in effect is evaded. Because of history's continuities, a default setting of 'more of the same, with only modest changes', generally serves well enough for an orderly performance in defence planning; at least it will appear to do so for a while. It is not that defence planners necessarily, indeed if at all, are blind to the possibility of extraordinary events apparently of a menacing kind, but rather that the politics of alarm cannot reliably be manufactured at official will, even when there is a prudent case to be made for unusual concern.

It would be difficult to exaggerate the importance for the defence planning function of the unavailability of evidence about the future from the future, and the pervasively political nature of the subject. These two elemental truisms tend to elude secure capture by comprehension, even by many people who should know better. When duly accepted, however reluctantly and regretfully, it begins to be possible to address the challenge of defence planning intelligently. Once one has accepted the permanent reality of a complete absence of direct data that might serve as reliable evidence about the future, one can focus as productively as may be on the only data that might do duty regarding the future—specifically, the past and the present. As for the political nature of the subject, this poses only a limited challenge once one acknowledges two foundational facts. First, politics is a collective noun referring to competition about relative power, it is innocent of particular policy content until such is added as fuel for the process. Second, political controversy about issues of defence planning must entail argument employing putative evidence as a tool in debate. Professional politicians and their variably attentive domestic publics cannot usually be relied upon to be swayed in their preferences by the apparent relative technical worth of the judgements of rival experts. However, the court of public opinion is apt to be swayed by claims and arguments that connect easily to longstanding traditional, indeed one can even say strategic cultural, attitudes and beliefs particular to individual societies. Strategic culture is not a concept that should be trusted to lend itself to exploitation in a search for a predictive quality of wisdom, but it is a large idea pointing to a source that politicians can aspire to mobilize for political support. When cultural icons are enlisted to serve as recruiting agents for strategic options, they can help mightily in creating and sustaining the public political mood that legitimizes and enables important ventures, even adventures, in defence planning.[3]

Public mood need not be rational and frequently it will seem unreasonable, but it is the depth of political conviction on which policy and its strategy must float. The concept of public mood is abstract, but in a democracy at least it can be plumbed as to its depth in a particular matter by standard methods of opinion and attitude polling. Politicians must listen to their electorate and support in governance what the mood of the day appears willing to tolerate. Defence planning must be shaped by expert analytical examination of alternatives, but a society chooses the general level of its current commitment to future defence preparation on the basis of what most usefully can be identified as its political mood. The electorate responds to what it senses is the condition of its national security, at least at the level of believing that the defence budget should be larger, smaller, or is probably at about the right level; in other words, in the last case just cited, it is deemed right enough.[4]

CONCEPTS OF PERIL

Four emotive concepts of menace in particular are commonly favoured in analysis and debate over defence planning; they warrant careful appreciation. Their individual inclusivity needs recognition, as does their subjectivity. The concepts of concern here are the abominable quartet composed of risk, threat, danger, and shock. These should not be understood as comprising categories with clear boundaries demarcating completely distinctive domains.

The abominable quartet make frequent appearances, both explicitly and implicitly, in the public documents that governments issue either episodically or routinely on national security policy and strategy.[5] The problematic nature of these concepts relates not so much to their distinctive meanings, but rather to their claims about strategic content. These four horsemen of the defence planners' Apocalypse all inhabit that foreign country, the future. Because ironically, that ethereal land has a climate of uncertainty always about it, reliable knowledge of its character must ever be problematic. Given that it is the professional duty of defence planners to prepare the nation to be able to protect itself in that uncertain future, it is no great surprise to learn that a contemporary shortage of plausible threat is not usually much of an intellectual or political hindrance to defence planning. My point is not to be critical of defence planners for anticipating threats that other citizens find less than convincingly worrying. Rather is it necessary to argue that there is always some risk and associated danger involved in international political relations; that simply is Man's Estate. Politics and the possibility of armed conflict in some variant of what reductively we oversimplify in the concept of war, cannot be eradicated. At least there is no convincing evidence that should incline us to believe that war is a behaviour of politics at all likely to disappear in the future. An important part of this argument pertains to the identification of threat, especially when the relevant theory is allowed historically specific humanized forms, notwithstanding standard oversimplification (for example, France, the French). Ken Booth hits the target and some of its associated structures, when he declaims and explains as follows:

> Strategy, like nature, abhors a vacuum: the field of strategy, be it a map, actual terrain, a sheet of paper or a mind (or set of minds), must be filled with enemies. Without enemies strategy is shapeless; it is like a house without walls. Strategy is in part a simplifying activity because strategists needs [sic] enemies. Strategists are most comfortable when relationships are polarising or polarised. Sometimes the enemies will be explicit; sometimes they will be implicit. Sometimes the assumptions of an enemy relationship will be justified; sometimes it will be misperceived. Sometimes the enemies will be real; sometimes they will be imagined. But enemies there must be: theory requires it while it gives purpose to day-to-day practice Both the theory and practice of strategy are simplified if an 'enemy' is assumed, rather than any of the more complicated relationships which exist between the poles of amity and enmity.[6]

Not only do defence planners, in common with the rest of us, inhabit a world amply stocked with potential risks that may well be dangerous to our national security, but also they are tasked specifically to seek to anticipate those risks and their dangers. It is necessary to understand that future risks, threats, and dangers—but possibly not shocks—will emerge in some interactive context. In other words, defence planning, with other instruments of grand strategy, ought not to be regarded strictly as a passive factor in security affairs. This is not to claim that collectively as a polity we will make our own security future. Strategic history is too rich in its continuities to yield the future to national constructivism unimpeded by the wishes, willpower, and capabilities of others, not to mention semi-organized chaos fuelled unpredictably by accident and friction. The future of strategic history is ours to influence, but assuredly not to control. This modest argument should alert us to the danger in erroneously objectifying the strategic future as a future context to which we can only adapt as best we will be able.

The awesomely troublesome conceptual quartet that is the focus here has no little value in irony. The hunt for, and near certain success in finding, risks, threats, and dangers, in a nation's future strategic context, may well fuel anxiety, but when generically regarded that reaction is by no means regrettable. After all, we know for certain that the twenty–first century will appear to offer many opportunities for state, or at least state-sponsored and licensed, behaviour that must be accounted variably risky. What we do not and cannot know is exactly which official or officially tolerated behaviours will fuel and trigger which particular risks. It follows that risks and dangers are going to prove inalienable features in the strategic future. For all countries there is no strategic future entirely free of risk and danger. This should mean that strategists doing defence planning ought not sensibly to be accusable of being more part of the problem than the solution. Unfortunately, this is not quite true. While there will be risks and dangers in a polity's strategic future, their frequency of occurrence and intensity are all too capable of being enhanced most unhealthily by the political consequences of imprudent threat identification and unwise defence preparation. In extreme form, such security mismanagement has become known as the 'security dilemma'.[7] In worst constructivist fashion, a polity may succeed in creating the enemies it anticipated and came to fear.

Some anxiety about the logic of the potential for the security dilemma is entirely appropriate to international relations, but it cannot be regarded as a legitimate show-stopper for defence planning. To cite the danger of the dilemma is indeed pertinent, but its peril is simply a price paid for performance in attempting to manage uncertainty in the essential, or at least partial, anarchy that is the context of future history. The conduct of international politics accompanied hopefully by prudent defence planning and strategy is really a mandatory duty in statecraft. The politics of national and international security do not offer risk-free, reliably safe, options that defence planners either can assume may be attainable, let alone could locate expediently yet expeditiously. In the words quoted above, Ken Booth identified what reasonably can be identified confidently as a core challenge for defence planning in many polities at most times. Polities nearly always find themselves placed by the consequences of strategic history somewhere between the 'poles of amity and enmity' in their security relations with other polities. Either condition, if dominant, is relatively unchallenging for the strategist as defence planner. Of course, confident belief in either may be unwarranted, but that is another matter. The two 'poles' are permissive: the condition of amity expressed largely in symbolic defence preparation, while that of enmity lends itself to expression in serious military measures. In the extreme case of a condition believed to be one of 'deep peace', it should not much matter what or how much military capability a society chooses to purchase, because it anticipates no strategic menace. The other 'pole', of enmity, greatly simplifies political choice meaning that believed needs for strategic success in war in the near-term future must dominate defence planning. If the strategic context is one of such extreme enmity that national survival is believed to be at stake, then prioritization for national defence becomes politically practicable because it is, and it appears plausibly to be, entirely legitimate. However, this is not to deny that overriding prioritization in favour of the demands on national resources for defence, bears no inherent guarantee of strategic prudence. One may be correct in identifying an objectively super-threat to national survival, and therefore in treating the contemporary struggle as a war of grimmest necessity, but national discretion may fail in examination demands by necessity in the field.

The experience of strategic history, however, has not usually been one marked by extreme conditions. It is common practice for governments to wobble on the spectrum of anxiety somewhere towards the centre insofar as it can be measured by resource allocation for defence. The national default setting for security concern in the main is uncertainty. The risks, threats, dangers, and shocks that may well appear in the decades immediately ahead, are not knowable with confidence in advance. We can and we should identify possible happenings that would have substantial first- and probably second-order negative consequences for our security, but the perils truly are incalculable. One can construct data, as with Delphi-type methods for collecting the best expert guesses about the future from notable sages, but the key quality in this case has to be its unscientific nature: it cannot offer reliable information attained through rigorous and repeatable testing.[8]

Frequent deployment of the commonplace concepts of risk, threat, danger, and shock (much less frequently) can have a numbing effect on our awareness of the need for judicious scepticism. I suspect that the repeated use of such popular terms as risk, threat, danger, and even shock, encourages in large effect a contempt based on under recognized ignorance. This is not to criticize politicians and officials for not knowing what they cannot possibly know about the future, but it is to suggest that these familiar terms of graded alarm are really only generic knowns, floating on a sea of largely unavoidable ignorance. Prudent defence planning need not, indeed cannot, eschew common terms that sound reassuringly knowable through their familiarity, but cannot possibly be reduced for manageably analytical examination ahead of their occurrence. Frank recognition of the limits of the knowable and mathematically analysable clears the methodological ground for careful analysis that does have a reasonably concrete objective base, even if only arguably so.

First, the concept of risk simply registers anticipation of uncertainty about the possible and probable consequences of action or inaction. Given that everything about the future is to some degree necessarily uncertain, assessment of future risk cannot help but be a leap in the dark, no matter how solemnly one seeks to dignify it as a process of risk assessment.

Second, threat is a concept that typically carries the baggage of an assumption of menace intended by the agent or agency causing concern. Threat can be implicit as well as explicit, and has subjective and objective potency. Since threat has to be perceived as a compounded product of capability and intention, it is easy to see why threat misperception, at the very least uncertainty, is all but ubiquitous and eternal in strategic history. The scope for discretionary interaction in the future by the generator and the recipient of threat means that the subject cannot usefully be examined scientifically. A threat may be discerned in material circumstances (for example, the PLAN as a hazard to possible US operations in support of Taiwan), but military capabilities always required interpretation as to their probable strategic meaning for political ends.[9]

Danger is the third concept of particular interest here; it is so familiar a concept that it all but invites loose usage. Because of the complexity of political affairs, danger can lurk just about anywhere in situations of risk. The concept carries the meaning of adversity of possible or probable consequences. Danger is a quality expected to inhere in some possible happenings, whether or not subsequent experience attests to the sense in the preceding anxiety. Perception and anticipation of danger is as important for defence planning as it is usually more than marginally problematic and therefore arguable. Danger, the risk of suffering harm, is a permanent neighbour of, if not always actually a resident in, the whole house of strategy. This concept is understood to have utility in the mobilization of concern among those who allegedly stand to be harmed. But, the values and interests of a society tend to be more important in the finding of dangers, than is empirical draft evidence requiring interpretation and perhaps translation. Strategic history is stocked generously with examples of menaces that proved dangerous, but relatively few would have seemed fully self-explanatory and commanding in the apparent logic of requisite response. Danger is so much clearer in retrospect than it was at the time. If one slips expediently into the habit of process-tracing history backwards from unique happening through the cast of people, to their probable interests, and the ever rich preceding context, one is likely to misunderstand the past heroically. When the finishing line (for example, the outbreak of war) is mis-employed as the sole objective in analysis, the historical narrative will be anti-historical in its probably under recognized determinism. The record of events needs to be a vital source of discipline upon the imaginative scholar, but for the education of defence planners it is shot through with peril. We cannot know the scale of future danger. We do not know whether happy enough political endings will reward our defence planning efforts, and we cannot know reliably what our successors will choose to regard as a good enough strategic performance for national security in a future of indeterminate date.

Shock, the fourth concept in the conceptual quartet of menace, has found favour since 11 September 2001, though it too merits careful scrutiny. Nassim Taleb's book, *The Black Swan* is foundational for the popularity of the concept of shock; his work is particularly useful in its brutal exposure of much of the nonsense that is presented with an unjustifiable claim to deserve the authority of science.[10] My argument is friendly to Taleb's logic, especially to his demolition of mathematical methodology that allegedly has value for prediction. The concept of strategic shock preferred here is close to Taleb's concept of a Black Swan happening, but it has some fuzziness that is more accurate historically. Here in this book, a strategic shock is understood to be an event that is not expected, not anticipated as at all probable by political authorities, and whose consequences are deeply consequential. This is not quite Talebian with respect to his concept of a Black Swan, because he identifies this rare bird as being one whose possibility was not even envisaged before it flew shockingly into view.[11] This extreme version of the requirements for shock is not sufficiently plausible to be convincingly relevant for this analysis. However, it is sensible to admit the possibility that the Talebian standard warrants respect, in which case we require some answer to the challenge cited by Donald Rumsfeld under the umbrella of 'unknown unknowns'. A reason for scepticism about the merit in his and Taleb's pure concept of what would amount to presumed black holes of deeply consequential peril, is that human political behaviour can be as great a shocking challenge as are the surprises born of ignorance. Another reason for declining to be thoroughly accommodating to the idea of the 'unknown unknown', is the admittedly arguable feasibility of meeting this extreme category of uncertainty with some intelligent preparation. I am not willing to concede that we are impotent in the face of what may well literally be unknowable.

By commonsense definition a strategic shock is an unanticipated event whose quality of surprise and quantity of consequence is unusual in the extreme. Although it is useful to retain a rigorous understanding of strategic shock, it is more sensible to be less demanding of such candidate happenings in order for them to qualify. In strategic historical experience there have been exceedingly few unambiguous strategic shocks, if one insists upon all elements of the definition I have offered. Many events are surprising and have shock effect, but it has been rare for strategically momentous occurrences to be utterly unanticipated. It is always likely that some few individuals in a defence community will have identified as a possibility, however dimly and inaccurately in detail, what comes in due course to be regarded as a surprise that should qualify as having made the grade as a strategic shock. This is a scholars' issue for which commonsense is needed, possibly at some cost in methodological rigour. The essential defining quality of a strategic shock should not be lost in the quest for academic precision. The reason is that a relatively relaxed understanding of the 'shock' concept is always potentially of high significance for defence planning.

It is important never to forget that strategy is all about the consequences of behaviour, not the behaviour itself, which is why 'so what' has to be regarded as the single most important question the strategist must ask of ideas and plans for threat and action. Considered strategically, shock is to be understood as an unexpected event that seems likely to have deep possible consequences. The surprise may not lie literally in its having been completely unanticipated by all, let alone unanticipatable, especially when reconsidered more comfortably in historical retrospect. But for the integrity of its status as a shock it must clearly have been officially unexpected. There is no strict requirement that a strategic shock should have appalling consequences, but it is prudent to anticipate such a probability. Major unexpected happenings will have a quality of ability in themselves to shock—think of 9/11—but also the possibility and even probability of triggering consequences in future strategic history. Such consequences will have primary first-order, and subsequently second- and third-order effects thereafter. It is necessary to acknowledge the historical reality of shocking events worthy of that categorization, because processes of defence planning nestled in systems of orderly peacetime governance are ill fitted to cope adequately with their sudden appearance. Indeed, there is merit in regarding as essential the ability of a defence planning system and process to cope with shock.

How can a defence planning process attempt to prepare against hostile strategic shocks, when one chooses prudently to regard such events rigorously? The beginning of prudence in this troubling case needs to be acceptance as a reliable assumption that the events will be entirely unexpected by socially and politically accepted expert assessment. This need not mean literally that no academic, journalist, novelist, or religious seer, will ever have speculated as to the happening's distant possibility. But, it would mean that any such speculation would be totally lacking in public credibility, let alone official acceptance. I am suggesting that a polity's defence planners should take seriously the possibility that their country, or community, will be the victim of strategically shocking events. In principle, at least, I do not exclude strategically beneficial shocking events from the logic of this discussion, but happy turns of fortune are not of primary importance to the purpose of this examination.

I emphasize the need for acceptance as an authoritative assumption of the unexpectedness of a strategic shock, because one dare not trust defence planners honestly to deny themselves the advantages of claims to be able to foresee the future. Recalling Ken Booth's apposite words quoted already on the necessity for enemies in the prospective battlespace for strategists and their planning, it is close to impossible for defence planning to be rigorously honest in its approach to hypothetical risks, threats, dangers, and especially shocks. To conduct defence planning without a cast of greater and lesser villains and villainies at least in mind, even if lightly and unconvincingly disguised in abstract or fictional designation, is not really feasible. By analogy, it would be akin to attempting to write a novel without permitting proper nouns to provide subject and plot identification.

The problem for defence planning is that the planners cannot know what is not knowable. I am suggesting that this condition should be acknowledged honestly, though not necessarily openly, and that such frank recognition be followed by an effort to guess about the future on the basis of what is known. The primary sources of such educated guesswork can only be the following: first, what we can extract from the vast if always contestable understanding of strategic history; and second, what we can imagine as not wholly improbable possibilities in the future. The first resource, strategic history, cannot, and must not be permitted to, provide detail, but certainly it yields a usefully rich arsenal of behaviours thoroughly appropriate to be regarded for education in preparation for the future. Understanding of strategic history can educate us as to possibilities, because it has been fuelled by the same ingredients that will make the future. Human nature, culture, politics, and strategy, will all be at work in the remainder of the twenty–first century; we can be sure enough of that. The argument here privileges strategic historical education, of course, not attempted analogical cherry-picking of allegedly compelling historical examples. As I have sought to insist already, detailed historical analogy cannot be useful because we do not know what specific situations will arise in the future for which specific historical analogy might be helpfully suggestive. However, analogy by category of behaviours and situations should be useful, provided one does not neglect to recognize the critical importance played by contingency and the cultural assumptions dominant for the period from which historical analogy may be drawn.[12]

It would be vain to expect defence planners to be able to identify causes for national strategic concern, even alarm in some cases, all the while never forgetting that these projections of fear are the products of well-educated imagination endeavouring to be prudent. It is close to impossible, as well as impracticable, to consider the near-term future as comprising anything much other than a version of today 'only more so'. It is not necessarily the case that the imagination fails, as rather the negative discipline of existentiality: we are where we are and approximately where we are bound to be for a while yet to come. In this book I have chosen not to allow the potent force of institutional and other inertia the influence that it can command, save in an historical context characterized by profound strategic shock. Such argument would have led me into fields that I choose to defer to another enquiry. What is highly pertinent to this discussion, however, is the temporal factor in defence planning.

Although unexpected happenings can be so surprising that they trigger reactions of shock and alarm, it is well to appreciate that the concept of strategic shock is more inclusive than one might think. Subsequent agreement that an event triggered shock and even alarm pertains not only to events that were all but unthinkable, though obviously not literally impossible. The launch of Soviet Sputnik 1 in 1957 was not entirely unanticipated, though certainly it was not expected when it occurred. Soviet deployment of intermediate range ballistic missiles to Cuba in 1962 was not anticipated, but neither was it deemed a political impossibility. Strategic shock is a concept able to accommodate both the extreme character of an event that was regarded previously as impossible, or so improbable that it attracted no political or analytical attention, as well as an occurrence that may have been somewhat anticipated but whose dire consequences had not been. The idea of shock virtually requires that one reduces the course of history conceptually to a moment of alarm, but such temporal reductionism is not really required. Apparently contrary to common sense understanding and usage, crisis and shock, shock effects at least, can be notably protracted. For a tendentious example, it is possible to argue that events in Iraq from late 2003 until 2007 comprised a strategic shock suffered cumulatively by a US military establishment that had been hoist on a petard of exaggerated self-confidence based on unduly high self-regard. The unexpected failures of post-war stabilization in Iraq and Afghanistan occasioned crises that shocked for years, not hours, days, or even months. However, one should not be over-alert to the phenomenon of strategic shock; this is a concept that attracts abusive overuse after the fashion of the like undisciplined contemporary overuse of 'iconic' as an indicator of alleged relative importance.

Black Swan theory tends to encourage undue recognition of the historical significance of true but extremely rare thoroughly unknown unknowns, sometimes at the heavy expense of under-anticipation of the possible ill consequences of events that are in some modest measure expected. Unexpected, even unanticipated, happenings may come as shocks to those unalerted by advance intelligence, but what can be traumatically shocking is just how bad for international security the consequences subsequently prove to be. The assassination of the heir to the throne of Austria–Hungary and his wife in Sarajevo on 28 June 1914 was a shocking outrage, but in no important sense was it a Black Swan event, something entirely unanticipatable previously.[13] By way of contrast, the cumulative consequences of the European balance-of-power war initiated in summer that year, triggered an unstoppable slow-motion strategic shock that indeed threatens to echo in eternity. It is important for defence planners not only to be alert to the undetectable Rumsfeldian surprises, but also to envisage unwelcome strategic shocks as events occurring in the continuous stream of time. Strategy is all about consequence; events are categorically tactical, no matter how immediately shocking they may be.

I have chosen not to trouble this text with much criticism of the continuing undue popularity of trend detection and projection.[14] Strategic history shows evidence of important continuities, which is why it has to be the primary basis for education in preparation for defence planning. However, history most emphatically is not linear. This readily detectable historical actuality means that trend spotters cannot be trusted, regardless of their popularity and self-confidence. It is a considerable methodological challenge simultaneously to be sufficiently alert to both the ever-present possibility of discontinuity, yet appreciative also of those themes in history that persist. Trend finding and analysis is unavoidable and ever desirable, but it needs to be done in full recognition of the condition of non-linearity imposed by human discretion and contingency. Because no reliable evidence can be provided today in support of the proposition that tomorrow will be very different, the path of prudence can be difficult to discern. Linear projection from today will seem the safe way to guard against what is unknowable, except, of course, when it is more prudent to prioritize the negative consequences of failure to adapt, albeit pre-emptively and therefore dangerously.

HOW TO MEET THE CHALLENGE OF UNCERTAINTY

The overriding purpose of this book has been to identify ways by which the challenge of uncertainty, inalienable from the context of defence planning, may be met successfully. I have striven to avoid writing here about the defence issues of today. It would have been agreeable had my research located an all but magical equation that might serve as a key to unlock the mysteries of prudent defence planning. Once metric methodology is recognized as largely irrelevant to the more challenging strategic issues of defence preparation, one is obliged to wade into the swamp and chaos of political and strategic judgement, more than marginally dependent upon expediency and a process of government that amounts to little more than 'muddling through'. Scientific certainty is not a noteworthy contributor to this enterprise. What now follows is a terse assemblage of the findings of this examination of the ways in which the great challenge of uncertainty may best be met by defence planners. These are presented as my 'findings'. I believe that those charged with the duty of defence planning would perform better than they otherwise might, were they to take some heed of these suggestions.

- *The architecture of the general theory of strategy is the basis for sound defence planning: it comprises ends, ways, means—and assumptions.* The whole subject is captured in this austere case of reductionism. Inattention to any of the four interdependent foundational elements can have lethal consequences.

- *Get the biggest things right enough.* Identify and satisfy the highest priorities; those for which compensation could not plausibly be found, if planning had erred. *Right enough*: a vital standard to meet, unscientific though it appears to be and indeed is.

- *Try only to make small mistakes.* Error is inevitable and unavoidable, but significant error may well be minimized even if it cannot be prevented.

- *The most important quality in defence planning is prudence.* To be prudent is above all else to be mindful of the potential harmful consequences of mistakes.

- *Thucydides explains what defence planning is all about: fear, honour, and interest.* Every motive that fuels defence planning is captured by this triptych. Fear and interest need no contemporary clarification, while *honour* is understood to encompass cultural preference and reputation.

- *Strategic history is by far the most useful source of education for defence planners and indeed for strategists generally.* The past is unique as the sole archive of our experience, incomplete and contested though it often is.

- *The future is not knowable in detail by any methodology.* Science, social science, and the arts and humanities are all of them useless for reliable information on the basis of which the future might be anticipated, forecast, or predicted. However, the humanities can and should be studied profitably for strategic education concerning what can happen, but not what will occur. Future strategic history, the subject of most interest to defence planning, is a realm fit only for historically educated guesswork.

- *The higher the levels of concern, policy and strategy in particular, the less utility there is to methodology allowing quantification.* Politics, policy, and strategy cannot be conducted by scientific methods in a quest for testably verifiable certainty of understanding.

- *Strategy is really politics, as readily is comprehended when the basic theoretical architecture for explanation consisting of political ends, strategic ways, and military means is appreciated fully.* Strategy cannot only be a compounded duopoly of ways and means; to make sense there has to be purpose that is necessarily produced in a political process.

- *Defence affordability nearly always is substantially discretionary. This means that the affordability of defence preparation is primarily a political, not an economic, matter.* Societies are able to choose how heavily they wish to invest in their defence planning for the future. Typically, political comment about 'what we can afford', simply ignores the fact that it is a question of choice.

- *Strategic thought and its reflection in societies' defence plans always has a more or less nationally distinctive cultural flavour to it.* Strategy is not all about culture, but neither is it prudent to ignore historical evidence of adversary preferences that warrant appreciation as cultural. Strategic culture lacks predictive quality, but then so does everything else.

- *Beware the curse of presentism! Remember that 'all world orders come to an end eventually'.* The present is transitory.[15] History, strategic and other, is a great stream of time. It features enduring elements (human nature, political process, strategic reasoning), continuities that enable us to make disciplined analogical use of it, but also discontinuities that are ever altering the context within which persisting factors must operate.

- *Rationality and reason cannot prudently be assumed to rule at home or abroad in the future; after all, they have not done so in the past.* The idea of Rational and Reasonable Strategic Man is not sound, because it is highly imprudent. Not only our own, but also Others' political and strategic leaders cannot be assumed to be certain to be both rational and reasonable. Defence planning in part is a 'hedging' effort to invest in insurance against unreasonable strategic proclivities on the part of nominally rational adversaries.

- *Rationality, let alone reasonableness, should no more be assumed of future leadership abroad than of that anticipated to be in positions of authority at home.* Even competence is not the guaranteed default quality setting for people in charge politically, economically, or strategically. Healthy self-doubt should animate defence planners and alert them to the near certainty of their proclivity to err. Even the biological and psychological mysteries permissive of individual genius are thwarted by the physics that preclude knowledge of the future.

- *Flexibility and adaptability are necessary virtues in defence planning, but also they can be mere 'buzzwords' intended to deceive the unwary.* These qualities are popular descriptors of alleged preparation for an unavoidably uncertain future. But their frequent repetition can numb faculties that should be critical, if not sceptical, because these essential and important virtues lend themselves too readily to undisciplined content-free deployment. It is all but meaningless to declare that we intend to be flexible and adaptable—to and for what? One must ask.

- *Play to one's strength, where and when possible.* For reasons of history, geography, and culture, many societies and their polities have traditions of relative excellence in the effectiveness of some, as opposed to other, instruments of national power theoretically employable in their grand strategy. Defence planning should seek hard to ensure the future availability of those particular military capabilities in which the polity and its culture takes a special pride deriving from (memories of!) historical experience of success with their employment. Many societies occasionally find themselves trapped by historical circumstance in the wrong war, in the wrong place, and so forth. But, even in that grim case, the course and outcome of conflict may well offer a range of possibilities and not be immune to the strategic effect of superior military performances of preferred kinds.

The 'findings' of this exploration and examination of defence planning have emphasized how privileged is the role of politics in strategy-making and implementation. I would like to be able to say that strategic history also holds a position of high privilege as the dominant source of strategic education, but I cannot write that with the necessary confidence. With a personal scholarly background in social science and a lengthy career doing strategic analysis in an intensely quantitative environment, with debate about nuclear exchanges and missile vulnerability and the like the lingua franca of the (Cold War) time and place (the United States), I approached this study of strategy and defence planning with a tolerably open mind. By pursuing issues of methodological suitability firmly in the necessary context of the general theory of strategy, I have sought to explain what is known and knowable and what is not, about the strategic history of the future. To close with a caveat: disciplinary tribalism should not be permitted to impede the dialogue that is necessary to enable us to grasp and grip for some control over the awesome challenge of uncertainty that inconveniently is inalienable from the conduct of defence planning.

NOTES

1. Raymond Aron, *Peace and War: A Theory of International Relations* (New York: Doubleday, 1966), 285.
2. Ken Booth, *Strategy and Ethnocentrism* (London: Croom Helm, 1979), 68.
3. In contemporary English usage, iconic means especially significant. There is and can be no scientific test for icons thus understood. An icon can be anything at all that is regarded as being of extraordinary importance. The dictionary definition lays stress on the word's erstwhile devotional meaning, but that understanding is now quite long gone. Obviously, iconic value today is a quality that is all but wholly subjective. For example, Gibraltar may well be iconic in its significance for the pride of Spaniards today, but that quality bears not at all on the intrinsic value of The Rock (or should it be the rock?). The value lies in what Spaniards are persuaded is the value for their dignity of what Gibraltar represents politically and culturally.

4. Although scholars have appreciated for generations that the level of national defence effort generally is set on the basis of what best can be characterized as the public political mood, this essential concept remains as vague as it is unquestionably useful; indeed its indeterminacy contributes to its widespread utility. Public political mood is so extensively comprehended, insofar as it probably can be, that its existence and importance are truisms. An outstanding study for which this concept is of central importance remains Warner Schilling, Paul Y. Hammond, and Glenn H. Snyder, *Strategy, Politics, and Defense Budgets* (New York: Columbia University Press, 1962). Helpful context is added in Gordon S. Barrass, *The Great Cold War: A Journey Through the Hall of Mirrors* (Stanford, CA: Stanford University Press, 2009). In fact, most of the decades since 1945 have been marked by cumulatively large shifts in public political mood about what is the right kind of level of national resource commitment to defence in the future. These shifts owed little to the cogitations of expert defence analysis. Public political relaxation or excitement has been appreciated at the time, but it has probably been deemed so obvious that it would be banal for scholars to elevate it in disciplined enquiry. The author of this book witnessed, felt, and participated in the consequences of public mood change on defence, when Ronald Reagan was elected in 1980, and then a decade later when the context of Cold War no longer had authority.

5. On 18 October 2010, the British government announced proudly 'for the first time the result of a National Risk Assessment process', as an integral part of its new National Security Strategy. The official summary of these results is reprinted as an Appendix. H. M. Government, *A Strong Britain in an Age of Uncertainty: The National Security Strategy* (London: The Stationery Office, October 2010), 'National Security Strategy: Priority Risks', 227. There is substantial reason to believe that the 'Strategy' in the document's title, and the 'National Security Risk Assessment process' advertised by the National Security Adviser, were more aspirational than methodologically rigorous and robust. The popularity of strategy and of risk assessment as terms of art is a fairly reliable indicator that their function is more decorative than in any real sense operational. Pertinent historical case studies on high-end risk assessment are presented and examined in Daryl G. Press, *Calculating Credibility: How Leaders Assess Military Threats* (Ithaca, NY: Cornell University Press, 2005). Press looked closely at risk and threat assessment in the late 1930s over appeasement in 1938–39, and at the Cold War crises over Berlin 1958–61, and Cuba 1962.

6. Booth, *Strategy and Ethnocentrism*, 24.

7. See Ken Booth and Nicholas J. Wheeler, *The Security Dilemma: Fear, Cooperation and Trust in World Politics* (Basingstoke: Palgrave Macmillan, 2008).

8. The core idea is the Delphi approach, which 'tries to improve the basis consensus method by subjecting the experts' views to each other's criticism without actual confrontation and all its psychological shortcomings... The Delphi technique replaces direct debate by a carefully designed program of sequential individual interrogations (best conducted by questionnaires) interspersed with information and opinion feedback derived by computed consensus from the earlier part of the program'. E. S. Quade, 'Methods and Procedures', in Quade, ed., *Analysis for*

Military Decisions: the RAND Lectures on Systems Analysis (New York: RAND McNally, 1964), 163; and 'When Quantitative Models are Inadequate', in W. I. Boucher and E. S. Quade, ed., *Systems Analysis and Policy Planning: Applications in Defense* (New York: American Elsevier, 1968), ch. 18.

9. See Jonathan Holslag, *Trapped Giant: China's Military Rise* (Abingdon: Routledge, for the International Institute for Strategic Studies, 2010), ch. 2.

10. Nassim Nicholas Taleb, *The Black Swan: The Impact of the Highly Improbable* (New York: Random House, 2010).

11. 'A gray swan concerns modelable extreme events; a black swan is about unknown unknowns'. Taleb, *The Black Swan, 2010,* 272.

12. The problem posed by contingency in strategic history for those who strive to locate 'lessons', is well explained in William C. Fuller, Jr, 'What is a military lesson?' in Thomas G. Mahnken and Joseph A. Maiolo, ed., *Strategic Studies: A Reader* (Abingdon: Routledge, 2008), 34–49. Fuller warns persuasively about 'the fallacy of the linear projection', 39.

13. See Christopher Clark, *The Sleepwalkers: How Europe Went to War in 1914* (New York: Harper Collins, 2013).

14. See Development, Concepts and Doctrine Center (DCDC), *Strategic Trends Programme: Global Strategic Trends-Out to 2040,* 4th edn. (London: Ministry of Defence, 2010). The then Director of DCDC, Major General Paul R. Newton offers a bold descriptive claim in the first sentence of his Foreword: 'The DCDC Strategic Trends Programme provides a comprehensive analysis of the future strategic context out to 2040'. It should be superfluous to comment that this impressive document passed instantly into *terra incognito* in its bold journeying. Even a notably friendly reader of the document could hardly fail to notice the frequency with which the word 'likely' was employed in italics.

15. Patrick Porter, *Sharing Power? Prospects for a US Concert-Balance Strategy* (Carlisle, PA: Strategic Studies Institute, April 2013), 10. Porter expands as follows on the words that I quote in my text: 'It would be foolish to dismiss the prospect of a power shift now because predictions were wrong in the past'.

APPENDIX

National Security Strategy: Priority Risks

Tier One: The National Security Council considered the following groups of risks to be those of highest priority for UK national security looking ahead, taking account of both likelihood and impact.

- International terrorism affecting the UK or its interests, including a chemical, biological, radiological or nuclear attack by terrorists; and/or significant increase in the levels of terrorism relating to Northern Ireland.
- Hostile attacks upon UK cyber space by other states and large scale cyber crime.
- A major accident or natural hazard which requires a national response, such as severe coastal flooding affecting three or more regions of the UK, or an influenza pandemic.
- An international military crisis between states, drawing in the UK, and its allies as well as other states and non-state actors.

Tier Two: The National Security Council considered the following groups of risks to be the next highest priority looking ahead, taking account of both likelihood and impact. (For example, a CBRN attack on the UK by a state was judged to be low likelihood, but high impact.)

- An attack on the UK or its Overseas Territories by another state or proxy using chemical, biological, radiological or nuclear (CBRN) weapons.
- Risk of major instability, insurgency or civil war overseas which creates an environment that terrorists can exploit to threaten the UK.
- A significant increase in the level of organised crime affecting the UK.
- Severe disruption to information received, transmitted or collected by satellites, possibly as the result of a deliberate attack by another state.

Tier Three: The National Security Council considered the following groups of risks to be the next highest priority after taking account of both likelihood and impact.

- A large scale conventional military attack on the UK by another state (not involving the use of CBRN weapons) resulting in fatalities and damage to infrastructure within the UK.
- A significant increase in the level of terrorists, organised criminals, illegal immigrants and illicit goods trying to cross the UK border to enter the UK.
- Disruption to oil or gas supplies to the UK, or price instability, as a result of war, accident, major political upheaval or deliberate manipulation of supply by producers.
- A major release of radioactive material from a civil nuclear site within the UK which affects one or more regions.

- A conventional attack by a state on another NATO or EU member to which the UK would have to respond.
- An attack on a UK overseas territory as the result of a sovereignty dispute or a wider regional conflict.
- Short to medium term disruption to international supplies of resources (e.g. food minerals) essential to the UK.

* Reprinted from H. M. Government, *A Strong Britain in an Age of Uncertainty: The National Security Strategy* (London: The Stationery Office, October 2010), 227.

Bibliography

Adamsky, Dimitry (Dima), 'The 1983 Nuclear Crisis—Lessons for Deterrence Theory and Practice', *The Journal of Strategic Studies*, 36 (February 2013): 4–41.

Arbella, Alex, 2008. *Soldiers of Reason: The RAND Corporation and the Rise of the American Empire*. Orlando, FL: Harcourt.

Aron, Raymond, 1966. *Peace and War: A Theory of International Relations*. New York: Doubleday.

Bacevich, Andrew J., 'America's Strategic Stupidity', *The Spectator* (London) (12 January 2013).

Bagehot, Sir Walter, 1867. *The English Constitution*. London: Oxford University Press, 1928.

Barrass, Gordon S., 2009. *The Great Cold War: A Journey Through the Hall of Mirrors*. Stanford, CA: Stanford University Press.

Bathurst, Robert B., 1993. *Intelligence and the Mirror: On Creating an Enemy*. London: SAGE Publications.

Bellamy, Christopher, 1990. *The Evolution of Modern Land Warfare: Theory and Practice*. London: Routledge.

Ben–Harim, Professor Yakov, 'Strategy and Uncertainty' (Technion–Israel Institute of Technology, 2012).

Bernstein, Alvin, 'The strategy of a warrior-state: Rome and the wars against Carthage, 264–201 BC', in Williamson Murray, MacGregor Knox, and Bernstein, eds., *The Making of Strategy: Rulers, States, and War* (Cambridge: Cambridge University Press, 1994: 56–84.

Best, Geoffrey, 2005. *Churchill and War*. London: Hambledon and London.

Biddle, Stephen, 2004. *Military Power: Explaining Victory and Defeat in Modern Battle*. Princeton, NJ: Princeton University Press.

Black, Jeremy, 'A Military Revolution? A 1660–1792 Perspective', in Clifford J. Rogers, ed. *The Military Revolution Debate: Readings on the Military Transformation of Early Modern Europe*. Boulder, CO: Westview Press, 1995: 95–114.

—— 2004. *Rethinking Military History*. Abingdon: Routledge.

—— 2012. *War and the Cultural Turn*. Cambridge: Polity Press.

—— 2013. *War in the Eighteenth Century*. Basingstoke: Palgrave Macmillan.

Bobbitt, Philip, 2013. *The Garments of Court and Palace: Machiavelli and the World that He Made*. New York: Grove Press.

Bond, Brian, 1980. *British Military Policy between the Two World Wars*. Oxford: Oxford University Press.

Booth, Ken, 1979. *Strategy and Ethnocentrism*. London: Croom Helm.

—— Bernard Brodie, in John Baylis and John Garnett, eds., *Makers of Nuclear Strategy*. New York: St. Martin's Press, 1991: 19–57.

—— and Nicholas J. Wheeler, 2008. *The Security Dilemma: Fear, Cooperation and Trust in World Politics*. Basingstoke: Palgrave Macmillan.

Brodie, Bernard, 1959. *Strategy in the Missile Age*. Princeton, NJ: Princeton University Press.

——1973. *War and Politics*. New York: Macmillan.

——"Strategy as a science", in Thomas G. Mahnken and Joseph A. Maiolo, eds., *Strategic Studies: A Reader*. Abingdon: Routledge, 2008: 8–21.

Brown, Seyom, 'Scenarios in Systems Analysis', in E. S. Quade and W. I. Boucher, eds., *Systems Analysis and Policy Planning: Applications in Defense*. New York: American Elsevier, 1968.

Bucholz, Arden, 1991. *Moltke, Schlieffen, and Prussian War Planning*. Providence, RI: Berg Publishers.

Bucknam, Mark and Robert Gold, 'Asteroid Threat? The Problem of Planetary Defence', *Survival*, 50 (October–November 2008): 141–56.

Bungay, Stephen, 2001. *The Most Dangerous Enemy: A History of the Battle of Britain*. London: Aurum Press.

Burleigh, Michael, 2010. *Moral Combat: A History of World War II*. London: Harper Press.

Buzan, Barry and Eric Herring, 1998. *The Arms Dynamic in World Politics*. Boulder, CO: Lynne Reiner Publishers.

Chandler, David, 1973. *Marlborough as Military Commander*. London: B. T. Batsford.

—— 1976. *The Art of Warfare in the Age of Marlborough*. London: B. T. Batsford.

Churchill, Winston S. 1947, *Marlborough: His Life and Times*, Book 2 (1933–8); London: George G. Harrap.

—— 1948. *The Gathering Storm*. London, Penguin 1985.

Cimbala, Steven J. ed., 2012. *Civil-Military Relations in Perspective: Strategy, Structure and Policy*. Farnham: Ashgate.

—— 'Interpreting Nuclear History: Lessons Retro—and Prospectively', unpub. Paper, July 2013.

Citino, Robert M. 2002. *Quest for Decisive Victory: From Stalemate to Blitzkrieg in Europe, 1899–1940*. Lawrence, KS: University of Kansas Press.

—— 2005. *The German Way of War: From the Thirty Years War to the Third Reich*. Lawrence, KS: University Press of Kansas.

Clark, Christopher, 2012. *The Sleepwalkers: How Europe Went to War in 1914*. London: Allen Lane.

Clausewitz, Carl von, *On War*, 1832–4 trans., Michael Howard and Peter Paret. Princeton, NJ: Princeton University Press 1976.

Cohen, Eliot A., 2002. *Supreme Command: Soldiers, Statesmen, and Leadership in Wartime*. New York: Free Press.

——and John Gooch, 1990. *Military Misfortunes: The Anatomy of Failure in War*. New York: Free Press.

Coker, Christopher, 2013. *Can War be Eliminated?* Cambridge: Polity Press.

Cornish, Paul, 1996. *British Military Planning for the Defence of Germany, 1945–50*. Basingstoke: Macmillan.

Creveld, Martin van, 1977. *Supplying War: Logistics from Wallenstein to Patton*. Cambridge: Cambridge University Press.

——1985. *Command in War*. Cambridge, MA: Harvard University Press.

Daddis, Gregory A., 2011. *No Sure Victory: Measuring U.S. Army Effectiveness and Progress in the Vietnam War*. New York: Oxford University Press.

Danzig, Richard, 'Driving in the Dark: Ten Propositions About Prediction and National Security'. Washington, DC: Center for a New American Security, October 2011.

Davis, Paul K. ed., 1994. *New Challenges for Defense Planning: Rethinking How Much is Enough.* MR–400–RC. Santa Monica, CA: RAND.

—— 2002. *Analytic Architecture for Capabilities-Based Planning, Mission-System Analysis, and Transformation.* MR–1513–OSD. Santa Monica, CA: RAND.

—— 'Uncertainty-Sensitive Planning', in Stuart E. Johnson, Martin C. Libicki, and Gregory F. Treverton, eds., *New Challenges, New Tools for Defense Decisionmaking,* MR–1576. Santa Monica, CA: RAND, 2003 : 131–51.

—— Lessons from RAND's Work on Planning Under Uncertainty for National Security, technical report. Santa Monica, CA: RAND, 2012.

Development, Concepts and Doctrine Center (DCDC), *Strategic Trends Programme: Global Strategic Trends-Out to 2040,* 4th edn. London: Ministry of Defence, 2010.

D'Este, Carlo, 2009. *Warlord: A Life of Churchill at War, 1874–1945.* London: Allen Lane.

Digby, James, 'Contributions of RAND to Strategy in the 1950s', in Andrew W. Marshall, J. S. Martin, and Henry Rowen, eds., *On Not Confusing Ourselves: Essays on National Security Strategy in Honor of Albert and Roberta Wohlstetter.* Boulder, CO: Westview Press, 1991: 17–28.

Dixon, Norman F., 1976. *On the Psychology of Military Incompetence.* London: Jonathan Cape.

Doughty, Robert A., 'France', in Richard F. Hamilton and Holger H. Herwig, eds., *War Planning 1914.* Cambridge: Cambridge University Press, 2010: 143–74.

Echevarria Antulio J., II, 'Dynamic Inter-Dimensionality: A Revolution in Military Theory', *Joint Force Quarterly,* 15 (spring 1997): 29–36.

—— 2007. *Clausewitz and Contemporary War.* Oxford: Oxford University Press.

—— 2007. *Imagining Future War: The West's Technological Revolution and Visions of Wars to Come, 1880–1914.* Westport, CT: Praeger Security International.

Enthoven, Alain C., and K. Wayne Smith, 2005. *How Much Is Enough? Shaping the Defense Program, 1961–1969.* Santa Monica, CA: RAND.

Fischer, David Hackett, 1970. *Historians Fallacies: Toward a Logic of Historical Thought.* New York: Harper and Row.

France, John, 2011. *Perilous Glory: The Rise of Western Military Power.* New Haven, CT: Yale University Press.

Freedman, Lawrence, 2004. *Deterrence.* Cambridge: Polity Press.

—— 2003. *The Evolution of Nuclear Strategy,* 3rd edn. Basingstoke: Palgrave Macmillan.

Freier, Nathan, 2008. *Known Unknowns: Unconventional 'Strategic Shocks' in Defense Strategy Development.* Carlisle, PA: Strategic Studies Institute, US Army War College, November 2008.

French, David, 1990. *The British Way in Warfare, 1688–2000.* London: Unwin Hyman.

Fuller, William C. Jr., 'What is a military lesson?' in Thomas G. Mahnken and Joseph A. Maiolo, eds., *Strategic Studies: A Reader.* Abingdon: Routledge, 2008: 34–49.

Gaddis, John Lewis, 'International Relations Theory and the End of the Cold War', *International Security*, 17 (Winter 1992–1993): 5–58.

——2002. *The Landscape of History: How Historians Map the Past.* Oxford: Oxford University Press.

——2005. *The Cold War.* London: Allen Lane.

——'What Is Grand Strategy?' lecture delivered at the conference on 'American Grand Strategy after the War', sponsored by the Triangle Institute for Security Studies and the Duke University Program in American Grand Strategy, 26 February 2009.

Gat, Azar, 2006. *War in Human Civilization.* Oxford: Oxford University Press.

Gentile, Colonel Gian, 2013. *Wrong Turn: America's Deadly Embrace of Counterinsurgency.* New York: The New Press.

Gerald of Wales (Giraldus Cambrensis), 1978. *The Journey Through Wales and the Description of Wales.* London: Penguin, 1978.

Gibbs, N. H., 1976. *History of the Second World War, Grand Strategy: vol. 1, Rearmament Policy.* London: Her Majesty's Stationery Office.

Gooch, John, 1974. *The Plans of War: The General Staff and British Military Strategy c.1900–1916.* London: Routledge and Kegan Paul.

Gray, Colin S. 'War Fighting for Deterrence', *The Journal of Strategic Studies*, 7 (March 1984): 5–28.

——'ICBMs and Deterrence: The Controversy Over Prompt Launch', *The Journal of Strategic Studies*, 10 (September 1987): 285–309.

——1992. *House of Cards: Why Arms Control Must Fail.* Ithaca, NY: Cornell University Press.

——1993. *Weapons Don't Make War: Policy, Strategy, and Military Technology.* Lawrence, KS: University Press of Kansas.

——1999. *Modern Strategy.* Oxford: Oxford University Press.

——2002. *Defining and Achieving Decisive Victory.* Carlisle, PA: Strategic Studies Institute, US Army War College, April 2002.

——2007. *Fighting Talk: Forty Maxims on War, Peace, and Strategy.* Westport, CT: Praeger Security International.

——2009. *Schools for Strategy: Teaching Strategy for 21st Century Conflict.* Carlisle, PA: Strategic Studies Institute, U.S. Army War College, November 2009.

——'Moral Advantage, Strategic Advantage?' *The Journal of Strategic Studies*, 33 (June 2010): 333–65.

——2010. *The Strategy Bridge: Theory for Practice.* Oxford: Oxford University Press.

——'Strategic Thoughts for Defence Planners', *Survival*, 52 (June–July 2010): 159–78.

——2011. 'Conclusion', in John Andreas Olsen and Gray, eds., *The Practice of Strategy: From Alexander the Great to the Present.* Oxford: Oxford University Press: 287–300.

——'The Strategist as Hero', *Joint Force Quarterly*, 62 (3rd Quarter, July 2011): 37–45.

——2012. *Categorical Confusion? The Strategic Implications of Recognizing Challenges either as Irregular or Traditional.* Carlisle, PA: Strategic Studies Institute, February 2012.

——'Clipping the Eagle's Wings: Explaining Failure and Success in the Battle of Britain, 1940', *Infinity Journal*, Special edn. (October 2012): 5–11.

——'Concept Failure? COIN, Counterinsurgency, and Strategic Theory', *Prism*, 3 (June 2012): 17–32.

——2012. *War, Peace and International Relations: An introduction to strategic history*, 2nd edn. Abingdon: Routledge.

——2013. *Perspectives on Strategy*. Oxford: Oxford University Press.

——'Dowding and the British Strategy of Air Defence, 1936–40', in Williamson Murray and Richard Hart Sinnreich, eds., *Successful Strategies: Triumphing in War and Peace from Antiquity to the Present*. Cambridge: Cambridge University Press, forthcoming.

Grazia, Sebastian de, 1994. *Machiavelli in Hell*. New York: Vintage Books.

Grygiel, Jakub, 'Educating for National Security', *Orbis*, 57 (Spring 2013): 201–16.

H. M. Government, A Strong Britain in an Age of Uncertainty: The National Security Strategy. London: The Stationery Office, October 2010.

Halperin, Morton H., 'Nuclear Weapons and Limited War', *The Journal of Conflict Resolution*, 5 (June 1961).

——1974. *Bureaucratic Politics and Foreign Policy*. Washington, DC: The Brookings Institution.

Hamilton, Richard F., and Holger H. Herwig, eds., 2010. *War Planning 1914*. Cambridge: Cambridge University Press.

Hammes, T. X., 'Assumptions—A Fatal Oversight', Infinity Journal, 1 (Winter 2010): 4–6.

Handel, Michael I., 2001. *Masters of War: Classical Strategic Thought*, 3rd edn. London: Frank Cass.

Hanson, Victor Davis, ed., 2010. *Makers of Ancient Strategy: From the Persian Wars to the Fall of Rome*. Princeton, NJ: Princeton University Press.

Harrison, Richard W., 2001. *The Russian Way of War: Operational Art, 1904–1940*. Lawrence, KS: University Press of Kansas.

Hastings, Max, 2009. *Finest Years: Churchill as Warlord, 1940–45*. London: Harper Press.

Herbig, Katherine L., 'Chance and Uncertainty in *On War*', in Michael Handel, ed. *Clausewitz and Modern Strategy*. London: Frank Cass, 1986: 95–116.

Herwig, Holger H., 'Conclusions' in Hamilton and Herwig, eds., *War Planning 1914*. Cambridge: Cambridge University Press, 2010.

Heuser, Beatrice, 2010. *The Evolution of Strategy: Thinking War from Antiquity to the Present*. Cambridge: Cambridge University Press.

Hill, Charles, 2010. *Grand Strategies: Literature, Statecraft, and World Order*. New Haven, CT: Yale University Press.

Hitch, Charles J. and Roland N. McKean, 1965. *Decision-Making for Defense*. Berkeley, CA: University of California Press.

——1966. *The Economics of Defense in the Nuclear Age*. New York: Atheneum.

Holslag, Jonathan, 2010. *Trapped Giant: China's Military Rise*. Abingdon: Routledge, for the International Institute for Strategic Studies.

House, Jonathan M., 2001. *Combined Arms Warfare in the Twentieth Century*. Lawrence, KS: University Press of Kansas.

Howard, Michael, 1972. *The Continental Commitment: The Dilemma of British Defence Policy in the Era of the Two World Wars*. London: Temple Smith.

——1983. *The Causes of Wars and other essays*. London: Counterpoint.

——1991. *The Lessons of History*. New Haven, CT: Yale University Press.

Howard, Michael, 2001. *The Invention of Peace and the Reinvention of War*. London: Profile Books.

Ikle, Fred Charles, 'Can Nuclear Deterrence Last Out the Century?' *Foreign Affairs*, 51 (January 1973): 267–85.

——'Nuclear Strategy: Can There Be a Happy Ending?' *Foreign Affairs*, 63 (Spring 1985): 810–26.

Isaac, Benjamin, 1990. *The Limits of Empire: The Roman Army in the East*. Oxford: Oxford University Press.

Jacobsen, Mark, Robert Levine, and William Schwabe, 1985. *Contingency Plans for War in Western Europe, 1920–1940*. Report from The RAND Strategy Assessment Center, R–3281–NA. Santa Monica, CA: RAND, June 1985.

Jervis, Robert, 'The Future of World Politics: Will It Resemble the Past?' *International Security*, 16 (winter 1991–2): 39–73.

Josephus, *The New Complete Works of Josephus*. Grand Rapids, MI: Kregel Publications, 1999.

Kahn, Herman, 1962. *Thinking the Unthinkable*. New York: Avon Books.

——1965. *On Escalation: Metaphors and Scenarios*. New York: Frederick A. Praeger.

——1960. *On Thermonuclear War*. New York: Free Press, 1969.

Kane, Thomas M., 2001. *Military Logistics and Strategic Performance*. London: Frank Cass.

Kaufman, William W., 'Limited Warfare', in Kaufman, ed., *Military Policy and National Security*. Princeton, NJ: Princeton University Press, 1956: 102–36.

Kennedy, Paul, 1979. ed., *The War Plans of the Great Powers, 1880–1914*. London: George Allen and Unwin.

——1991. ed., *Grand Strategies in War and Peace*. New Haven, CT: Yale University Press.

——'British "Net Assessment" and the Coming of the Second World War', in Williamson Murray and Allan R. Millett, eds., *Calculations: Net Assessment and the Coming of World War II*. New York: Free Press, 1992: 19–59.

——2013. *Engineers of Victory: The Problem Solvers Who Turned the Tide in the Second World War*. London: Allen Lane.

Kent, Glenn A., 2008. *Thinking About America's Defense: An Analytical Memoir*. Santa Monica, CA: RAND.

Khalilzad, Zalmay M., 'Strategy and Defense Planning for the Coming Century', in Khalilzad and David A. Ochmanek, eds., *Strategic Appraisal 1997: Strategy and Defense Planning for the 21st Century*, MR–826–AF. Santa Monica, CA: RAND, 1997.

Krepinevich, Andrew F. Jr., 1986. *The Army and Vietnam*. Baltimore: Johns Hopkins University Press.

——'Transforming to Victory: the US Navy, Carrier Aviation, and Preparing for War in the Pacific', in Talbot C. Imlay and Monica Duffy Toft, eds., *The Fog of Peace and War Planning: Military and Strategic Planning under Uncertainty*. Abingdon: Routledge, 2006:179–205.

——2009. *7 Deadly Scenarios: A Military Futurist Explores War in the 21st Century*. New York: Bantam Books.

Krulak, Charles, 'The Strategic Corporal: Leadership in the Three–Block War', *Marines Magazine*, 28 (May 1999): 28–34.

Kuklick, Bruce, 2006. *Blind Oracles: Intellectuals and War from Kennan to Kissinger.* Princeton, NJ: Princeton University Press.

Lasswell, Harold D., 1936. *Politics: Who Gets What, When, How?* New York: Whittlesey House.

Lawrence, T. E., *Seven Pillars of Wisdom: A Triumph.* New York: Anchor Books, 1991.

Lieber, Keir A., 2005. *War and the Engineers: The Primacy of Politics over Technology.* Ithaca, NY: Cornell University Press.

Luttwak, Edward N., 2001. *Strategy: The Logic of War and Peace*, rev. edn. Cambridge, MA: Harvard University Press.

——2009. *The Grand Strategy of the Byzantine Empire.* Cambridge, MA: Harvard University Press.

Machiavelli, Niccolo, *The Prince*, 1532. trans. Peter Bondarella and Mark Muna. Oxford: Oxford University Press, 1998.

Marshall, A. W., 'A Program to Improve Analytic Methods related to Strategic Forces', *Policy Sciences*, 15 (November 1982): 47–50.

McKean, Roland N. 1987. ed., *Issues in Defense Economics.* New York: National Bureau of Economic Research.

McMaster, H. R., 'Learning from Contemporary Conflicts to Prepare for Future War', in Richmond M. Lloyd, ed., *William B. Ruger Chair of National Security Economics Papers, No. 3, Defense Strategy Air Forces: Setting Future Directions.* Newport, RI: Naval War College, November 2007: 71–94.

Melvin Mungo, 2010. *Manstein: Hitler's Greatest General.* London: Weidenfeld and Nicolson.

Mintzberg, Henry, 2000. *The Rise and Fall of Strategic Planning.* Harlow: Pearson Education.

——Bruce Ahlstrand, and Joseph Laupel, 2009. *Strategic Safari: The complete guide through the wilds of strategic management,* 2nd edn. Harlow: Pearson Education.

Mombauer, Annika, 'German War Plans', in Richard F. Hamilton and Holger H Herwig, eds., *War Planning 1914.* Cambridge: Cambridge University Press, 2010: 48–79.

Morgan, Patrick M., 2003. *Deterrence Now.* Cambridge: Cambridge University Press.

Murray, Williamson, 'History, War, and the Future,' *Orbis*, 52 (Fall 2008): 544–63.

——2011. *Military Adaptation in War: With Fear of Change.* Cambridge: Cambridge University Press.

——'Thoughts on Grand Strategy', Murray, Richard Hart Sinnreich, and Jim Lacey, eds., *The Shaping of Grand Strategy: Policy, Diplomacy, and War.* Cambridge: Cambridge University Press, 2011: 1–33.

——'The Battle of Britain: The Nazis Stopped (1940)', in James Lacey and Murray, eds., *Moment of Battle: The Twenty Clashes That Changed the World.* New York: Bantam Books: 292–317.

——Richard Hart Sinnreich, and James Lacey, eds., *The Shaping of Grand Strategy: Policy, Diplomacy, and War.* Cambridge: Cambridge University Press.

——'The American Civil War', in John Andreas Olsen and Colin S. Gray, eds., *The Practice of Strategy: From Alexander to the Present.* Oxford: Oxford University Press, 2011: 199–218.

Murray, Williamson, 2011. *War, Strategy and Military Effectiveness*. Cambridge: Cambridge University Press.

Nagl, John A., 2002. *Learning to Eat Soup with a Knife: Counterinsurgency Lessons from Malaya and Vietnam*. Chicago: The University of Chicago Press.

Neilson, Keith, 'Great Britain', in Richard F. Hamilton and Holger H. Herwig, eds., *War Planning 1914*. Cambridge: Cambridge University Press, 2010: 175–97.

Neustadt, Richard E. and Ernest R. May, 1986. *Thinking in Time: The Uses of History for Decision-Makers*. New York: Free Press.

O'Hanlon, Michael, 2009. *The Science of War: Defense Budgeting, Military Technology, Logistics, and Combat Outcomes*. Princeton, NJ: Princeton University Press.

Olsen, John Andreas and Martin van Creveld, 2011. eds., *The Evolution of Operational Art: From Napoleon to the Present*. Oxford: Oxford University Press.

Osgood, Robert Endicott, 1957. *Limited War: The Challenge to American Strategy*. Chicago: The University of Chicago Press.

Otte, T. G., and Keith Neilson, 2006. eds., *Railways and International Politics: Paths of Empire, 1848–1945*. Abingdon: Routledge.

Overy, Richard J. 1995. *Why the Allies Won*. London: Jonathan Cape.

——2009. *1939: Countdown to War*. Allen Lane: London.

——2009. *The Morbid Age: Britain and the Crisis of Civilization, 1919–1939*. London: Allen Lane.

Payne, Keith B., 1996. *Deterrence in the Second Nuclear Age*. Lexington, KY: University Press of Kentucky.

——2001. *The Fallacies of Cold War Deterrence and a New Direction*. Lexington, KY: University Press of Kentucky.

——2008. *The Great American Gamble: Deterrence Theory and Practice from the Cold War to the Twenty-First Century*. Fairfax, VA: National Institute Press.

——2013. (Study Director), *Minimum Deterrence: Examining the Evidence*. Fairfax, VA: National Institute Press.

——2013. ed., *Understanding Deterrence*. Abingdon: Routledge.

Pearsall, Judy and Bill Trumble, eds., *Oxford English Reference Dictionary*, rev. 2nd edn. Oxford: Oxford University Press, 2002.

Pinker, Stephen, 2011. *The Better Angels of Our Nature: The Decline of Violence in History and Its Causes*. London: Allen Lane.

Platias, Athanassios G. and Constantinos Koliopoulos, 2006. *Thucydides on Strategy: Athenian and Spartan Grand Strategies in the Peloponnesian War and Their Relevance Today*. Athens: Eurasia Publications.

Pois, Robert and Philip Langer, 2004. *Command Failure in War: Psychology and Leadership*. Bloomington, IN: Indiana University Press.

Porter, Patrick, 2009. *Military Orientalism: Eastern War Through Western Eyes*. London: Hurst.

——2013. *Sharing Power? Prospects for a US Concert-Balance Strategy*. Carlisle, PA: Strategic Studies Institute.

Press, Daryl G., 2005. *Calculating Credibility: How Leaders Assess Military Threats*. Ithaca, NY: Cornell University Press.

Quade, E. S., and W. I. Boucher, 1964. ed., *Analysis for Military Decisions: the RAND Lectures on Systems Analysis*. New York: RAND McNally.

—— 1968. eds., *Systems Analysis and Policy Planning: Applications in Defense*. New York: American Elsevier Publishing Company.

Rahe, Paul A., 'Thucydides as educator', in Williamson Murray and Richard Hart Sinnreich, eds., *The Past as Prologue: The Importance of History to the Military Profession*. New York: Cambridge University Press, 2006: 95–110.

Rees, Martin, 2003. *Our Final Century: Will Civilization Survive the Twenty-First Century?* London: Arrow Books.

Ritter, Gerhard, 1958. *The Schlieffen Plan*. London: Oswald Wolf.

Rodger, N. A. M., 'The Perils of History', The Hattendorf Prize Lecture, *Naval War College Review*, 66 (Winter 2013): 7–15.

Rosen, Stephen Peter, 'Net Assessment as an Analytical Concept', in Andrew W. Marshall, J. J. Martin, and Henry S. Rowen, eds., *On Not Confusing Ourselves: Essays on National Security Strategy in Honor of Albert and Roberta Wohlstetter*. Boulder, CO: Westview Press, 1991: 283–301.

—— 2005. *War and Human Nature*. Princeton, NJ: Princeton University Press.

—— 'The Impact of the Office of Net Assessment on the American Military in the Matter of the Revolution in Military Affairs', *Journal of Strategic Studies*, 33 (August 2010): 469–82.

Rumsfeld, Donald, 2011. *Known and Unknown: A Memoir*. New York: Sentinel.

Ryan, Alan, 2012. *On Politics: A History of Political Thought from Herodotus to the Present*. London: Allen Lane.

Sawyer, Ralph D., 1999. (tr.), *The Tao of War: The Martial 'Tao Te Ching'*. Boulder, CO: Westview Press.

Schelling, Thomas C., 1960. *The Strategy of Conflict*. New York: Oxford University Press.

—— 1966. *Arms and Influence*. New Haven, CT: Yale University Press.

Schilling, Warner, Paul Y. Hammond, and Glenn H. Snyder, 1962. *Strategy, Politics, and Defense Budgets*. New York: Columbia University Press.

Schwartz, Peter, 1998. *The Art of the Long View: Planning for the Future in an Uncertain World*. Chichester: John Wiley.

Shields, Christopher, 'Aristotle', in the *Stanford Encyclopaedia of Philosophy* <http://plato.stanford.edu/entries/aristotle-ethics/>.

Showalter, Dennis E., 1986. Hamden, CT: Archon Books.

Simpson, Emile, 2012. *War from the Ground Up: Twenty-First-Century Combat as Politics*. London: Hurst.

Singer, P. W., 2009. *Wired for War: The Robotics Revolution and Conflict in the 21st Century*. New York: The Penguin Press.

Steel, Duncan, 1995. *Rogue Asteroids and Doomsday Comets: The Search for the Million Megaton Menace That Threatens Life on Earth*. New York: John Wiley and Sons.

Steiner, Barry H., 1991. *Bernard Brodie and the Foundations of American Nuclear Strategy*. Lawrence, KS: University Press of Kansas.

Steiner, Zara, 2011. *The Triumph of the Dark: European International History, 1933–1939*. Oxford: Oxford University Press.

Stevenson, David, 1996. *Armaments and the Coming of War: Europe, 1904–1914*. Oxford: Clarendon Press.

Stevenson, David, 'Strategic and Military Planning, 1871–1914', in Talbot C. Imlay and Monica Duffy Toft, eds., *The Fog of Peace and War Planning: Military and Strategic Planning under Uncertainty*. Abingdon: Routledge, 2006: 75–99.

Stoker, Donald, 2010. *The Grand Design: Strategy in the U.S. Civil War*. Oxford: Oxford University Press.

Strachan, Hew, 2011. *The First World War, Volume 1: To Arms*. Oxford: Oxford University Press.

—— 'Strategy in the Twenty-First Century', in Strachan and Sibylle Scheipers, eds., *The Changing Character of War*. Oxford: Oxford University Press, 2011: 503–23.

Taleb, Nassim Nicholas, 2007. *The Black Swan: The Impact of the Highly Improbable*. New York: Random House.

Thucydides, ca. 400 BC. *The Landmark Thucydides: A Comprehensive Guide to The Peloponnesian War*, ed. Robert B. Strassler, rev. tr. Richard Crawley; New York: Free Press, 1996.

Thurnher, Jeffry S., 'Legal Implications of Fully Autonomous Targeting', *Joint Force Quarterly*, 67 (4th quarter 2012): 77–84.

Triandafillov, V. K., 1929. *The Nature of the Operations of Modern Armies*. Ilford: Frank Cass, 1994.

Tuchman, Barbara W., 1984. *The March of Folly: From Troy to Vietnam*. New York: Ballantine Books.

Tzu, Sun, *The Art of War*, c. 490 BC. trans. Samuel B. Griffith; Oxford: Clarendon Press, 1963.

Urban, Mark, 2010. *Task Force Black: The Explosive True Story of the SAS and the Secret War in Iraq*. London: Little, Brown.

Vivanti, Corrado, 2013. *Niccolo Machiavelli: An Intellectual Biography*, trans. Simon MacMichael. Princeton, NJ: Princeton University Press.

Waldman, Thomas, 2013. *War, Clausewitz and the Trinity*. Farnham: Ashgate,

Walton, C. Dale, 2002. *The Myth of Inevitable U.S. Defeat in Vietnam*. London: Frank Cass.

Watt, Donald Cameron, 1989. *How War Came: The Immediate Origins of the Second World War, 1938-1939*. New York: Pantheon Books.

Wheeler, Nicholas J. and Ken Booth, 2008. *The Security Dilemma: Fear, Cooperation and Trust in World Politics*. Basingstoke: Palgrave Macmillan.

Williams, Paul D., 2013. ed., *Security Studies: An Introduction*, 2nd edn. Abingdon: Routledge.

Winters, Harold A., 1998. *Battling the Elements: Weather and Terrain in the Conduct of War*. Baltimore, MD: Johns Hopkins University Press.

Winton, Harold R., 'An Imperfect Jewel: Military Theory and the Military Profession', *The Journal of Strategic Studies*, 34 (December 2011): 853–77.

Yarger, Harry R., 2008. *Strategy and the National Security Professional: Strategic Thinking and Strategy Formulation in the 21st Century*. Westport, CT: Praeger Security International.

Yuen, Derek M. C., 'The System of Chinese Strategic Thought', *Comparative Strategy*, 29 (July–August 2010): 245–59.

Zabecki, David T., 2008. ed., *Chief of Staff: The Principal Officers Behind History's Great Commanders, Vol. 1, Napoleonic Wars to World War I, Vol. 2, World War II to Korea and Vietnam.* Annapolis, MD: Naval Institute Press.

Zellen, Barry Scott, 2012. *State of Doom: Bernard Brodie, the Bomb, and the Birth of the Bipolar World.* New York: Continuum.

Zuber, Terence, 2011. *The Real German War Plan, 1904–14.* Stroud: The History Press.

——2002. *Inventing the Schlieffen Plan: German War Planning, 1871–1914.* Oxford: Oxford University Press.

Index

Printed and bound by CPI Group (UK) Ltd, Croydon, CR0 4YY